Teach in Canada

Stephen B. Lawton
George J. Bedard
Duncan K. MacLellan
Xiaobin Li

Detselig Enterprises Ltd.

Calgary, Alberta Canada

Teachers' Unions in Canada
© 1999 Stephen B. Lawton

Canadian Cataloguing in Publication

Teachers' unions in Canada

Includes bibliographical references and index.
ISBN 1-55059-192-4

1. Teachers' unions—Canada. I. Lawton, Stephen B.
LB2844.53.C3T42   1999   331.88'113711'00971   C99-910392-X

Detselig Enterprises Ltd.
210-1220 Kensington Rd. N.W.
Calgary, Alberta T2N 3P5
Phone: (403) 283-0900 / Fax: (403) 283-6947
e-mail: temeron@telusplanet.net
www.temerondetselig.com

Detselig Enterprises Ltd. appreciates the financial support for our 1999 publishing program, provided by Canadian Heritage and other sources.

All rights reserved. No part of this book may be reproduced in any form or by any means without permission in writing from the publisher.

Printed in Canada
ISBN 1-55059-192-4
SAN 115-0324
Cover design by Dean Macdonald

Contents

List of Tables iv
List of Figures iv
Preface v
 1 Introduction 7
 2 The Rise of Teachers' Unions 13
 3 Labor Relations Legislation 41
 4 Canadian Teachers' Unions as Organizations 61
 5 Contesting the Neo-Conservative Agenda 75
 6 Province-wide Bargaining in British Columbia 87
 7 The Battle over Ontario's Bill 160 103
 8 Teachers' Unions in Anglo-Democracies 123
 9 Teachers' Unions, Salaries and the Cost of Education . 135
10 Teacher Pension Plans in Canada 167
11 Who Benefits? 183
12 Choices 199
Index 211

List of Tables

Table 2.1: Historical Development of Teacher Education in Canada 16

Table 2.2: Teachers' Organizations: 1861-1970 23

Table 2.3: Canadian Teachers' Federation Member Organizations, 1996 30

Table 3.1: Provincial Employment Relations Legislation for Teachers 53

Table 4.1: Annual Membership Fees for Teachers' Unions 70

Table 4.2: 1996/1997 Budget for Nova Scotia Teachers' Union 72

Table 4.3: 1996/1997 Budget for Alberta Teachers' Association 73

Table 9.1: Expenditures per Pupil by Province in Constant 1986 Dollars, 1991-1996 136

Table 9.2: Salary Grid for a British Columbia School District, June 30, 1994 146

Table 9.3: Average Employment Income of School Teachers as a Percentage of Selected Occupations (Constant 1990 Dollars), Age 15 and over 157

Table 9.4: Percentage of Persons Aged 15 to 65 with a University Degree in Selected Occupations 159

Table 9.5: Hay Control Points and Salary Range for Ontario Educators, 1972 161

Table 9.6: Average Family Income and Average Teacher Income by Province, 1995 163

Table 10.1: Summary of Teacher Pension Plans Across Canada, 1998 170

List of Figures

Figure 9.1: The Labor Market for Teachers 138

Preface

We wish to acknowledge the generous support of the Donner Canadian Foundation for the resources that made this work possible. The formal title of the project, "Impact of Teachers' Unions on Public Finance and Schooling," was funded as Grant No. C-10-96. We appreciate, as well, the opportunities offered by the Foundation to participate on several occasions when they sponsored visits by important scholars and analysts to Toronto. The occasion with Dr. Myron Lieberman, who has published extensively about teachers' unions, was particularly appreciated given the topic of the present study.

The staff of the Foundation has been supportive throughout, including the executive director, Patrick Luciani, program officer Sonia Arrison and previous program officer Adrian Snow.

Near the end of the project, the first author had an opportunity to participate in a conference, "Teacher Unions and Education Reform," at the Kennedy School of Government, Harvard University. The conference proved very timely in that it brought together specialists and officials from a variety of perspectives. The Program on Education Policy and Governance and the Taubman Center for State and Local Government organized the conference. The Center and the John M. Olin Foundation provided funding.

A draft of this manuscript was reviewed by a number of knowledgeable individuals who helped to refine arguments, provide examples and counter examples, and suggest additional material. We appreciate the contributions of: Nina Bascia, Associate Professor, OISE/UT; Harold Press, Director of Corporate Planning and Research, Newfoundland and Labrador Department of Education; Kenneth Wm. Thornicroft, Associate Professor of Law and Labour Relations, University of Victoria; and Judge Marvin Zuker, Associate Professor, OISE/UT. The authors are, of course, fully responsible for the use made of their advice.

The four authors worked as a team on this project. Meetings were stimulating occasions as we debated not just our research but also the unfolding drama in Ontario education as the conflict between teachers' unions and government increased. Different individuals did commit their energies to particular activities and chapters. Specifically, Lawton and Bedard jointly drafted chapters 1 and 12; MacLellan prepared chapter 2; chapters 3, 6, 8, 10 and 11 are by Lawton; chapters 4, 5, and 7 are by Bedard; and chapter 9 is by Lawton and Li.

Ultimately, the authors are responsible for the accuracy of the information included here. The first author, as principal investigator on the project, bears full responsibility for the perspective provided as to the implications of this information for education and public policy.

Stephen Lawton
George J. Bedard
Duncan K. MacLellan
Xiaobin Li

Toronto, Ontario
February 1999

1

Introduction

> *Pressures like those that led to the transformation of the private sector industrial relations systems in the 1970s and 1980s are now affecting the public sector.*
>
> Belman, Gunderson and Hyatt, 1996.

The current struggles over education in Canada are being mirrored in countries around the world. One wonders if ever there was a time that this was not so, but it does seem that the intensity of the conflict is peaking. At the centre of the battle are teacher unions and their leaders who have become some of the best known figures in provincial politics. Even the union of provincial teachers' unions, the Canadian Teachers' Federation, has entered the fray, staking out territory to defend or expand. But while much is written about education, politics and government, there is a relative dearth of recent literature on teachers' unions. What we do know of these combative opponents that confront representatives of governments and often trustees on television and in the newspapers? Why the intensity? What is at stake that is so valuable that teachers either leave their classrooms to strike, sacrificing their love of teaching and significant income, or are locked-out on the streets by trustees who are charged with ensuring the provision of sound educational services? Is it a question of greed or power, as some would have it? Or is it driven by commitment to a social vision or political cause that demands forceful action?

To answer these and other questions it is first necessary to understand what teachers' unions are, how and why they were created, and the laws that govern – and change – them. It is possible to collect many facts, although not as many as we would like since some important information is not public and there is a lag between current events and the publication of official statistics. Having facts does not answer questions, in any case; that takes interpretation, which is invariably based on assumptions and, to a degree, beliefs. While the majority of the literature on teachers' unions praises their contributions and promise, there is a growing literature that expresses skepticism as to the overall value of their contributions. Surprisingly to us, some of their harshest critics today were once their visionaries or helpful negotiators. American journalist and scholar Myron Lieberman promoted unionism in the post-war years (1956; 1966), but now believes that teacher unions have become so destructive that they must be abolished or circumvented so that civil society might reclaim the education of its children (1993; 1997). Ontario lawyer Leon Paroian assisted teachers' unions with collective bargaining for many years, but concluded that existing legislation was too favorable toward their side of the table in a report he authored for the government of Ontario (1996).

This volume's perspective derives from a concern about a public need to understand the balance of interests influencing education today. To this end, we collected, analyzed and commented upon reports, statements and observations available in print or electronic media. Field research involving interviews were avoided because of ethical challenges, in that any negative information reported could jeopardize the informant.

Concern about the balance of interests means that one questions official accounts of actions and seeks other motives that may also explain the actions of individuals and groups. Evidence to support alternative interpretations is then sought to provide validation. Selection of statistical data to give a fair perspective on matters such as costs and compensation present a particular challenge. Data series on teachers' annual salaries are a bit like data on mutual funds: careful selection of a base year can produce a chart supporting or undermining any assessment. Readers should bring their own skepticism to the tables and graphs in the chapters that follow. We have endeavored to be fair and balanced but our conclusions are always subject to reevaluation in light of new or refined statistical data.

Teachers' unions are first and foremost teachers' agents. That is, the unions act for individual teachers in negotiating salaries, handling grievances and resolving many problems. We may not be used to thinking about unions in this way but their role is similar to that of the agents of movie stars, musicians and athletes who negotiate contracts, book events, handle publicity and help to guide the careers of these pop-culture stars. When you next see the president of a teachers' union on CBC Newsworld, listen carefully and you will hear a promoter who is out to get the best deal possible for his or her clients.

But you will also hear more. You will hear another agenda. It varies from time and place, but it is the second agenda that may count most in the long run. It is a social or political agenda that is being advanced by engaging in political debate. Often opposition parties are praised, but not the government. Certain trustees congratulated and others are condemned. Links to labor groups receive praise while school-business partnerships are denounced as creeping corporatism. One may argue these dichotomies are part of the game of bargaining in order to make the best deal for the client. But does insulting your employer's agent – for provincial governments and trustees are the agents of the people – make sense? Do the agents for the stars publicly slander the producers who employ the performers? This pattern of behavior on the part of unions does not make sense in terms of normal economic relationships between buyers, sellers, and agents, who have continuing relationships. It is a pattern of behavior that needs a deeper understanding that only can come from knowing the place of teachers' unions in our social, political and economic system.

To develop this understanding we delve into the history of teachers' unions, tracing their origins back into the last century (chapter 2). Today's teachers' unions were founded not as unions, but as benevolent associations under their province's laws governing benevolent societies serving the needs of their members. The collective impulse to help one another reflects both the unprotected lives lived by most teachers at that time and recognition of the benefits of sharing risk. Much the same motivation gave rise to mutual insurance companies, farmer cooperatives and credit unions. Also present, though, were a sense of being aggrieved and a demand for just treatment. During the earlier years, this demand translated into a quest for tenure laws to prevent arbitrary dismissal, for minimum salary standards and the beginnings of professional training and certification. Much later, this impulse helped to drive a quest for power so that greater desires could be fulfilled.

Collective bargaining laws and the negotiated agreements that they engender create a set of binding obligations for school districts as great as any provincial education act. In some cases, collective agreements include such minutiae that one may wonder why the details are worth writing down. Provincial laws and board bylaws are recapitulated in agreements, presumably to ensure that the rules remain in force should the laws or bylaws change. Nothing, it seems, can be left to chance. The dimensions of these agreements, and the legislation that gives them force, form an institutionalized order that is invisible to typical citizens and parents yet governs many elements of students' education (chapter 3).

The internal operations of teachers' unions, inferred from public documents and existing research, demonstrate the organizational form that developed in order to implement the mission of achieving for teachers the best possible contractual relationships. Supporting the primary economic agenda are professional training programs for teachers and legal units that provide services to protect and defend incumbents' positions. Also evident, though, is a certain distance between classroom teachers and their official representatives in terms of values and objectives (chapter 4). The sense of being aggrieved, allied with traditions of social unionism, translates into an ambitious partnership for domestic and international social change that is broad in scope (chapter 5).

The combination of union history, legal frameworks for labor relations, and the emergence of fiscally responsible governments of all political stripes – Progressive Conservative, Liberal and New Democratic – have created a crisis for public sector unions in general and teacher unions in particular. Typically, these new regimes are referred to as neo-conservative if they emphasize business interests and choice in public services and neo-liberal if they emphasize efficiency, a sound economy, equity and client-centred services. Both groups tend to endorse "re-inventing" government, including contracting out and privatization of some services that government has traditionally provided. Such initiatives are supported by neo-conservative Premiers Mike Harris in Ontario and Ralph Klein in Alberta, neo-liberals like Prime Ministers Jean Chrétien and the U.K.'s Tony Blair, and even Ontario's former NDP Premier Bob Rae. Teachers' unions and their allies see these schemes as scourges of the earth to be fought at every turn. Case studies of British Columbia's difficulty in implementing a new form of province-wide bargaining and Ontario's fight over Bill 160, the *Education Quality Improvement Act*, illustrate the dynamics that new political philosophies have created (chapters 6 and 7). These dynamics are not unique to Canada, as a review of the experiences of teachers' unions in other Anglo-democracies demonstrates (chapter 8).

Successful agents should make deals that satisfy the clients' hopes and expectations. How well have teachers' unions done? One measure is teacher compensation. Has it leapt forward since teacher federations converted into full-fledged unions in the 1970s and 1980s? Since 61 percent of the $35 billion Canada committed to elementary and secondary education in 1996 – or about $21 billion – went to pay teachers' salaries and benefits, this matter is a significant issue (chapters 9 and 10) (Lawton, 1996, pp. 129-134). On the other hand, if the agents have not won better deals for their clients, what is one to make of the tens of millions of dollars that they, as agents, are paid each year for representing their clients, Canada's school teachers? Value for money is as common a demand by clients these days as it is by governments.

Reflecting on the relationship between teachers and their agents stimulates a variety of possibilities and concerns. How satisfied are teachers with their representation? How and why have they chosen the leaders they have? Do all teachers agree with the current arrangements? What does one do if one does not? Freedom of association is a human right guaranteed by the *Canadian Charter of Rights and Freedoms* and the *International Declaration of Human Rights*, but what of forced association? That is, in becoming a member of a profession or government agency, does one lose the right to choose *not* to join in an association with one's workmates? What of the person who appreciates the union's economic contribution but differs from it on social and political positions that it, in the name of the teachers, advocates on the provincial, national and world stages (chapter 11)?

We believe that the current initiatives, which include school district amalgamation, changes in school finance systems, provisions for more explicit curriculum, and systematic assessment are only now beginning to affect the system. Depending upon the province, implementation of the most recent round of changes began just one, two or three years ago. Some are being contested in court and others have yet to begin. As a result, the changing roles that teachers' unions will assume are not yet fully evident. We believe that there are choices to be made and sketch several alternative paths that the administration and governance of educational systems may follow and the implications of these paths for teachers' professionalism and teachers' unions (chapter 12). Given the importance of maintaining and developing strong, publicly-supported systems of education, discussion and debate are needed about possible paths toward the future. It is evident part of this interchange ought to include identifying opportunities to refine the employment arrangements for teachers.

References

Belman, D., Gunderson, M. & Hyatt, D. (1996). Public sector employment relations in transition. In D. Belman, M. Gunderson & D. Hyatt (Eds.), *Public sector employment in a time of transition* (pp. 1-20). Madison, WI: Industrial Relations Research Association.

Lawton, S. B. (1996). *Financing Canadian education*. Toronto: Canadian Education Association.

Lieberman, M. (1956). *Education as a profession*. Englewood Cliffs, NJ: Prentice-Hall.

Lieberman, M. (1966). *Collective negotiations for teachers*. Chicago: Rand McNally.

Lieberman, M. (1993). *Public education: An autopsy*. Cambridge, MA: Harvard University Press.

Lieberman, M. (1997). *The teacher unions: How the NEA and the AFT sabotaged reform and hold students, parents, teachers and taxpayers hostage.* New York: Free Press.

Paroian, L. (1996). *Review of the school boards'/teachers' collective negotiations process in Ontario.* Toronto: Ministry of Education and Training.

2

The Rise of Teachers' Unions

> *Don't talk to me about teachers' unions. They're what gave me a middle-class standard of living.*
>
> A Canadian school superintendent.

The history of teachers' unions[1] in Canada is a story of increasingly influential activity by groups of educators dedicated to advancing the social and economic status of teaching as an occupation. While Canada's experience is not unique, it does provide an interesting case in the study of teacher unionism for three reasons. First, Canada is a federation of provinces and territories, each with its own laws, rules, unions and government bargaining agencies; second, it is a society with both English- and French-speaking provinces, schools and unions; and third, some provinces delegate substantial power to local educational authorities. The Canadian education system offers an example of decentralized, complex and multilevel decision-making, all in the absence of a strong national educational presence (Cooper, 1992; Muir, 1969).

The Division of Powers in Canada

A prerequisite for the discussion of the evolution of teachers' unions in Canada is a brief account of the division of powers within the nation. This review includes a description of the division of powers in regard to education, background information with respect to labor legislation and a summary of the evolution of collective bargaining in the educational sector.

In 1867, the Dominion of Canada came into existence with the passage of the *British North America Act (BNA)*, now the *Constitution Act, 1867*. The Fathers of Confederation adopted a federal form of union with sovereignty divided between the provinces and the federal parliament, with the exercise of legislative powers of each limited to subject matters allotted to them by the constitution (VanLoon & Whittington, 1987).

The federal government and the provincial governments are each in possession of exclusive and sovereign powers that cannot be encroached upon by the other level of government. The legislative powers of the federal parliament are, for the most part, defined in section 91 of the *Act*. This section is in two parts. The first is a broad and general grant of power, giving Parliament the authority to make laws for the "Peace, Order, and Good Government of Canada" in relation to all matters which are not assigned to the legislatures of the provinces. The second part includes 31 enumerated matters such as "the Public Debt and Property" and the "Regulation of Trade and Commerce" among others (Lawton, 1989; Smiley, 1980; VanLoon & Whittington, 1987). Also, the courts have recognized that the federal government has emergency powers to override provincial authority, as occurred with the anti-inflation wage controls in the 1970s.

The legislative powers of the provinces are for the most part set out in section 92. In each province, the legislature may exclusively make laws in relation to matters pertaining to the areas that are specified in this section but not included in section 91. The intention of sections 91 and 92 is to give the federal and provincial levels exclusive power to make laws which relate to their respective areas of jurisdiction[2] (Smiley, 1980).

The subject of education is normally considered to rest within the exclusive jurisdiction[3] of the provincial legislatures by section 93.[4] Section 93 places certain limitations and conditions on the exercise of this power by the provinces. First, it states no provincial law shall "prejudicially affect any right or privilege with respect to denominational schools" that existed at the time of union. Second, it states that the rights of the separate schools in Upper Canada (now Ontario) shall continue after the union and shall apply equally to Protestant separate schools in Lower Canada (now Quebec).[5] The third clause of section 93 establishes a right of appeal to the Governor General in Council if the education rights of a Protestant or Catholic minority are abrogated by a provincial legislature. Finally, in the event that the province does not respond positively to an appeal that is allowed by the Governor General in Council, provision is made for the Parliament of Canada to "make remedial Laws for the due Execution of the Provisions of this Section" (Axelrod, 1997; Lawton, 1989).

The significance of this section is that it gives the federal government the power and responsibility to protect the education rights of religious minorities from encroachment by the provinces. Consequently, separate (primarily Roman Catholic) schools persist in Ontario. While all schooling was officially non-sectarian in the three Maritime provinces, following considerable debate and conflict, arrangements were made during the 1870s to maintain religious instruction in Nova Scotia and New Brunswick on the basis of local community initiatives. However, public school acts of the

1870s entrenched the Maritime provinces' non-sectarian school systems.

Manitoba entered Confederation in 1870 with a dual school system of denominational (Protestant and Roman Catholic) schools, while British Columbia joined Canada one year later committed to a completely non-sectarian process of public schooling. At the other end of the spectrum were Quebec and Newfoundland. Provincial funding was divided among Roman Catholic and Protestant church authorities that, subject to certain guidelines, governed their respective schools.[6] Education in Canada at the time of the passage of the *BNA (1867)* reflected a mix of private, public and religious forces, as well as particular ethnic and linguistic tensions (Axelrod, 1997; Manzer, 1994). More recently, section 23 of the *Charter of Rights and Freedoms* strengthens the language rights of linguistic (French and English) minorities by guaranteeing their right to an education in their own language in all provinces and territories.

Shortly after Confederation, steps were also taken to formalize and standardize the certification of teachers throughout the provinces. In the early 19th century, there were few regulations governing teaching applicants' scholarly credentials, although one's perceived moral character, nationality and religion would be questioned and considered. Axelrod notes,

> *The campaigns for school expansion were top-down projects, with social and religious elites controlling the agendas and determining the process of educational change. Their role was unmistakably central, but ordinary citizens had their own reasons for favouring the development of state-supported schooling (p. 32).*

At this point in history, the majority of Canadians lived in rural communities. Many farm families recognized the value of formal education in light of the industrial changes that were sweeping the country and some Protestant denominations, particularly Methodists and Presbyterians, were keen on extending literacy for religious reasons. Building schools in rural communities gave the children of these families opportunities to either apply what they learned in school on farms or as employees in the emerging urban centers of Canada (Axelrod, 1997).

As public schooling was extended, pressure mounted to elevate the quality of school teaching and to enhance its occupational credibility. What followed was the establishment by provincial educational officials of "normal schools"[7] for teacher training. While the first of these was set up in Toronto in 1847, New Brunswick, Nova Scotia, Prince Edward Island and Quebec followed suit

Table 2.1
Historical Development of Teacher Education in Canada

1822	British and Canadian School Society established in Montreal to train persons to teach.
1836	Two normal schools established in Lower Canada.
1847	Normal schools established in Canada West and New Brunswick.
1850	Teachers' Institutes provide in-service teacher training in Ontario.
1850-1900	Provincial Departments of Education established with responsibility for teacher training; teachers were required to have education beyond elementary level.
1855	Teachers' Institutes created to provide in-service teacher training in New Brunswick.
1856	Teachers' Institutes created to provide in-service training in Prince Edward Island.
1882	Normal School established in Manitoba and Regina.
1897	Professional training made obligatory for high school teachers in Ontario.
1898	Bishop's University first to offer professional training to high school teachers.
1901	Normal Schools established in British Columbia.
1906	Normal Schools established in Alberta.
1907	Professional training for high school teachers offered at universities in Ontario.
1923	Professional training for high school teachers offered at the University of British Columbia.
1928	Professional training for high school teachers established in Saskatchewan and Alberta.
1935	Professional training for high school teachers established in Manitoba.
1946	Saskatchewan initiated four-year undergraduate program, but still retained normal schools as an option.
1950s	Normal Schools became teachers' colleges in Ontario, New Brunswick, Nova Scotia, Saskatchewan and Manitoba, but still did not grant college degrees.
1953	McGill University began four-year Bachelor of Education program.
1956	British Columbia moved all teacher training from normal schools to the University of British Columbia and Victoria College.
1962	Teachers required to complete a two-year course in Nova Scotia and New Brunswick.
1963	Teachers' training transferred to universities in Saskatchewan and Manitoba.
1968	Dalhousie University approved four-year Bachelor of Education program for teachers. Ontario began phasing out teachers' colleges. A two-year university program and, later, a four-year program replaced teacher college programs.

Source: King and Peart, 1992.

within the decade. The aim of the normal school was to engage incoming teachers in the principles and practices of teaching according to established rules that were to be exemplified in the schools. Table 2.1 provides a chronological summary of teacher education in Canada (King & Peart, 1992; Axelrod, 1997; Paton, 1962).

Public school enrollment rose steadily in the last four decades of the 19th century, increasing from 600 000 in 1861 to 1.1 million in 1901. Over the same period, the Canadian population, fueled by immigration, grew from 3.2 million to 5.3 million (Axelrod, 1997). There was an increasing demand for teachers to cope with the growing numbers of students who were entering Canada's school system. The expansion of secondary education, the consolidation of schools, and the reorganization of school districts created both the political and the institutional foundations that led teachers to look for organizations that would "oversee" their needs.

The Establishment of Teachers' Federations: 1850-1930

Educational organizations in Canada developed on a provincial basis, since constitutional responsibility for education resides at this level. The first provincial educational association was the Teachers' Association of Canada West, organized in 1861 with Dr. McCaul, President of the University of Toronto, as its leader. In 1892 it merged with the Provincial Association of Public and High School Trustees, started in 1887, to form the Ontario Educational Association (OEA). The OEA was the forerunner of other educational associations that subsequently developed in many provinces prior to the turn of the century. The Provincial Association of Protestant Teachers of Quebec (PAPT) was founded in 1864. Other early examples were the Educational Association of Nova Scotia (1863) and the Teachers' Federation of Prince Edward Island (1880) (Manzer, 1994).

These associations were, for the most part, organized and sponsored by officials within the departments of education and served three purposes. They provided general in-service training for teachers, the majority of whom had little or no professional training. They offered an opportunity for people with an interest in education to meet annually to discuss common educational concerns. Finally, they created a forum for departments of education to make public pronouncements (Smaller, 1988).

It is important to note that these educational associations were an amorphous group of people interested in the schools and in education, some lay and some professionals. They were not, in the strict sense, organizations of teachers speaking for teachers directly to the authorities who controlled the school laws and regulations. The teachers themselves appear to have had a relatively minor role in these associations and institutes. Typically, teachers respected and apparently followed without question their superiors in education; the teachers knew their place and refrained from any kind of self-assertive action (Paton, 1962). In many cases, while they appeared to be independent, these teachers' associations and institutes were usually tied into the larger state agenda of solidifying the system, often to the disadvantage of teachers' material concerns (Johnson, 1964; Smaller, 1988).

In the case of Nova Scotia, the Nova Scotia Teachers' Union (NSTU) traces its origin to 1896[8] when, as part of the Nova Scotia Provincial Education Association, it was made up of normal school instructors, department officials, school trustees and teachers. In its early years, the NSTU met more or less as an adjunct to the Provincial Educators' Association (Paton, 1962). The Teachers' Protective Union of Nova Scotia was formed in October 1895 with the aim of exerting an influence in gaining better salaries[9] and to aid teachers in securing better results in their school work. Those in attendance at the meeting agreed that the teaching profession, like other professions, should have a union for at least defensive purposes. The Protective Union, it was thought, would do much for educational reforms, such as developing a code of ethics to prevent underbidding and promoting legislation to protect individual teachers from the petty tyranny of some trustees.

The constitution of the Protective Union stated the following five objectives:

1. to elevate and unify the teaching profession in Nova Scotia;
2. to bring the claims of the profession before the public and legislature of Nova Scotia as occasion may require;
3. to watch the educational outlook and trends of thought in other parts of the world with a view to keeping the profession in Nova Scotia abreast of the time;
4. to endeavor to advance salaries by increasing the capability of the teachers and improving the quality of the work; and
5. to protect teachers, who, through errors in agreements or otherwise, are in danger of being defrauded by unscrupulous employers (Parker, 1962).

A number of the teachers' associations followed in the footsteps of the Teachers' Protective Union of Nova Scotia and structured their constitutions to reflect similar objectives.

In Prince Edward Island a Provincial Teachers' Association, formed in 1880, became strong enough to secure an *Act of Incorporation* in 1895, six years after the Provincial Association of Protestant Teachers of Quebec. The Newfoundland Teachers' Association (NTA), founded in 1889, aimed to establish a pension plan and increase salaries – indicating that the founders were primarily concerned with their own welfare. Of interest is the representation of the province's three major religious denominations on the original slate of NTA officers: Church of England, Methodist and Roman Catholic. The NTA established the practice of choosing at least one representative from each of the three religions for the top four or five NTA positions (Cuff, 1985). The New Brunswick Teachers' Association (NBTA) was founded in 1902 in a merger of county associations; however, the NBTA, like its Atlantic counterparts, went into the doldrums until after the First World War.

After World War I, at a time of economic turmoil that engendered the Winnipeg General Strike of 1919, teachers began to support the establishment of special-interest teachers' organizations to assert a degree of occupational self-control (Bascia, 1994; Smaller, 1995). Teachers faced changing social and economic conditions, including the new bureaucratic organizations of urban education. Many teachers began to feel that the time was right for them to assert themselves within the educational arena. Existing institutes and associations lacked the ability or desire to represent teachers' primary needs. With little action being taken to address their problems, they began to form separate organizations of their own (Muir, 1969). Johnson (1968) notes the feelings of British Columbia teachers towards the Institutes:

> The Institute, while serving as a forum of teacher opinion on some academic and professional aspects of their work, nevertheless denied teachers the opportunity to discuss openly their economic problems and other grievances. The paternal eye of the Department was always upon them (p. 239).

The majority of today's teachers' associations in Canada were founded between 1914 and 1920. The decline in the economic security of teachers during and immediately after the First World War reflected the reduction of teachers' salaries by school boards. As well, additional teachers were needed to meet the expansion of elementary and secondary education. The new associations promoted political and professional objectives that differed from those sought by educational institutes and associations controlled by the departments of education (Manzer, 1994).

The Saskatchewan Union of Teachers, established in 1914, was the first of what Paton (1962) refers to as the "new-style" associations. This association came into being after Saskatchewan's Minister of Education in 1913-14 rejected the teachers' presentation of grievances, which included three requests: the security of job tenure, more adequate salaries and superannuation (retirement) allowances. The Union became the Saskatchewan Teachers' Alliance in 1919 and increasingly militant attitudes developed, resulting in the famous Moose Jaw strike,[10] said to be the first recorded action of its kind by teachers (Paton, 1962; Tyre, 1968).

During this same period of time, the Alberta Teachers' Alliance, which enrolled over half of the province's teachers as members, set out demands for material benefits including tenure, sick leave and a pension scheme. Also sought were political objectives such as larger administrative units, collective bargaining and representation of teachers on committees controlling conditions of work. Over the next two decades, the ATA was notably successful in having these demands met by school boards and the Department of Education (Chalmers, 1968; Paton, 1962).

The Manitoba Teachers' Society (MTS), established at a meeting of teacher-examiners in July 1918, became incorporated by an *Act* of the provincial legislature adopted one year later. Similar to its counterparts in Saskatchewan and Alberta, the MTS was a united and closely-knit organization of teachers which from the beginning was able to avoid divisions based on geography, gender or language (Chafe, 1969; Paton, 1962).

In Ontario, the school system evolved differently and divisions based upon elementary and secondary, male and female, public and separate (Roman Catholic), French and English became rooted in the administration of schools. The Toronto Teachers' Association (TTA) and the Women's Teachers' Association (WTA) were at the forefront of organizing teachers; however, these two organizations differed with respect to their foci. The TTA conducted its semi-annual meetings along the lines of the Ontario Educational Association's, with speeches by experts and discussions related to pensions. The WTA, in contrast, focused on developing and implementing strategies to improve the working conditions of its members (Dixon, 1994; Smaller, 1988).

Shortly after the end of World War I Ontario teachers leaned toward the formation of an effective, province-wide union, an objective that was being pursued by the WTA in Toronto. The Federation of Women Teachers' Association of Ontario (FWTAO) and the Ontario Secondary School Teachers' Federation (OSSTF) were the first two Ontario provincial teachers' associations to become permanent, province-wide organizations in 1918 and 1919 respectively. One of the key items that emerged from the first meeting of the FWTAO was a concern by its leaders that "something be done towards having a fixed minimum salary that shall be more adequate than present" (Smaller, 1988, p. 272).

High school principals initiated the establishment of the OSSTF, beginning with secret letters to all high school principals in the province asking them "to send a male delegate as a representative" to a meeting. Differences quickly emerged between classroom teachers and school principals during this meeting. Classroom teachers realized that, in agreeing to the plan of action being proposed by the principals, teachers would no longer be allowed to resign from their posts for the following academic year after a certain date each spring. Eventually, this motion was carried in favor of the principals' position. Smaller (1988) notes that in many ways this debate and its outcome symbolized and foreshadowed in a significant way the direction of the provincial associations during the ensuing two decades.

On the West Coast, the British Columbia Teachers' Federation (BCTF) was incorporated under the *Benevolent Societies Act of 1917*, but there was no obligation on the part of either the local school boards or the Department of Education to recognize or bargain with the BCTF. In 1919, the Victoria Teachers' Association went on strike for two days. The school board appealed to the Department of Education to take action against the teachers but the Department refused and instead mediated the dispute, effectively recognizing the teachers' right to bargain.

As a direct result of this strike, the British Columbia government amended *The Public Schools Act* to enable a school board to enter into agreement with its teachers and to provide a weak form of voluntary arbitration. A strike by the Westminster Teachers' Association in 1921 pointed out the shortcomings of voluntary arbitration for teachers. There were no provisions for compulsory arbitration; no recognition of the local teachers' association or the BCTF; and no provision enabling or compelling a board to pay the additional salaries awarded by the arbitration board (Johnson, 1964).

The reasons leading to the establishment of these "new-style" teachers' unions were grounded in the teachers' unwillingness to mutely accept the indignities that had traditionally been the lot of the public school teacher. There was evidence of a new pride in their role and of a determination to win the recognition they felt their profession deserved (Cuff, 1967; Johnson, 1964; Muir, 1969). The acute economic difficulties that followed World War I accentuated the increasing gap between existing conditions and the expectations held by both teachers and the general public.

Among the concerns of the teachers' occupational associations were improving teachers' salaries and working conditions; establishing a code of ethics and a system of discipline as the basis for their profession; and winning a place for their associations in the educational power structure. During the next two decades, teachers' unions lobbied to advance this agenda with limited success. Table 2.2 provides a summary of the establishment of provincial teachers' unions (Smaller, 1988).

A review of the average salaries for the year 1925-26 suggests that teachers' unions were beginning to have a positive influence on teachers' salaries. British Columbia teachers earned an annual salary of $1430, followed in order by Ontario, Manitoba, Alberta and Saskatchewan, the latter with an average salary of $1119. Corresponding figures for New Brunswick and Nova Scotia were $807 and $660 (Paton, 1962).

During the early years, unions sought to improve the economic position of teachers while, at the same time, they advocated higher levels of certification. As a result, the economic status of teachers changed from that of unorganized, poorly paid individuals to that of a highly organized group demanding, and receiving, a relatively good level of remuneration (Muir, 1969). By the end of the 1920s, education had become a leading sector of the Canadian public economy and teachers had become one of the largest groups of public employees. This achievement was short-lived, however. Spending on public education declined in relative importance as the Great Depression took its toll across Canada and teachers' unions came under renewed pressure to act on behalf of their members (Manzer, 1994).

The Growth of Teachers' Federations: 1930-1960

During these three decades, one of the major changes altering the relationship between the school boards and the teachers' unions was the move toward collective bargaining. Three approaches to collective bargaining were taken: inclusion of teachers under provincial labor laws, protection of teachers' rights to bargain under specific legislation or sections of the education act, or voluntary recognition by school boards (Manzer, 1994). Before delving into these three approaches, a review of the evolution of labor relations in Canada will help to set the stage.

The *British North America Act* did not allocate responsibility for matters relating to labor relations. As a result, the courts have been

Table 2.2
Teachers' Organizations: 1861-1970

Year	Organization
1861	Teachers' Association of Canada West
1864	Provincial Association of Protestant Teachers (Quebec)
1880	Association of Prince Edward Island Teachers
1889	Newfoundland Teachers' Association
1895	Nova Scotia Teachers' Union
1903	New Brunswick Teachers' Association
1914	Saskatchewan Union of Teachers
1917	British Columbia Teachers' Federation
1918	Alberta Teachers' Alliance Federation of Women Teachers' Associations of Ontario
1919	Manitoba Teachers' Society Ontario Secondary School Teachers' Federation Saskatchewan Teachers' Alliance
1920	Canadian Teachers' Federation Newfoundland Teachers' Association Prince Edward Island Teachers' Union (now Prince Edward Island Teachers' Federation)
1921	Ontario Public School Men Teachers' Federation (later Ontario Public School Teachers' Federation)
1933	Saskatchewan Teachers' Federation
1935	Alberta Teachers' Association
1939	Association de l'enseignant français de l'Ontario (now Association des enseignantes et des enseignants franco-ontariens)
1944	Ontario English Catholic Teachers' Association
1946	Corporation générale des instituteurs catholique du Québec (since 1974 Centrale de l'enseignement du Québec)
1953	Northwest Territories Teachers' Association
1955	Yukon Teachers' Association
1969	Provincial Association of Catholic Teachers (Quebec)
1970	Association des enseignantes et enseignants francophone du Nouveau Brunswick

Source: King and Peart, 1992.

relied upon to distribute this responsibility. The federal government first assumed this role when it passed *The Industrial Disputes Investigation Act* in 1907. The constitutionality of the federal government's jurisdiction was tested and upheld in 1921, but was again challenged in the courts in the case of *Toronto Electric Commission v. Snider* (Russell, Knopff & Morton, 1993). The court found that the federal government could not bind employers within exclusive provincial jurisdiction. This decision effectively gave major responsibility for labor relations to provincial governments.

This responsibility has been affected by the *Charter of Rights and Freedoms,* which the Supreme Court of Canada has recognized as applying to public employees in their employment relations.[11] Although the provinces proceeded to model their labor laws on the federal legislation, over time they modified the laws and somewhat altered the principles originally established.

Nationally, there is still a strong similarity in the underlying philosophy on which public policies on labor relations are grounded, although the approach varies from one province to another. For example, the provinces of New Brunswick, Prince Edward Island, Ontario and Saskatchewan specifically excluded teachers from the provision of their respective labor acts. In the provinces of Newfoundland, Nova Scotia and Manitoba, teachers are not referred to in the labor acts and by practice are excluded. In British Columbia, teachers come under both the British Columbia *Labour Relations Code* and the *Public Education Labour Relations Act.* Only in Quebec and Alberta were teachers specifically included under the provisions of the labor acts (Muir, 1969). Recent legislation in Ontario has added it to the list of provinces in which teachers are included under the province's labor relations act, as recounted in chapter 7.

Canada's initial statutory framework was modeled after the United States' Wagner Act (*The National Labor Relations Act of 1935*) which granted private-sector unions recognition and bargaining rights, including the right to strike. Canadian labor policies have gone further in regulating bargaining than have those in the United States and today present more of a patch-work quilt of laws and policies. Collective bargaining tends to be fragmented and decentralized in both the private and public sectors (Grant, 1993).

As the teachers' unions moved through the 1930s, their treasuries were bare, fees were modest, and their members were required to renew and forward fees each year. The leaders of these unions sought to protect members from unnecessarily large salary cuts as the Depression deepened, and worked to maintain association membership, since dues were crucial to the unions' continued existence. Many of the provincial teachers' unions challenged cuts that were made to teachers' salaries during this period. In 1932, close to bankruptcy, Newfoundland, then a colony of Great Britain, cut expenditures drastically. Government employees' salaries were reduced by 25 percent for civil servants, 33 percent for Ministers of the Crown, and 50 percent for teachers. Furthermore, civil service pensions were cut 20 percent, while those for teachers were slashed by 50 percent. Enraged, the NTA Executive Council authorized a petition which 1100 teachers signed. The NTA succeeded in having the teachers' pensions fully restored, but the 50 percent cut in salaries remained in effect for a year (Cuff, 1985).

One significant consequence of the economic turmoil was the implementation of automatic or compulsory membership obtained from the provincial legislature by the Saskatchewan Teachers' Federation in 1935. The impetus for requesting automatic membership was the STF's loss of approximately 1000 members between 1921 and 1933.

In 1933, the Minister of Education told STF that if it could raise membership from 40 percent to 70 percent of Saskatchewan's teachers, he would see that they got their professional act. By the end of 1934, the STF had a paid-up membership of 73 percent of the province's teachers. When over 91 percent of the affected teachers declared themselves in favor of the proposed legislation, the battle was over and statutory membership for the teachers of the province became law in February 1935. The law stated that all Saskatchewan teachers in schools that received school grants from the legislature would henceforth be required to be members of the STF as a condition of their employment (Paton, 1962; Tyre, 1967). Saskatchewan teachers were the first in Canada to be granted, by provincial legislature, statutory membership with payroll deduction of membership fees.

The STF also concentrated its efforts on obtaining a statutory minimum for teachers' salaries through the provincial government, since bargaining with the large number of individual school boards in the province was extremely difficult. In 1940, over three-quarters of the teachers in Saskatchewan signed a pledge that they would not accept a teaching contract for less than $700 per year. The strategy was successful and the legislature amended *The Saskatchewan School Act* to provide the first minimum salary for teachers in Canada – $700 per year.

Following on the heels of Saskatchewan, the Alberta Teachers' Association gained compulsory membership in 1936 after the election of the Social Credit government the previous year. *The Alberta Teaching Professional Act* granted statutory membership to the Alberta Teachers' Association and established the ATA[12] as a body corporate and politic, giving a major foothold for the ATA's move toward advancing and promoting the cause of education in Alberta (Chalmers, 1968).

The ATA was the first Canadian association to obtain the specified right to bargain collectively with school boards on behalf of its teachers. This right came with the passage in 1941 of *The Industrial Conciliation and Arbitration Act*. As a result of considerable lobbying by the ATA, the Act specifically included teachers as "employees," which for the first time gave the ATA, their "bargaining agent," the specified right to bargain with school trustees on matters relating to teachers' salaries and working conditions (Chalmers, 1968; Manzer, 1994; Muir, 1969).

In 1935, three of the teachers' federations in Ontario – the Ontario Secondary School Teachers' Federation, the Federation of Women Teachers' Associations of Ontario, and the Ontario Public (Men)[13] Teachers' Association – created the Ontario Teachers' Council (OTC). The Council was composed of representatives from these federations and focused most of its attention on issues related to tenure, contracts, salary and membership.[14] At this time, membership in the teachers' federations in Ontario was voluntary and the Council believed that in order for teachers to have an effective voice in education, teaching must be looked upon as a profession that required mandatory membership. The Council lobbied the provincial government during the late 1930s and early 1940s to support this request from the teachers but the provincial government did not respond (OTF, 1965).

In 1943, the election of a minority Conservative government with George Drew as Premier and Minister of Education gave the Council renewed hope that his government would support the proposal for a teaching profession act. Premier Drew, concerned over the successful efforts of the Cooperative Commonwealth Federation (CCF) to attract teachers to its party and the possibility of teacher strikes, initiated steps to support legislation to ensure the continuation of professional development among teachers in the province (Smaller, 1988). Drew requested that the Department of Education study the OTC proposal and, in April 1944, the *Teaching Profession Act* (R.S.O. 1990, c.T2) received passage, leading to the creation of the Ontario Teachers' Federation that was composed of representatives from the five federations. In 1945, Drew led the Conservatives to an election victory, taking 66 of the legislature's 90 seats.[15] One could infer that Drew's strategy for attracting teachers away from the CCF was successful.

The five teaching affiliates associated with the Ontario Teachers' Federation in 1944 were the Federation of Women Teachers' Association of Ontario, the Ontario Public School Men Teachers' Federation, the Ontario Secondary School Teachers' Federation, L'association des enseignants franco-ontariens and the Ontario English Catholic Teachers' Association. The affiliates each represented a different teacher constituency based on religion, sex, language or level of teaching. Each teacher in Ontario was mandated to be a member of one of these affiliates and of the Ontario Teachers'

Federation. Teachers are forbidden by law to reconsider this situation, and/or to select alternatives (Smaller, 1988).[16] Although this legislation did not give teachers the right to collective bargaining, local branches of the federations often began to act as bargaining agents for their members (Muir, 1969). Each affiliate works within its own constitution and sends representatives to the OTF Board of Governors, which is the governing body of the Ontario Teachers' Federation.[17]

Prior to the passage of Ontario's *Teaching Profession Act* in 1944, officials of the Department of Education did not necessarily accept teachers' organizations as representing the collective views of teachers. However, automatic membership and dues payment included within the *Act* changed the operational basis of these teachers' federations almost overnight. Teachers' federations became union bureaucracies offering a wide range of services and benefits to their members (Spaull, 1991; chapter 4 this volume). The OTF Board of Governors established basic policies with regard to salary negotiations, including equal pay for equal qualifications, the right of each affiliate to establish its own salary schedule and general procedures to be followed in salary negotiations.

The Manitoba Teachers' Society received bargaining rights in 1948 with the passage of *The Labour Relations Act*. Teachers bargained along with industrial employees under this *Act* until 1956, when *The Public Schools Act* was amended to transfer teachers' bargaining rights from *The Labour Relations Act* to *The Public Schools Act* with the provision for compulsory, binding arbitration (Chafe, 1970).

Quebec teachers chose not to bargain under their province's 1944 *Labour Relations Act* for several reasons: Roman Catholic teachers' associations were dominated by teachers who were members of religious orders and who opposed such procedures; Protestant teachers felt such action to be "unprofessional"; and *An Act Respecting Municipal and School Corporations* gave the Roman Catholic teachers access to compulsory arbitration. While many of the Catholic teachers' association locals became certified under the *Labour Relations Act*, it was not until this *Act* was replaced by the *Labour Code of 1964* that locals of the Protestant teachers' association applied for certification. Thus it was not until 1965 before the majority of teachers in Quebec legally obtained the right to bargain (Grant, 1993).

In 1937 the British Columbia government passed an act which provided compulsory arbitration in teacher salary disputes, plus an implicit recognition of teachers' right to bargain. In that year, arbitration became a right for the teachers rather than a privilege sometimes granted by a school board. In 1958, reacting to a provision of the *Public Schools Act* that gave the trustees a right to fix salaries, the British Columbia Teachers' Federation forced 58 school districts into arbitration under the *Act*. This was enough to persuade the provincial government to amend the legislation to provide teachers the right to bargain for salaries (Johnson, 1964; Muir, 1969).

In Nova Scotia there were virtually no negotiations between teachers and trustees prior to 1953. After considerable pressure by the NSTU, *The Nova Scotia Teachers' Union Act* was amended to incorporate permissive machinery for negotiating teachers' salaries. This Act was again amended in 1956 to make conciliation mandatory at the request of either party. Thus, although negotiations machinery was included in the *Act* in 1953, the teachers of Nova Scotia did not obtain the right to bargain until 1956 (Parker, 1962).

While each province's own teaching profession act differs from others to some extent regarding statutory membership requirements,[18] all provinces require that school boards deduct association membership fees from the payroll of member teachers. Only the provinces of Alberta, Ontario and New Brunswick have followed the Saskatchewan policy of requiring that all teachers, as a condition of employment, be members of their association. The provinces of Manitoba, Quebec, Nova Scotia, Prince Edward Island, Newfoundland and British Columbia[19] provide automatic membership, though not compulsory. Teachers are allowed to opt out of the association each year during a stipulated "escape" period (Muir, 1969).

In 1935 it is doubtful that many people fully considered the significance of the breakthrough that had been made in Saskatchewan. Obtaining professional statutes and statutory membership has played a crucial role in providing the means for teachers to exercise a significant influence in provincial educational discussions. Furthermore, the "closed shop" imposed and enforced by statute has a powerful influence on the operation of the collective bargaining process (Muir, 1969; Smaller, 1988). The advantage of this type of legislation to teachers' organizations soon became evident and within two decades virtually every Canadian province had passed similar bills. In all provinces, amended versions of these acts remain in force to this day, regulating the working relations of teachers across the country (Smaller, 1995).

Beginning in the 1950s and extending over the next two decades, there was a rapid increase in demand for teachers across Canada to meet the needs of the post-war "baby boom" generation. In the case of Ontario, the 1950 *Report of the Royal Commission on Education* (The Hope Commission) stressed that consideration must be given to the effect on school enrollment of growth in total population and, consequently, to the number of additional teachers required.

> The steadily increasing school enrollment in the elementary schools has such implications with reference to the supply of teachers that, in our opinion, emergency measures are imperative. (Ontario Department of Education, 1950, p. 210)

With increased numbers of teachers at the elementary and secondary levels, teachers' federations also experienced unparalleled growth.[20] Table 2.3 contains an overview of the membership of each of the teachers' federations. With the passage of provincial professional acts or comparable legislation, teachers' organizations began to assume a new role in Canadian education. These associations began to see themselves as the "voice" of their members when it came to discussing issues related to education (Flower & Stewart, 1958). Provincial organizations of teachers and of trustees moved closer towards being viewed as legitimate channels for representation of advice to provincial policy-makers, enjoying close relationships with ministers and officials.

During the 1950s, the teachers' federations expanded their areas of interest beyond "the welfare of their members" and devoted more attention to the improvement of education. They commissioned studies related to the development of curriculum and the application of new teaching techniques and aids, supported educational research and studied merits of increasing the level of teacher qualifications (Flower & Stewart, 1958). Alberta, for example, witnessed a remarkable development in specialist associations (e.g., in English, Mathematics, etc.) sponsored by the Alberta Teachers' Association. Similarly, in 1959, the British Columbia Teachers' Federation spent $10 000 to improve the understanding and teaching of the new mathematics curriculum being introduced into the public school system. The New Brunswick Teachers' Association introduced a scholarship program to award teachers-in-training (Paton, 1962). Manzer (1994) notes that the teachers' federations were not yet, however, regarded as legitimate participants in educational policy-making, an area that remained the preserve of premiers, ministers and senior department officials.

Table 2.3
Canadian Teachers' Federation Member Organizations, 1996

Affiliate	Membership
British Columbia Teachers' Federation	31 488
Alberta Teachers' Federation	27 565
Saskatchewan Teachers' Federation	10 940
Manitoba Teachers' Society	12 877
Ontario Teachers' Federation	128 393
Provincial Association of Protestant Teachers of Quebec	5300
New Brunswick Teachers' Association	5485
Association des enseignantes et des enseignants du Nouveau Brunswick	2750
Nova Scotia Teachers' Union	10 500
Prince Edward Island Teachers' Federation	1433
Newfoundland and Labrador Teachers' Association	7689
Northwest Territories Teachers' Association	1295
Yukon Teachers' Association	427
Total	246 142

Source: Canadian Teachers' Federation, 1996.

The primary reason for the development and growth of teachers' organizations in Canada was to provide a vehicle through which teachers could improve their economic position. Teachers recognized that the economic improvements they sought could be achieved more easily through the united efforts of all teachers as a group rather than individual action. Increasing professional standards was a key part of their strategy, since higher standards could legitimize their expectations and demands. The teachers of the four western provinces, of Ontario and, to a lesser degree, Protestant Quebec and the three Maritime provinces, achieved organizational strength and some considerable success in reaching their economic goals.

New Challenges for Teachers' Federations: 1960-1998

The expansion of employment in the educational sector during the 1960s and 1970s was coupled with more liberal educational policies that arose from the release of three important provincial reports. The report of the Royal Commission of Inquiry on Education in the Province of Quebec was released in 1967 and is usually referred to as the Parent Report, after the Commission's chair, Alphonse Parent. *Living and Learning,* the report of The Provincial Committee on Aims and Objectives in the Schools of Ontario, was published in 1968 and is referred to as the Hall-Dennis Report; the

Commission's co-chairs were Justice Emmett Hall and Mr. Lloyd Dennis. The final member of this trilogy, the Worth Report (1969), was the work of the Commission on Educational Planning in Alberta chaired by Walter Worth. Each of these reports proposed a comprehensive reform of school organization and curriculum in its respective province. Their recommendations for educational reform became the framework for educational policy development across Canada for the next decade (Manzer, 1994). The changes brought on by these reports helped to support the growth of services offered by teachers' federations. Dixon notes that,

> The 1960s were the boom years, marked by a strong economy, optimism, expanding school systems, positive and growing psychological and financial support for education, higher salaries for the teaching profession, a progressive Hall-Dennis Report and new educational programmes. The 1970s represented in many ways a mirror image of the vibrant 1960s. They were an age of decline in the economy, the birth rate, and the funding of education (p. 269).

The unionization movement that swept through the private sector in North America during the 1930s and 1940s now embraced the public sector. The move to extend full collective bargaining rights to public employees started with Quebec teachers in the 1960s where, in 1964 and 1965, the private sector model was extended to the public sector. Following a period of labor strife and special legislation, Quebec established a separate bargaining system for public services. The province then established a set of procedures that highly centralized and controlled bargaining (Grant, 1993).

In New Brunswick, teachers did not have the right to bargain. They were excluded from the *New Brunswick Labour Relations Act* and no other statute gave them bargaining rights. Many school boards had, however, agreed to bargain informally with the teachers. In 1967 the responsibility for education was moved from the municipal to the provincial level and, under the 1968 *Public Service Labour Relations Act*, the New Brunswick Teachers' Association obtained the right to bargain with the government on behalf of the teachers in the province.

In December 1973, 80 000 teachers across Ontario joined together to protest the introduction of Bill 274, legislation designed to deny them the right to collective resignation.[21] At the same time, teachers did not have the right to strike. Instead, teachers' federations dealt with intransigent boards by having their members submit their resignations en masse, a tactic that was used with some success as a negotiating weapon in 17 school boards. The spreading of its use was anticipated. After a number of mass rallies across the province to protest the bill, but before Bill 274 was passed, the Legislature adjourned.

In a situation reminiscent of 1943, the 1975 election in Ontario left the Progressive Conservative party to head a minority government, which then moved to give teachers the right to strike by introducing Bill 100.[22] *The Teachers and School Boards Collective Negotiations Act*[23] passed in 1975 and provided the foundation for negotiations that endured for a quarter century. Supporters of Bill 100 believed it had created an effective regime that maintained good labor relations during difficult times; detractors believed it had tilted the playing field in favor of teachers' unions.

In practice, *The Teachers and School Boards Collective Negotiations Act* regulated collective bargaining procedures for the teachers and the school boards. It provided for the negotiation of all working conditions, established the right of teachers to strike after a series of compulsory steps, and offered voluntary binding arbitration and binding final-offer-selection as alternatives to strikes and lockouts. The legislation created a five-person Education Relations Commission to supervise disputed negotiations (R.S.O. 1990, c. S. 2, s. 60(1)). It is notable that when bargaining rights were enacted for teachers in Ontario, it was done, not as part of *The Teaching Profession Act* or as part of the province's *Labour Relations Act*, but rather as a separate and distinct piece of legislation pertaining only to teachers. Changes in 1997, however, placed collective bargaining for teachers under the provincial *Labour Relations Act*, as recounted in chapter 7. By the mid-1970s, virtually all the provinces had followed the lead of Quebec and enacted legislation giving unions the right to organize public sector workers (Smaller, 1995).

The economic recession of the early 1980s had a chilling effect on the propensity to strike among union members. Many provincial governments followed the federal lead of adopting fiscal restraint measures. The Parti Québécois government in Quebec imposed a 19 percent rollback in wages for teachers, nurses and other public sector professionals after their refusal to reopen contracts during a fiscal crisis. In British Columbia, fiscal restraints took the shape of dramatic staff cuts in the civil service and a reduced funding of school boards and municipalities. Pupil-teacher ratios were increased to their level of a decade before. Wage restraints and cuts by governments dramatized the government's determination to limit their deficits (Grant, 1993).

A number of government-sponsored reports at the time surveyed the state of elementary and secondary education in Canada. The reports[24] pointed to a shift in the economies of industrialized countries from a primary emphasis on the production of goods and resources extraction to a reliance on the provision of services based on the use of human knowledge and research. They concluded that, to compete in this new arena, provinces would require better-educated work forces. The reports recommended that provincial governments adopt policies to determine the allocation of resources in public education, the content of a common or core curriculum, provincial standards of educational achievement and mechanisms of accountability. Management, they argued, should be decentralized to schools, school councils and teaching staff, while ensuring that accountability to the policy-determining centre was preserved. They supported widening the variety of groups participating in educational decisions to include business interests that could assist schools in adapting to technological changes and deciding upon appropriate school outcomes.

In the early 1990s, another severe recession saddled governments with mounting deficits that led a series of initiatives to control and reduce expenditures, including a "Social Contract"[25] in Ontario and salary roll-backs in a number of provinces including Alberta, Nova Scotia and New Brunswick. Other reductions implemented on a permanent basis caused school boards to reduce the number of consultants and support staff that aided teachers in the classroom. Subsequent initiatives in most provinces shifted power away from school boards toward tighter provincial control of finances, curriculum and overall management of their school systems.[26] While funding for educational programs has been reduced, teachers find that they are still expected to attain better results.

Conclusions

This chapter provided an overview of the evolution of teachers' unions in Canada and highlighted a number of the key issues that have played an important role in the unfolding of teacher unionism in Canada. Teachers' unions have affected education through negotiating formal contracts, initiating changes in the nature of relationships between teachers and administrators, and reshaping the political context of school policy-making (Kerchner & Mitchell, 1983).

Unionism has altered the role of teachers as they interact with schools and what actions they take when dissatisfied. Unionism has also changed the definition of teacher loyalty and the interaction of teachers with social and education reforms. In education, as in the case of most occupations, rules help to define the nature of work. Unionization has had a major impact on the rule-making machinery in education and on the specification of the web of rules that govern teaching. In addition to affecting the work of teachers and teaching as an occupation, unionization has shifted the relationship between teachers and the organizations in which they work. Principally, the teacher/school district relationship was altered by the new rules of how one behaved when dissatisfied, unhappy or angry. Before unionism, teachers had the option of accepting their employment setting as it was, of leaving to find another job or requesting generosity from the employer. Teachers' unions gave dissatisfied workers an authoritative voice for issuing their complaints and proposing changes that would better accommodate their needs (Kerchner, 1986; King & Peart, 1992; Muir, 1969).

In Canada there are 14 provincial teachers' associations, all but one of which is affiliated either directly or indirectly with the Canadian Teachers' Federation.[27] The current interests and activities of teachers' organizations across Canada are varied but common themes do emerge. The original objectives of these associations were to improve teachers' salaries and working conditions, to establish codes of ethics and systems of discipline as the basis for their profession, and to win a place for the association in provincial educational power structures. Many teachers' federations have attained considerable success in collective bargaining for salaries and, while there is evidence of greater co-operation between teachers' organizations, trustees and provincial authorities in addressing problems, economic crises repeatedly test these relationships to the full – sometimes leading to their disruption (Johnson, 1968; King & Peart, 1992; Muir, 1969; Smaller, 1988).

Achievements of teachers' organizations include improved teacher-training programs, greater disciplinary powers for federations, and better pension schemes. In many provinces, teachers' organizations participate in curriculum design and school building programs and have deepened support for smaller class sizes, particularly at the elementary level (Flower & Stewart, 1958; Muir, 1969; Grant, 1993).

While the successes of teachers' unions have been significant, giving teachers a recognizable voice on issues outside of their classrooms, the events of the past few years point to a shift in the locus of educational policy making away from the educational arena in which teachers, trustees and government officials prevailed into the political arena in which major provincial parties compete. Teachers look to their unions to protect teachers' interests and to ensure that there are adequate resources available to local school districts. Provincial teachers' unions have been outspoken in their criticism of educational decisions of many governments during the past decade as the resources allocated to education, as well as other public services, have declined. Overall, the current climate of relations between teachers' unions and their respective provincial governments is in a state of flux. Whether or not this situation continues depends on economic trends, political negotiations and the creation, perhaps, of better structures and processes for resolving disputes.

References

Althouse, J. (1967). *The Ontario teacher 1800-1910.* Toronto: Ontario Teachers' Federation.

Axelrod, P. (1997). *The promise of schooling: Education in Canada 1800-1914.* Toronto: University of Toronto Press.

Bacharach, S. & Mitchell, S. (1989). *Strategic choice and collective action: Organizational determinants of teacher militancy.* Washington, D.C.: National Institute of Education.

Bascia, N. (1994). *Unions in teachers' professional lives: Social, intellectual, and practical concerns.* New York: Teachers' College Press.

British Columbia. (1988). *Royal Commission on Education. A legacy for learning: The report of the Royal Commission on Education.* Victoria: Queen's Printer for British Columbia.

Chafe, J. (1969). *Chalk, sweat, and cheers: A history of the Manitoba Teachers' Society commemorating its 50th Anniversary 1919-1969.* Saskatchewan: The Hunter Rose Company.

Chalmers, J. (1968). *Teachers in the Foothill Province.* Toronto: University of Toronto Press.

Chalmers, J. (1968). Battle of long ago. *ATA Magazine, 49* (1), 17-19.

Clarke, S. (1968). Wither the Alberta Teachers' Association. *ATA Magazine, 49* (1), 45-48.

Corsetti, C. (1992). Benchmarks and assessments in Ontario. *The Reporter: The Magazine of the Ontario English Catholic Teachers' Association, 17* (3), 35-36.

Cuff, H. (1967; 1985). *A history of the Newfoundland Teachers' Association 1890-1930.* St. John's: Creative Publishers.

Downie, B. (1978). *Collective bargaining and conflict resolution in education: The evolution of public policy in Ontario.* Kingston: Queen's University Press.

Downie, B. (1992). *Strikes, disputes, and policy making: Resolving impasses in Ontario education.* Kingston, ON: IRC Press.

Fergusson, N. (1970). The first twenty-five years of the Nova Scotia Teachers' Union. *Province of Nova Scotia Journal of Education, 19* (3), 31-43.

Flower, G. & Stewart, G. (1966). *Leadership in action: The superintendent of schools in Canada.* Toronto: W.J. Gage Limited.

French, D. (1968). *High button bootstraps: Federation of Women Teachers' Associations of Ontario, 1918-1968.* Toronto: Ryerson Press.

Glegg, A. (1992). Five years of teacher self-governance: The British Columbia College of Teachers. *Journal of Educational Administration and Foundations, 7* (2), 46-61.

Grant, M. (1993). Canada. In B. Cooper (Ed.), *Labor relations in education: An international perspective* (pp. 29-50). Westport, CN: Greenwood Press.

Johnson, F. (1964). *A history of public education in British Columbia*. Vancouver, BC: University of British Columbia Publication Center.

Kerchner, C. (1986). Union-made teaching: The effects of labor relations on teaching work. *Review of Research in Education, 3*, 317-352.

Kerchner, C. & Mitchell, D. (1983). Labor relations and teacher policy. In L. Shulman & G. Sykes (Eds.), *Handbook of Teaching and Policy*. New York: Longman Publishers.

King, A. & Peart, M. (1992). *Teachers in Canada: Their work and quality of life*. A National Study for the Canadian Teachers' Federation. Kingston, ON: Social Program Evaluation Group.

Lawton, S. (1989). Public, private, and separate schools in Ontario: Developing a new social contract for education. In W. Boyd & J. Cibulka (Eds.), *Private schools and public policy: International perspectives*. NewYork: The Falmer Press.

Lawton, S. (1995). Ontario's "Social Contract": Tightening the screws on education. *Journal of Education Finance, 20*(3), 302-311.

Lawton, S. (1996). *Financing Canadian education*. Toronto: Canadian Education Association.

Manzer, R. (1994). *Public schools and political ideas: Canadian educational policy in historical perspective*. Toronto: University of Toronto Press.

Muir, J. (1969). Canada. In A. Blum (Ed.), *Teacher unions and associations: A comparative study*. Chicago: University of Illinois Press.

Nason, G. (1965). The Canadian Teachers' Federation: A study of its historical development, interests, and activities from 1919 to 1960. *Ontario Journal of Educational Research, 7* (3), 297-302.

Noel, S. (Ed.). (1997). *Revolution at Queen's Park*. Toronto: James Lorimer & Company, Publishers.

Ontario. (1950). *Report of the Royal Commission on Education in Ontario* (The Hope Commission). Toronto: Printer to the King.

Ontario. (23 April 1993). Ministry of Finance News Release. Toronto: Queen's Printer, 2.

Ontario Teachers' Federation. (1965). *OTF at 20: Recollections of the First Two Decades of the Ontario Teachers' Federation*. Toronto: Ontario Teachers' Federation.

Parker, T. (1963). *A history of the Nova Scotia Teachers' Union: Its struggles and achievements 1950-1963*. Halifax, NS: Nova Scotia Teachers' Union.

Paton, J. (1962). *The role of teachers' organizations in Canadian education*. Toronto: W.J. Gage Limited.

Paton, J. (1961). *The professional status of teachers*. Ottawa: Canadian Conference on Education.

Radwanski, G. (1988). *Ontario study of the relevance of education, and the issue of dropouts*. Toronto: Ministry of Education.

Russell, P., Knopff, R. & Morton, T. (1993). *Federalism and the Charter: Leading constitutional decisions*. Ottawa: Carleton University Press.

Smaller, H. (1988). *Teachers' protective associations, professionalism and the "state" in nineteenth century Ontario*. Unpublished doctoral dissertation. University of Toronto.

Smaller, H. (1995). The teaching profession act in Canada. In C. Gonick, P. Phillips & J. Vorst (Eds.), *Labour gains, labour pains: Fifty years of PC 1003, Socialist Studies, 10*. Winnipeg: Manitoba: Society for Socialist Studies.

Smiley, D. (1980). *Canada in question: Federalism in the eighties*. Toronto: McGraw-Hill Ryerson Limited.

Smiley, D. (1987). *The federal condition in Canada*. Toronto: McGraw-Hill Ryerson Limited.

Spaull, A. (1991). Fields of disappointment: The writing of teacher union history in Canada. *Historical Studies in Education, 3* (1), 21-48.

Stamp, R. M. (1982). *The schools of Ontario, 1876-1976*. Toronto: University of Toronto Press.

Tanguay, A. B. (1997). "Not in Ontario!" From the Social Contract to the Common Sense Revolution. In Sid Noel (Ed.), *Revolution at Queen's Park*, (pp. 18-37). Toronto: James Lorimer & Company, Publishers.

Tyre, R. (1968). *Tales out of school: A history of the Saskatchewan Teachers' Federation*. Toronto: W.J. Gage Limited.

The Teachers and School Boards Collective Negotiations Act. R.S.O. 1990 c. S. 2: as amended S.O. 1996, c. 1, Schedule Q, s. 5, 1996, c. 12, s. 66 [Repealed 1997, c. 31, s. 178].

VanLoon, R. & Whittington, M. (1987). *The Canadian political system: Environment. structure, and process*. Toronto: McGraw-Hill Ryerson.

Notes

[1] A number of authors, including Bachararch (1989), Bascia (1994) and Kerchner (1986), employ the terms union, organization and association interchangeably. Their precedent is followed in this chapter.

[2] Section 95 established concurrent federal-provincial powers in matters of agriculture and immigration. Amendments to the Act in 1951 and 1964 added a third concurrent power in the area of pensions.

[3] Manzer (1994) notes that the *BNA* assigned general legislative and administrative jurisdiction over education to the provinces, but did not erect any constitutional impediments to federal expenditures for educational purposes where the provinces agreed to accept federal aid or if federal transfer payments were made directly to individuals. There are three areas where the federal government does have constitutional jurisdiction: public education in federal territories, federal schools for defense establishments and federal schools for Native children. The intervention by the federal government into provincial jurisdiction over elementary and secondary education has consisted of a series of incentive grants designed to promote the expansion of vocational education and the teaching of French and English as second languages.

[4] Since education in Canada is a provincial responsibility, one needs to consider that schools in the provinces and territories are not similarly structured with regard to grade organization. In Quebec, elementary school extends from kindergarten to grade 6 and secondary from grade 7 to grade 11. At the end of grade 11, Quebec students attend a CEGEP where they are prepared in two years for university or in two- or three-year programs for careers. In Ontario, secondary school begins in grade 9 and is typically five years. Courses for university admission are designated as Ontario Academic Credits (OACs). In the remaining provinces and territories, Grade 12 is the final year of secondary school

(King & Peart, 1992). Ontario plans to phase in a four-year secondary school program commencing in 1999.

[5] Quebec schools were realigned along linguistic lines in 1998 after passage of a constitutional amendment.

[6] Newfoundland's schools became non-denominational in 1997 after passage of a constitutional amendment.

[7] The mission of normal schools was to elevate the tone of school training. Provincial education officials contended that consistent certification rules were required to achieve these ends. However, incoming teachers were not always required to attend normal schools in order to ensure their suitability for teaching. For example, in Nova Scotia in the 1860s, candidates were examined in five subject areas by a provincial board. Individuals would then be licensed with a certificate grade ranging from A to E, depending on how well they had performed on the exam (Axelrod, 1997).

[8] The Nova Scotia Teachers' Union as we know it today was not organized until 1920.

[9] Dr. J. G. Althouse, in *The Ontario Teacher, 1800-1910*, stated the salary of a teacher in 1855 was equal to the wages of a driver of an oxen. Dr. W. Parmelee reported that in 1911 the average teacher's salary in the rural county of Stanstead, Quebec, was $162 per year, or $13.59 per month for 12 months (Paton, 1962).

[10] The Moose Jaw strike closed all the schools in the City of Moose Jaw and was the first teachers' strike in Saskatchewan. The strike was due to teachers' dissatisfaction with the salary schedule that was being offered by their local board. Refer to Tyre (1967) for an account of the Moose Jaw strike.

[11] See *McKinney v. University of Guelph* (1990), 76 D.L.R. (4th) 545; and *Lavigne v. O.P.S.E.U.* (1991), 81 D.L.R. (4th) 545.

[12] The Alliance became the Association and the terms of the Act restated the aims and objectives of the organization that had been laid down in 1918.

[13] The Ontario Public Men Teachers' Federation removed the word Men from its title in 1982.

[14] The matter of security of tenure and establishment of a proper contract pre-dates the formation of OTF. The *Teachers' Board of Reference Act* became law in 1938 and the basic, standard permanent contract was adopted in Regulations in 1943. The major work was done through the Ontario Teachers' Council from which the OTF evolved in 1944. The *Board of Reference Act* made it possible for either party to the contract to request the Minister of Education to grant a board of reference. Nothing in the legislation made the findings of a board of reference mandatory.

[15] After the 1943 election, Conservatives held 38 seats, Liberals 16, CCF 34 and others 2. In the election of 1945, Conservatives claimed 66 seats, the Liberals 14, the CCF 8 and others 2. The CCF was the precursor to the New Democratic Party (Tanguay, 1997, p. 22). See also Stamp (1982, pp. 179-181).

[16] Compared to other unions, teachers' unions typically possess a high degree of influence which permits a federation and its local affiliates to "regulate" members through tribunals and disciplinary committees for infractions of ethics and or/etiquette (Smaller, 1988). With the establishment of the Ontario College of Teachers in 1998, this situation is in a state of flux in Ontario.

[17] Lam (1990) refers to the OTF as a "paper tiger" because the five teachers' affiliates are very autonomous in the day-to-day running of their organizations.

[18] While the legislation varies in detail in the different provinces, it is essentially the same in principle. In actual practice, it requires persons entering teaching to become members of their professional teachers' organization, or society, as the case may be, with respect to compliance with a code of ethics and other established regulations (Flower & Stewart, 1958). Creation of colleges of teachers to oversee the profession in British Columbia and Ontario provide for a separation of professional and economic interests. See footnote 16.

[19] In 1987, the British Columbia Social Credit government announced that compulsory membership legislation for teachers would be replaced to allow teachers to decide between professionalism and unionism. Under the new *Teaching Profession Act*, teachers across British Columbia would be required to select one of the two structures. Over 95 percent of all teachers re-joined the British Columbia Teachers' Federation as individual and voluntary members and voted for union rather than professional status. Remaining teachers were then required to join BCTF or be dismissed. The new *Act* also excluded principals and vice-principals from union membership by designating them as administrative officers, and created the College of Teachers (Glegg, 1992; Smaller, 1995). See chapter 6 for a detailed analysis of British Columbia.

[20] Ontario Ministry of Education statistics report that in 1965 the number of full-time teachers at the elementary and secondary level was 61 195 compared with 119 706 in 1993. In comparing these data, consideration needs to be given to the extension of public funding to Roman Catholic Secondary schools beginning in 1985 (Ontario Ministry of Education, 1993).

[21] Events leading up to the passage of this *Act* included an increase in the level of conflict between teachers and employers. The strike of secondary school teachers in Windsor in 1974 set a precedent in Ontario. For the first time in the history of the province, teachers in a school system by collective decision deemed themselves to be on strike despite personal contracts with the boards which obliged them to be in their classrooms. When the dispute was settled, it gave Windsor teachers the most lucrative contract in the province and it also established conditions which granted them some determination of school policy and management (Harp & Betcherman, 1980).

[22] In 1975, the Tories won 51 seats, the Liberals 36 and the New Democratic Party 38. An election two years later, unlike that of the 1945 election, did not return to a majority Conservative government. In 1977, the Progressive Conservatives won 58 seats, the Liberals 34 and the NDP 33 (Tanguay, 1997, p. 22).

[23] It is notable that while the province of Alberta passed legislation in 1937 requiring local boards to bargain collectively with teachers, the same guarantee came to Ontario 38 years later.

[24] *Ontario Study of the Relevance of Education, and the Issue of Dropouts* (Radwanski, 1988). This report was followed by *People and Skills in the New Global Economy* (Queen's Printer, 1990) and the Economic Council of Canada's *A Lot to Learn: Education and Training in Canada* (Ottawa: Supply and Services, 1992). The Economic Council of Canada report found that young people were lacking in the basic skills needed for

lifelong learning and work in a technological society and that these shortcomings could be attributed to the public educational system. These reports recommended a shift in educational philosophy from one that was individually based to one embracing a general curricula not structured for the individual interests of students. The child-centered approach was an integral aspect of the 1968 report entitled *Living and Learning*. This report stressed that a school should serve all of its children comfortably and humanely in child-centered programs and should develop learning experiences that would match the needs of each.

[25] The NDP adopted multiple approaches which included a $2 billion increase in income taxes, an increase in sales taxes by $1.6 billion, a $4.4 billion reduction in government spending which was expected to eliminate about 10 000 positions in the public sector, and a $2 billion in compensation negotiated through a "social contract" with the public service (Ontario, 1993).

[26] In Ontario, key recommendations were made by the Royal Commission on Learning, co-chaired by Monique Bégin and Gerald Caplan. Other members were Manisha Bharti, Avis Glaze and Dennis Murphy. Their report was titled *For the Love of Learning*. The Ontario College of Teachers, which was proclaimed into law in July 1996 and commenced operation in 1997, was recommended in the report.

[27] In Quebec there was one Protestant association, an English association and a French Catholic association (which was not affiliated with the Canadian Teachers' Federation). On January 1, 1998, after passage of a constitutional amendment, Quebec's schools were realigned along linguistic lines.

3

Labor Relations Legislation

... a just share of the fruits of progress to all.

Canada Labour Code

Today's powerful teachers' unions evolved from weak associations of educators formed early in this century. Their most rapid development took place during the peak of the baby boom years of the 1960s and 1970s when, after a period of intense political conflict, provincial governments granted full collective bargaining rights including, in most cases, the right to strike.

The purpose of this chapter is to explore the nature of collective bargaining and the laws that govern it in elementary and secondary education in Canada. These laws, probably taken as part of a static legal framework by the average citizen or teacher, are in fact subject to change. They provide the rules of the game to be abided by during a process that can be wracked with tension. Their purpose, as in any game, is to keep the players moving toward their goals without having ritualized conflict deteriorate into civil disorder.

Collective Bargaining Laws

The intent of laws governing the relations between employers and employees reflects both pragmatics of civil government and the ideals of particular social visions. The Preamble of the *Canada Labour Code*, the original model for provincial labor legislation applicable to teachers, provides an informative example. It emphasizes:

1. The "promotion of the common well-being through the encouragement of free collective bargaining and the constructive settlement of disputes."
2. Recognition and support of "freedom of association and free collective bargaining as the bases of effective industrial relations for the determining of good working conditions and sound labour-management relations."
3. A belief that the "development of good industrial relations to be in the best interests of Canada in ensuring a just share of the fruits of progress to all."

Underlying the emphasis on good relations is recognition that labor disputes, reflecting at times fundamental conflicts of interest, can deteriorate into dangerous confrontation. At the same time, endorsement of collective bargaining as a mechanism for ensuring that all receive a "just share of the fruits of progress" reflects a view that both labor and owners have implicit rights to the profits that the economic system can generate. While tax laws, particularly the progressive income tax, and broad public services, particularly in education and health, are also mechanisms for achieving this aim, labor laws govern what is perhaps the most direct means of allocating national income: the compensation of employees.

Ross (1978) classifies the various sections usually included in labor legislation into 12 sections; though derived from an analysis of state laws and regulations applicable in the United States, the framework is appropriate for Canadian laws in most regards. The 12 sections consider the intent of legislation, who is covered by the law, the definition of bargaining units, oversight of the collective bargaining process, management rights, the scope of bargaining, the resolution of disputes, grievance procedures, and a number other matters. Each of the 12 areas is described in some detail. Subsequently, a tabular analysis of current Canadian labor relations laws for teachers is provided.

Statement of Intent

A labor law's purpose embodies ideals in an overarching vision that gives form to the entire piece of legislation. While not stated in concrete terms, as are other parts of the law, the intent of the legislature in passing the law, as expressed in its preamble, can be critical in legal interpretations of the law by the courts. Alterations in statements of intent may reflect changes in social philosophy, concerns about imbalances in power between unions and management, or a perceived need to adapt legislation to changing economic circumstances.

Coverage and Definitions

The designation of types of employees who are covered under the law, together with the identity of the bargaining agent for management, are specified in order to define the scope of the law. There may be separate legislation for the public and private sectors; within the public sector, there may be separate legislation covering different sectors, such as elementary and secondary education, municipalities, etc. Typically restrictions are stated in clauses that, for example, deny bargaining rights to senior level administrators who report directly to governing boards or to support staff who handle confidential material related to the management side of bargaining. Definitions provide explanations for terms such as "collective agreement," "bargaining agent" and "arbitrator."

Bargaining Unit Designation

A bargaining unit may be designated by statute or may result from a result of a certification process that requires some form of expression of support by the majority of the qualifying employees. In the latter case, some agency, such as a labor relations board, oversees the process and grants certification for a period of time during which the unit has the exclusive right to represent and negotiate on behalf of the group of employees represented.

Bargaining Unit and Union Security

One of the crucial issues and problems in labor relations is defining who is, and who is not, in a particular bargaining unit. In some cases, a general labor law may cover all employers and employees in a province, and allow employees to sort matters out for themselves. In others, legislation may define the members of a bargaining unit by specifying all those working for an employer (or a group of employers) who hold similar positions or certification. Usually, "bargaining units must be 'appropriate' and reflect a 'community of interest'" (Ross, 1978, p. 3). Collective agreements apply only to the specific units for which they are negotiated. Different units working for the same employer may, as a result, have very different contracts.

The "community of interest" that a unit embodies does not extend to management, which includes those whose incumbents act as employers for the purposes of hiring and dismissing employees, assigning responsibilities and the like. The line between management and labor is often not clearly drawn and is often a matter for dispute in and of itself. In such cases, a labor relations board ultimately may decide the issue.

Union security refers to the protection that a union is offered by specific clauses that may appear in collective agreements, in regulation, in legislation, or in legal judgements. Examples include the automatic collection of dues by the employer for the unit, access to the employers' mail systems for distribution of materials, etc. When these and other privileges are subject to collective negotiations, union membership by bargaining unit members and payment of dues are matters of high priority for unions. The weakest arrangement, from a union perspective, is the "open shop" in which membership in the union and payment of dues are not required of bargaining unit members covered by a negotiated contract. If membership of all of the employees who are covered is not required, but dues or fees must be paid to the bargaining unit, then the arrangement is termed an "agency shop." A "union shop" exists when anyone hired into a position covered by a negotiated contract must join the union within a specified period of time; with a "closed shop" all new employees in a bargaining unit must already be dues-paying union members. In Canada, union shops are the norm for elementary and secondary teachers; at the post-secondary level, a variety of arrangements exist – non-union, agency shops and union shops. However, in Canada open shops do not exist; if a bargaining unit is certified, an agency shop is created due to the application of the so-called "Rand Formula," discussed in more detail later. Conversely, in the United States, both union and closed shops are banned, for all practical purposes, since the courts have held that "membership" carries with it only the obligation to pay dues, creating the so-called "financial core members" over which unions have negligible disciplinary authority. Their only sanction is for non-payment of dues. That is, they have no legal manner of punishing those who ignore directives to participate in strikes or other actions against employers (Thornicroft, 1990).

Middle-Management Provisions

Mid-level management may or may not be included within a bargaining unit for professional categories of staff, such as teachers. If they are not in a comprehensive unit by definition, they may have the right to decide to join that unit or not, or the right to form a bargaining unit of their own, or they may be barred from collective bargaining altogether. In elementary and secondary education, the boundaries of middle management may be unclear – whether it reaches down to department heads in schools or up to assistant superintendents of education. Ross (1978, p. 3) notes, "There are some who feel that administrators such as principals and assistant principals should be allowed bargaining rights, lest they be squeezed out by teachers and school boards during the bargaining process. The other side of this point of view is that these classifications are definitely 'management' and should not bargain, unless as part of the management team."

Administration of Bargaining Process

In Canada, responsibility for labor relations is split between the federal and provincial levels. Federal responsibility, covered by the

Canada Labour Code, concerns enterprises with national operations, including banks, transportation companies, federal civil service and the like, and includes only about 10 percent of the workforce. The remainder of the workforce, including those in education which is a provincial responsibility under the *Constitution Act (1867/1982)*, come under the jurisdiction of provincial and territorial legislation, creating a "crazy quilt" pattern of legal structures for labor relations (Gunderson & Hyatt, 1996).

Administering the federal law is the Canada Labour Relations Board. Labor legislation in the provinces or territories designates one or more agencies similarly responsible to provide assistance and decision-making procedures to those engaged in the bargaining process (Table 3.1). This assistance may include recognition, deciding unit composition, settling of disputes that reach an impasse (including fact-finding, conciliation and arbitration), grievance procedures, ruling on unfair practices, appeal processes, and the collection and distribution of information useful in facilitating the bargaining process (Ross, 1978).

Scope of Bargaining and Management Rights

The intent of labor relations laws, that is, to ensure good working conditions and a "just share of the fruits of progress," are open to many different interpretations. To ensure sharper focus and to reflect a particular philosophy of administration, these terms typically are refined to include or exclude specific matters, although even these refinements are further interpreted by regulations, previous decisions by labor relations boards and the courts. In some cases, legislation for collective bargaining in education specifies that wages, benefits, class size, preparation time, length of the school day and the like are to be bargained. In other cases, bargaining may be restricted to salaries and benefits; in yet others, the boundaries are not specified or are specified by defining some areas that are not to be bargained; i.e., that are reserved as "management rights."

Impasse Procedures

Impasse may occur during bargaining over interests – e.g., compensation – or in settling disputes over employee or employer rights, e.g., a grievance. When a bargaining unit and management cannot agree on a contract, either party may decide to use sanctions against the other. To prevent these actions whenever possible, procedures to facilitate a settlement are normally outlined by law, regulations or, when legislation is silent on the matter, in individual contracts. Typical procedures begin with mediation or conciliation and may move to fact-finding and arbitration. Mediation is the use of a third party to "meet with the two parties on the dispute, together and/or separate, in order to perform a catalytic function in an effort to reach an agreement" (Ross, 1978, p. 61). Fact-finding is a "process of determining accurate facts and information to be used as a basis for recommendations for the resolution of a contract dispute." A fact-finder's report may be confidential or, after a period, released to the public with a view toward placing public pressure on the parties to resolve their dispute. Arbitration, the strongest of the three, is a procedure that involves the use of a third party to decide the issues at hand. "The arbitrator(s) will study the problems and, in accordance with mandated or agreed-upon procedures, come up with a final decision . . ." (Ross, 1978, p. 4) which, depending on procedures, may be the "final offer" of either party or a settlement composed of decisions on each item in dispute. Arbitrators may be limited to deciding certain issues only (e.g., wages) and may make binding decisions or be limited to advising the labor relations board.

Usually, a timeline is set out indicating when bargaining should commence and when it should be completed. If an impasse occurs, there is also a time line for moving through each stage from mediation to arbitration.

Gunderson and Hyatt (1996, p. 263) report that, between 1987 and 1994, 51 percent of public sector negotiations in Canada were settled at the bargaining table, 23 percent were settled through conciliation and mediation, 5 percent through arbitration, 3 percent with strikes and subsequent agreements, and 16 percent with legislation, including "social contracts" – that is, with government-mandated public sector agreements. While interest arbitration is relatively rare, rights arbitration is widespread, being guaranteed by statute in all jurisdictions.

Grievance Procedures

Grievances, in labor relations parlance, refer to complaints by labor or management related to, especially, the application and/or interpretation of negotiated agreements. Internal grievance procedures provide for a series of steps for the parties to follow in order to reach a settlement by negotiation or by the decision of an internal body. External grievance procedures involve an independent third party to make a binding, nonconsensual decision.

Traditionally, if there were no clause in an agreement that clearly pertained to a complaint, then it normally was not a candidate for the grievance process. Recent Supreme Court of Canada decisions in *Weber v. Ontario Hydro* [1995] 2 S.C.R. and *New Brunswick v. O'Leary* [1995] 2 S.C.R. (see www.droit.umontreal.ca) have, however, greatly extended the jurisdiction of the grievance arbitrator. Persons may grieve as individuals or as members of a bargaining unit; if they choose the latter route, they may have the full fiscal and legal support of the bargaining unit. The procedures themselves may be outlined in law, regulation or policy, or be set down as part of a negotiated agreement. As with impasse resolution, the process may include mediation and arbitration, although mediation is relatively rare. British Columbia has an experimental program that has had some success.

Grievance procedures are critical to unions as they often serve as the central mechanism for enforcing clauses in an agreement to ensure that they are not violated. Filing and pursuing grievances may be used as a tactic to press management to change its behavior between periods of collective negotiation. It is common for unresolved issues originally raised in grievances to appear in clauses that union representatives place on the table for negotiation.

Unfair Labor Practices and Sanctions

Since a major objective of labor law is to prevent disruptions that may lead to violence or public danger – i.e., to promote the common well being – legislation typically outlaws some disruptive behaviors but permits others with some restrictions. Unfair labor practices of the employer generally include interference with employees' and/or employees' organization's rights under the bargaining law. This infringement may include "hiring and employment discrimination, dismissal of employees because they exercise their rights under the law, communication with employees other than through their authorized representative(s) during the bargaining process, and refusal to bargain in good faith and violations of written contracts" (Ross, 1978, p. 5). Given that Canadian teachers belong to certified bargaining units as a matter of law, unfair labor practices meant to weaken unions that are common in the private sector are unusual in the education sector. However, in the case of province-wide bargaining, if matters are not going well, governments can legislate solutions to which teachers have little or no recourse. Laws that normally offer protection may be over-ridden and, if teachers refuse to obey, severe financial penalties may be imposed on individuals and unions alike.

Strikes, slowdowns and lockouts by employers may be allowed, permitted on a restricted basis or considered as an unfair labor practice. A strike typically is defined as a cessation of work or a refusal to work by employees acting in concert or a slowdown that is designed to reduce or limit output. Under this definition, "working-to-rule" by teachers might be considered a strike if teachers refuse to mark examinations or supervise co-curricular activities that are considered by management to be part of their continuing responsibilities. As a result, their employer could withhold full or partial payment of wages. Although teachers and teachers' unions may believe such activities are not contractual obligations, much is not spelled out in the "hand shakes" that seal employment contracts, particularly where professionals are concerned. The full range of obligations covered by teachers' contracts is a gray area that is subject to legal judgements, arbitration, mediation, negotiations and legislation.

In 1995, eight provinces allowed teachers to strike; two, Manitoba and Prince Edward Island, did not, instead ending disputes by binding arbitration at the request of either party (and sometimes by Minister's order) (Gunderson & Hyatt, 1996, p. 251). In contrast, municipal workers were allowed to strike in all ten provinces, but police in only four (British Columbia, Saskatchewan, Manitoba and Nova Scotia). Elsewhere, police disputes go to arbitration. Evidently, a police strike is generally seen to be a greater threat to "common well-being" than is a strike by teachers. Gunderson and Hyatt note that even when the strike is allowed, "general legislation often exists stipulating that employees providing essential services may be [or will be] required to continue working during a strike. . . . . Furthermore . . . having the right to strike can mean little, if in fact the government constantly invokes back-to-work legislation, wage controls or the suspension of the collective agreement" (p. 151-2).

Penalties for unfair labor practices may be trivial or substantial. Typically, a charge of unfair labor practices results in an investigation by the labor relations board, a finding of who is at fault, cease and desist orders and/or a court injunction. Employees, their organizations and employers may be subject to fines, dismissal and imprisonment if unfair practices do not stop once court orders have been made.

Open Meeting Provisions

Most public bodies, such as school boards and municipal councils, are considered corporate bodies that can only engage in their public duties during open sessions. Conferring or decision-making out of the public's eye may be considered collusion. While this issue is not normally treated in labor legislation, the legitimacy of closed-door collective bargaining sessions has been viewed as a violation of democratic principles by writers such as Fuller (1997). In practice, as long as the beginning and end of the process – the end being ratification by the public body – are in public sessions, the public interest is viewed as being protected. The give-and-take of negotiations is typically conducted in private sessions – a practice often defended either out of pragmatics or on the basis that negotiations represent personnel matters that should be shielded from public view. When negotiations are confined to financial matters, this issue is not critical; but when they are of broad scope and include issues that touch upon the core educational services, this issue is fundamental to the provision of local democratic oversight for schools.

Final Form and Timeline

Legislation may require that the negotiated contract be placed in written form and be made available to employees. Timelines are set out that may determine the term of the contract, its beginning and ending date, and the like. Terms of contracts are particularly critical in the public sector since the annual budgetary process requires coordination between revenue generation and expenditures on operations according to fixed schedule mandated by law.

Provincial Legislation

Table 3.1 reports eight traits of provincial labor laws as they apply to elementary and secondary teachers in each province. These eight characteristics include the legal reference, coverage of bargaining units, number and type of bargaining units, scope of bargaining, bargaining impasse procedures, the right to strike and educational funding mechanisms.

Five provinces have special legislation for elementary and secondary teacher collective bargaining or include relevant legislation within their public schools acts. One, New Brunswick, includes collective bargaining for teachers under public-sector labor relations legislation. Four provinces, Quebec, Ontario, Alberta and British Columbia, have general labor relations legislation that encompasses both the public and private sectors, including of course teachers. However, in all cases, additional legislation that is part of the education act clarifies the nature of bargaining units and the agent with which the units bargain. In New Brunswick bargaining is done between the teachers' union and the ministry of finance, which represents the executive branch of government in negotiations. In Newfoundland, centralized tri-partite negotiations include the teachers' union, government represented by the Departments of Treasury Board and Education, and school boards, represented by the Newfoundland and Labrador School Boards Association. In British Columbia, Nova Scotia and Saskatchewan, committees representing trustees and government at a central table negotiate major issues such as salary, while relatively minor issues are bargained locally. Ontario, Manitoba and Alberta retain local collective bargaining between teachers' unions and school trustees, even though both Ontario and Alberta now fund education provincially. Quebec has a unique system with several stages, with a three-year cycle of negotiations that cascades from the entire public sector, to education, to local school districts.

Centralized bargaining does not by any means solve labor relations issues. Trustees in Saskatchewan have deferred participation in their shared central bargaining process which, in their view, has led to settlements that are unaffordable at the local level. As well, the first two rounds of province-wide bargaining in British Columbia (see chapter 6) ended in stalemate, with the province stepping in to conduct negotiations.

In all provinces, essentially all elementary and secondary school teachers are specifically covered by labor relations legislation of one type or another. Other employees of school districts, in contrast, typically fall under general labor relations legislation – which means that their bargaining units are not specified in law as are those for teachers. As a result, various unions may offer their services as agents to one or more groups of employees. Formerly, bound by a philosophy linked to traditional craft or contemporary professional unionism, teachers preferred to have their own exclusive organization. As teachers' unions have adopted the industrial union model whose "distinguishing characteristic is membership based upon employment in an industry regardless of occupation or skill, rather than employment in a particular skilled occupation, as in a craft union" (OCAW, n.d), they have become more likely to form alliances with associations serving job categories other than teaching or to simply enter into the fray and attempt to organize employees themselves. Industrial unionism, whose strength is based on numbers, arose in response to demands by unskilled and semi-skilled workers in the factories and mines of the industrial age. Craft unionism, which traces its history to medieval guilds, gains power through the critical nature of the skills practiced by specialists within and across large enterprises. Some writers believe that the adoption of the industrial model by teachers' unions is driven by existing legislation which discourages excessively close relations between labor and management in order to preserve labor's independence and prevent union leadership from "selling out" to management (e.g., Kerchner, 1998).

Established unions across Canada are very competitive in offering their services to potential clients. Surprisingly, the fastest growing union in Canada is now the United Steelworkers of America, which gained 30 000 members between 1996 and 1997 while other unions were stable or declining (Human Resources Development Canada, 1997). It recently won the loyalty of support staff workers at the University of Toronto, in competition with the Canadian Union of Public Employees, which has traditionally organized public educational institutions. Unlike school teachers, most employees in Canada are able to select their bargaining agents based upon a competitive process.

In six provinces labor relations for teachers are administered by labor relations boards of some type. Comprehensive boards are responsible in Newfoundland, Ontario, Alberta and British Columbia. New Brunswick's Public Service Relations Board is responsible for educators in that province, where all educators are now civil servants in light of the province's decision to abolish elected school boards in the early 1990s. Saskatchewan maintains an Education Relations Board to oversee labor relations in education. Ontario's Education Relations Commission formerly administered the labor law for teachers. After recent legislative changes, detailed in chapter 7, the Commission lives on in a reduced capacity, collecting and analyzing work force data. In other provinces, the minister of education or labor is responsible for the fair administration of labor relations legislation for education.

The scope of bargaining is specified in the legislation of only six provinces, as far as we could determine. In two- or three-tier bargaining, salaries and major benefits are invariably negotiated centrally, with non-financial matters left to the local level. Where specified, the scope of bargaining is relatively narrow, specifically excluding, as in the case of New Brunswick and Ontario, discussion of class size and preparation time. Under general labor legislation working conditions, including workload, would normally be a negotiable issue.

When impasses occur, all provinces provide for conciliation or mediation. Arbitration is available as well, with compulsory binding arbitration the final stage in Prince Edward Island and Manitoba, and in Quebec between the three-year cycle of province-wide negotiations. Otherwise, arbitrators' decisions do not carry the force of law. Where binding arbitration is not the final stage of an impasse resolution procedure, the employees have the right to strike that is matched by the employers' right to lock out employees. Strikes and lockouts do not resolve disputes in and of themselves; in fact, they may make matters worse, destroying what trust and good will existed between employees and employers. Withdrawal of services is most effective when employees play a critical function and where no other suppliers exist. The failure of a service interruption to provide sufficient economic or political damage to employers may lead to attempts to impose other sanctions, such as sympathy strikes, boycotts or different forms of intimidation. Courts, in considering requests for injunctions to force employees to return to work, and legislatures entertaining back-to-work legislation, are likely to be influenced by collateral damage which may threaten the general welfare.

Underlying the bargaining process is the political and economic allocation of resources, including the levying of taxes and distribution of revenue. Traditionally, Canadian provinces, like U.S. states, have operated shared systems of school finance, with provinces "topping up" local tax revenue. Often school grant systems were designed to stimulate local spending by reducing the cost to local taxpayers of funding. While successful in many ways, these grant schemes sometimes encouraged profligacy in some quarters while, elsewhere, a lack of adequate local resources meant that the provincial incentive to spend more went unheeded. In the name of equity and cost control, increasing numbers of provinces have moved toward full provincial funding. At last count, only Quebec, Manitoba and Saskatchewan had left independent taxing powers in the hands of local trustees. Whether centralized school finance necessarily leads to centralized bargaining is as yet an unanswered question. In any case, when no table is set aside for formal bargaining, interested parties will turn to lobbying legislatures to realize their hopes and forestall their fears.

Table 3.1
Provincial Employment Relations Legislation for Teachers

	NEWFOUNDLAND & LABRADOR	PRINCE EDWARD ISLAND
Legal Reference	<u>Newfoundland Teacher Collective Bargaining Act, 1973, No. 114.</u> Prov. bargaining. Mgmt. team & chief negotiators chosen by Minister of Treasury Board with trustee & admin. representation.	<u>School Act, 1993 c. 35 (Bill 31)</u> and Regulations. Provincial bargaining with representation from school boards.
Coverage	All K-12 teachers.	All K-12 teachers
Employee Classification	11 school boards: 10 Anglophone & 1 Francophone.	3 school boards: 2 Anglophone and 1 Francophone.
Bargaining Unit	One bargaining unit for all teachers. Newfoundland Labour Relations Board may exclude persons deemed "part of management."	Bargaining unit comprises "instructional personnel," (teachers employed by regional school boards & designates of Minister of Education). Excluded: superintendents & assistant superintendents.
Type of Representation	Newfoundland and Labrador Teachers' Association	Prince Edward Island Teachers' Federation.
Administration	Newfoundland Labour Relations Board	Minister of Labour
Scope of Bargaining	Not specified.	Not specified.
Bargaining Impasse Procedures Grievance Procedures	1. Conciliation officers and 2. Conciliation Board 3. Arbitration Board (voluntary) Either party may apply in writing to Chair of LRB to appoint a conciliator from the Dept. of Manpower and Industrial Relations whose Minister may order a board to be appointed. Both Parties must request arbitration.	Minister of Labour may appoint a conciliation officer and arbitration board. Either party can request arbitration or Minister of Labour may opt for arbitration. Compulsory binding arbitration is the final stage of negotiations.
Strikes	Strikes are legal 7 days after report of Conciliation Board.	No strikes.
Education Funding	Entirely funded by province from general revenues.	Provincial funding from general revenues with a provincial tax levy.

	NOVA SCOTIA	NEW BRUNSWICK
Legal Reference	Teachers' Collective Bargaining Act, 1974 c.23. Two-tiered system with provincial and local bargaining.	Public Service Labour Relations Act, RSNB, 1973. Provincial bargaining.
Coverage	All K-12 teachers.	All K-12 teachers.
Employee Classification	7 school boards: 6 Anglophone and 1 Francophone.	No school boards. Parent councils at schools with regional and provincial advisory committees. Anglophone and Francophone schools.
Bargaining Unit	Local bargaining units of teachers. Excluded from bargaining unit: superintendents, supervisors of schools and principals.	One provincial unit. Excluded from bargaining unit: a person who has executive duties in policy development and administration.
Type of Representation	Nova Scotia Teachers' Union.	New Brunswick Teachers' Federation.
Administration	Minister of Labour and Manpower (Chief Justice of Nova Scotia in default.)	Public Service Relations Board (Chair).
Scope of Bargaining	Provincial jurisdiction: salary and allowances. Local jurisdiction: sick leave, sabbatical leave, education leave.	Negotiable: rates of pay, hours of work, standards of discipline. Not negotiable: preparation period, class size, leave of absence for professional activities, educational leave, retirement allowance.
Bargaining Impasse Procedures Grievance Procedures	Conciliation officer is appointed by Ministry of Labour and Manpower. Mediation officer may be appointed by Minister of Labour and Manpower.	At the request of either party in writing, the Chair of PSLRB may appoint a conciliator or a commissioner. If the parties are unable to reach an agreement they may submit to binding arbitration by notice to secretary of the PSLRB.
Strikes	Legal at provincial level and illegal at local level.	Legal if one or more of nine conditions are met.
Education Funding	Funded by province from general revenues and mandatory property taxes collected by municipalities.	Provincial 100 percent funding from general revenues including provincial property tax.

	QUEBEC	ONTARIO
Legal Reference	An Act Respecting the Process of Negotiation of Collective Agreements in the Public and Private Sectors 1985, c.12; The Labour Code RSQ 1977. Provincial bargaining under employer committees.	Labour Relations Act and the Education Quality Improvement Act (1997) (Bill 160). Local bargaining.
Coverage Employee Classification	All employees: teachers, non-teaching professionals & support staff. School boards now organized on linguistic lines. Employers organized into Anglophone and Francophone management committees.	K-12 Teachers & support staff may be in same union but are separate bargaining units. 116 school boards: 31 Anglophone & 4 Francophone public, 30 Anglophone & 7 Francophone Catholics, plus 44 isolates.
Bargaining Unit Type of Representation	Bargaining units include employees except those in a supervisory or representative position.	Local bargaining units of teachers in one or more of 4 unions, as of July 1, 1998. Occasional teachers in bargaining units. Principals, vice-principals & supervisory staff (board level) excluded from teacher bargaining units.
Administration	Minister of Labour	Ontario Labour Relations Board
Scope of Bargaining	3 bargaining tables: Central: salaries, parental leaves, pension plans, regional disparities. Sectorial: work load, job security, other major working conditions. Local: major and minor working conditions.	Working conditions such as preparation time, length of work day/year and class size removed from local bargaining by Bill 160. Local bargaining: mainly non-financial issues but includes school staffing.
Bargaining Impasse Procedures Grievance Procedures	Compulsory mediation can be requested by either party; will be held for not more than 60 days. If no agreement, the mediator will report & make recommendations to the Minister of Labour. Arbitration award must provide written reasons for the decision. If mediator/arbitrator makes no decision, he/she must still make recommendations. Award is binding for 1 to 2 years.	Provisions under Ontario Labour Relations Act prevail: time lines, precedents, conditions, etc. LRA provides that notice to bargain be served by either party within 90 days before the existing collective agreement ceases to operate. Thereafter, the parties must meet within 15 days to bargain in good faith. May seek conciliation services, and may be assisted by a conciliation board and/or mediation services.

Strikes	Strikes or lockouts permitted only for provincially negotiated items after compulsory mediation followed by a 20-day cooling off period.	No strike or lockout may occur until 16 days have elapsed following a no-board report by Ministry of Labour. Strikes allowed if they follow provincial Labour Relations Act. Principals and Vice-principals not permitted to strike. No provision in LRA for work-to-rule.
Education Funding	84 percent from provincial grant and 11 percent local property tax levies.	Provincial funding from general revenues including a provincial levy on property.

	MANITOBA	SASKATCHEWAN
Legal Reference	Public Schools Act, RSM 1987, c.p.250 (Bill 72) Local bargaining.	The Education Act, 1995 Provincial and lcoal collective bargaining. Two-tiered system with provincial government & trustee bargaining committee.
Coverage	All K-12 teachers.	All K-12 teachers.
Employee Classification	57 school boards: 56 public and 1 Francophone.	124 school boards: 89 public, 21 Catholic, 8 Francophone and 6 joint.
Bargaining Unit	The bargaining unit includes all teachers defined as holders of certificates and employed by a board. Not included in the bargaining unit: superintendents, assistant superintendents.	The Education Relations Board may include or exclude persons as teachers for the purpose of collective bargaining based on their duties and responsibilities and the criteria for inclusion/exclusion developed for provincial bargaining.
Type of Representation	Manitoba Teachers' Society.	Saskatchewan Teachers' Federation.
Administration	Minister of Education	Chairman of Education Relations Board (ERB)
Scope of Bargaining		At provincial level, salaries & benefits, including pensions, are negotiated. Local bargaining on local issues and working conditions.
Bargaining Impasse Procedures Grievance Procedures	Mediator/Arbitrator appointed at request of either party after 60 days of notice is given (precludes possibilities of conciliation). If either conciliation or mediation is unsuccessful, compulsory binding-arbitration follows. Excluded from arbitration: staffing, staff evaluation, class size, schedule of recesses, mid-day lunch break. Local ability to pay must be taken into account. Bill 72 imposes duty of fairness and a failure to comply can be changed through the grievance process set out in collective agreement.	Either party may request in writing that the Chair of ERB establish a conciliation board. ERB may appoint mediator at any time. Arbitration is compulsory if both parties select mediation-arbitration option. Arbitration is voluntary if conciliation-strike option selected.

Strikes	Strikes are illegal.	Strikes are legal at provincial and local levels if conciliation-strike option selected but illegal if mediation-arbitration option selected.
Education Funding	Primarily provincial funding out of general revenues and provincial levy on property. School board levied local property taxation provides 25 percent of funding.	Province provides 40 percent through provincial grants; boards generate 60 percent of funding from property tax base through locally determined levies.

	ALBERTA	BRITISH COLUMBIA
Legal Reference	Labour Relations Code, 1988, c.L-1.2 (Bill 22). School Act, c.S-3.1, 1988. Local collective bargaining.	Labour Relations Code 1992, c.82 (Bill 84). Public Education Labour Relations Act, c.21 1994 (Bill 52). Provincial and local collective bargaining.
Coverage	All K-12 teachers.	All K-12 teachers.
Employee Classification	66 school boards: 42 public, 21 Catholic and 3 Francophone.	59 school boards: 58 public & 1 Francophone educational authority.
Bargaining Unit	ATA represents all teachers in local bargaining units. LRC excludes persons from coverage who exercise management functions or who are employed in a labor relations capacity. But the Alberta School Act provides that inclusion of administrative, supervisory or consultative positions in collective bargaining may be negotiated between parties.	BCTF is agent for province-wide bargaining unit. BCTF bargains with employers' association. Excluded from teacher bargaining units: assistant superintendents or administrative officers (directors of instruction, principals or vice-principals.)
Type of Representation	Alberta Teachers' Association.	British Columbia Teachers' Federation.
Administration	Labour Relations Board and Minister of Labour.	Labour Relations Board and Ministry of Labour.
Scope of Bargaining		All major economic issues must be negotiated provincially: salaries, benefits, workload including class size restrictions, hours of work and paid leaves.
Bargaining Impasse Procedures Grievance Procedures	1. Disputes Inquiry Board (DIB). 2. Mediator. 3. Single Arbitrator or Arbitration Board (Voluntary). DIB may be established at request of Ministry of Labour before strike or lockout. Parties to a dispute may agree in writing to refer matters in dispute to either a single arbitrator or a 3-member arbitration board.	Conciliation: 1. Fact Finder. 2. Industrial Inquiry Commission. Mediation: 1. Mediation Officer. 2. Special Mediator. LRC encourages mediation. The Code added new options to improve the grievance arbitration process, including expedited arbitration and informal mediation-arbitration.

Strikes	Legal. Mediation is compulsory prior to supervision of strike vote by LRB, with 14-day cooling-off period.	Legal only on provincial basis but must meet four conditions. Strikes prohibited during collective agreement.
Education Funding	Province provides all funding under block grant system. Equal amounts come from general revenue sources and property taxes levied by the province. School boards may seek elector approval to levy tax on property to a maximum of 3 percent of budget allocation.	Provided entirely by province under a block grant system. Access to property tax through referenda (not used in practice).

References

Canada Labour Code, R.S.C. 1985, c.L-2.

Fuller, H. L., Mitchell, G. A. & Hartmann, M. E. (October 1997). *The Milwaukee Public Schools' Teacher Union Contract: Its history, content, and impact on education.* Milwaukee: Institute for Transformation of Learning, Marquette University.

Gunderson, M. & Hyatt, D. (1996). Canadian public sector employment relations in transition. In D. Belman, M. Gunderson & D. Hyatt (Eds.), *Public sector employment in a time of transition* (pp. 243-281). IRRA Series 1996. Madison, WI: Industrial Relations Research Association.

Human Resources Development Canada Workplace Information Directorate. (1997). *1997 Directory of labour organizations in Canada.* Ottawa: Canadian Government Publishing.

Kerchner, C. T. (1998). Organizing around quality: Examples and policy options from the frontiers of teacher unionism. Paper presented at the "Teacher Unions and Educational Reform Conference," September 24-25, Kennedy School of Government, Harvard University.

OCAW (Oil, Chemical and Atomic Workers International Union). (n.d.). *The OCAW and labor movement histories*: http://ext.ilr.cornell.edu/labor/ocaw/6.htm#OCAW

Ross, D. J. (October 1978). *Cuebook – State education collective bargaining laws.* Report No. 1, 578-9. Denver, CO: Education Commission of the States.

Thornicroft, K. W. (December 1990) Unions, union dues and political activity: A Canada/U.S. comparative analysis. *Labor Law Journal*, 41(12), 846-855.

4

Canadian Teachers' Unions as Organizations

We dedicate ourselves to the professional excellence and personal well-being of teachers.

Newfoundland and Labrador Teachers' Association

How do Canadian teachers' unions function as organizations? What are their goals and objectives, organizational structures, day-to-day activities, politics and stances on public issues? To answer these questions, we describe, in generic terms, what teachers' unions tell us about themselves through their various publications and through the Internet sites that most unions maintain. Such documentation is in some cases detailed and transparent and in others quite modest in terms of the amount of information available to the researchers. Specific examples are used to add concreteness to this detail. What emerges from this description is a composite picture of teacher unions, a pastiche of what we know about them as they exist on the cusp of the 21st century.

One should bear in mind that no two teachers' unions are alike and that their histories, sizes, memberships and contexts differ not only across Canada but also in some cases within a single province. Teachers in most provinces belong to a single provincial professional organization that enrols teachers of all levels, from kindergarten through secondary school. Some have specialized sub-associations for primary teachers, administrators and so forth, but in some provinces, such as Ontario, membership is parcelled out to several different entities divided on panel (elementary or secondary), religion (public secular or Separate Roman Catholic) and language (English- or French-speaking). Until July 1998 gender was also the basis of two different unions that represented educators in Ontario public elementary schools. Because of Ontario's plurality of associations, an umbrella organization, the Ontario Teachers' Federation, helps to coordinate association activity with provincial executives, but this does not limit the autonomy of any association to act independently if its provincial executive feels such a course is in the interest of its membership.

Who is included in union membership also varies. While most provincial teacher unions include principals and vice-principals in their bargaining units, recent legislation in British Columbia and Ontario has excluded them from bargaining units on the principle in labor law, widely applied in other sectors, that their supervisory roles preclude such inclusion. Many teacher associations also have members who hold non-teaching positions in custodial, maintenance and office support services. The inclusive term "educational workers" sometimes is used to refer to teaching and non-teaching personnel. For example, 41 percent of the British Columbia Teachers' Federation membership are educational assistants, clerical, administrative officers, other professionals and other support staff. Some associations, such as the Nova Scotia Teachers' Union, also represent post-secondary educational workers such as community college personnel. Non-teacher unions such as the Canadian Union of Public Employees (CUPE) also represent a large contingent of educational support workers in several provinces.

In Ontario, membership drives for non-teaching personnel have led to charges of "raiding" against the Ontario Secondary School Teachers' Federation by other unions. This broadening of membership beyond individuals with teaching certificates, who are required by statute to belong, reflects a shift in philosophy of some federations away from professional or craft unionism, that emphasizes specialized skills and apprenticeship, to industrial unionism, which emphasizes the number of members. The different types of unionism reflect different and sometimes incompatible philosophical, political and technical foundations for employee collective organizations. On the need for teacher unions to expand their membership in order to fund further struggles with the provincial government and school districts, Earl Manners, the President of the Ontario Secondary School Teachers' Federation, declared:

> Through the ravages of the Social Contract and the downsizing and restructuring initiatives of the Harris Tories, we have suffered losses in our membership and fee income. While we are confident that, in the longer term, OSSTF's record of service will continue to make OSSTF the union of choice for educational workers in all job classes and all parts of the education sector, we must be prudent in managing our resources so that our ability to respond to any sudden challenge remains unimpaired. We must not minimize the magnitude of the challenge before us. We must continue an aggressive campaign of organizing new members and bringing new bargaining units into our Federation (President's Address to the OSSTF Annual General Meeting, March 14, 1998).

Mission Statements

Teacher unions' documents typically begin with a mission statement and a statement of principles that provide an entry point to understanding how their members articulate the basic purposes of their professional organizations and the values and principles that anchor these activities. While some of these statements are part of the historical legacy of teacher organizations that have remained constant from the first days of collective association, other statements are more recent, reflecting the adoption of new values and assumptions about appropriate methods for serving their members.

Mission statements reflect the underlying purpose of teachers' unions, encapsulating the basic services, duties and tasks that such organizations perform on behalf of their members. Each union has a general mission, mandate or objectives statement and each sub-unit, such as collective bargaining or professional development, may have a specialized mission or mandate statement.

The six objectives of the Saskatchewan Teachers' Federation (STF) are consistent with those of other teacher unions and generally reflect the belief that the basic purposes of teacher unions are to promote better working conditions and compensation for their members, and to protect the legal rights of teachers. To achieve these ends, they work to enhance the professionalization of teachers, to influence public opinion on public education and to shape public policy on matters educational and beyond. Implicit in these statements is the assumption that what is good for teachers through advocacy, lobbying and negotiating is good for public policy. Implicitly and explicitly, they hold that benefits accruing to teachers also benefit the clients of publicly funded education: the students, their parents and guardians, and taxpayers who support this public service. The specific purposes of the STF are

1. to promote the cause of education in Saskatchewan;
2. to raise the status of the teaching profession;
3. to promote and safeguard the interests of teachers and to secure conditions that make possible the best professional service;
4. to influence public opinion regarding educational problems;
5. to secure for teachers a greater influence in educational affairs;
6. to afford advice, assistance and legal protection to members in their professional duties and relationships.

The Newfoundland and Labrador Teachers' Association mission statement reads: "Through educational leadership and service, we dedicate ourselves to the promotion of the professional excellence and personal well-being of teachers, through support, advocacy and the development and delivery of outstanding programming."

The mission and principle statements of the Ontario English Catholic Teachers' Association (OECTA), while in accord with the six STF objectives, adds particular features that recognize how their membership differs from their secular brothers and sisters. They state that, "Recognizing our uniqueness as teachers in Catholic schools, we are an Association committed to the advancement of Catholic education. As teacher advocates we provide professional services, support, protection and leadership." OECTA, unlike its secular counterparts, declares that it will "promote Catholic values" and "promote spiritual growth in our members." It usually falls to local separate school boards or districts to fashion mission statements that apply to Catholic teachers in provinces such as Saskatchewan and Alberta where there are provisions for public funding of a separate school system, but where Catholic teachers are not organized into separate unions. The Alberta Teachers' Association's mission statement reads: "[The ATA], as the professional organization of teachers, promotes and advances public education, safeguards standards of professional practice and serves as the advocate for its members."

Structure

Like other professional associations, teachers' unions must operate in accord with the formal legal requirements set out in provincial frameworks pertaining to the formation of corporations. Formal legal recognition is often provided in provincial legislative acts, chiefly school, teacher or education acts, as described in chapter 3. Each association is governed by a constitution that outlines the objectives or goals of the organization, the services to be offered to members, and the internal committee structure. Also included are descriptions of who is to be eligible for membership, a listing of officers and where the head office is to be located, a description of the annual or biannual general meetings and the rules for deliberation and debate, such as *Robert's Rules of Order*. An amending formula for the constitution and sometimes a detailed description of the roles and duties of important officials, such as the president and the general secretary, are included. By-laws usually spell out the powers of the association, various types of membership (e.g., statutory, voluntary, life and honorary) and formal affiliations. Teacher associations are required to release annual reports that detail yearly activities, amendments to the constitution, a description of the budget and an audited statement reporting revenues, expenditures, and surpluses or deficits.

The by-laws describe where and when the general meeting(s) or convention is to be held and the nature of its business. Agendas may include action items calling for the approval of goals and objectives, setting of membership fees, and receiving and approving financial statements. General policies may be adopted or modified, resolutions proclaimed, a provincial executive elected and reports received from the standing committees, work groups, networks and councils. Other business deemed necessary also is transacted. At the general meeting, voting members include unit presidents and delegates from local units, whose numbers are stipulated in the by-laws, as is the percentage of voting delegates that constitutes a quorum.

At the annual general meeting the provincial executives are nominated and elected, often for two-year terms. Provincial executives may consist of the president; the immediate past-president; first, second and third vice-presidents; treasurer; and councillors. All of these are collectively called table officers. Also on the executive is the general secretary or executive director and deputies, and in some cases district representatives. The larger the association, the longer the hierarchy. Provincial presidents and first vice-presidents usually serve on a full-time basis for a two-year period, with the former acting as the chief spokesperson and representative of the association. Usually, the president is a member of all provincial committees, work groups, networks and project teams, calling and presiding over meetings of the association and provincial executive. In the absence of the president, the vice-presidents and councillors, in hierarchical fashion, perform the required duties. The treasurer keeps the financial records in good order for internal and external scrutiny.

The main tasks of provincial executives are to provide leadership on educational issues and to oversee the formulation and implementation of policy. Policy guidelines are usually in written form and included in association handbooks along with other salient documents such as the constitution and by-laws. Provincial executives also interpret the application of policy, guiding staff and committees in areas where policy guidelines do not exist. Executives also direct permanent staff in developing programs, receive and deliberate reports and recommendations from representatives and staff, deal with problems directed to them, and strike and disband committees, panels and task forces as needed. Provincial executives exert much energy in preparing budgets and responding to resolutions adopted at annual general assemblies. Discipline investigations, grievances and other teacher employment problems, including negotiations, are central functions, as is the appointment of executive staff. Provincial executives are also charged with representing associations to governments, liaison with provincial organizations and national organizations, and with the representation to the Canadian Teachers' Federation.

In 1997, the Provincial Executive Council of the Alberta Teachers' Association met a total of 18 days in eight regular meetings and one special meeting. Clearly, the day-to-day direction of the ATA, and other associations, is entrusted in the hands of its full-time elected executives such as the president, executive assistants and non-elected permanent staff who support the president's work, and the elected table officers.

While the assembly of delegates, known as the annual general meeting, is the supreme governing body, it is difficult to assess how much leverage the assembly actually has. For most associations the assembly is a hectic two-day affair with electioneering for a new executive and an array of committees, speech-making, sabre-rattling, declaring and debating of resolutions, procedural wrangling, and of course socializing and partying. Ministers of education, presidents of school board associations, and the president of the Canadian Teachers' Federation bring greetings. In addition, financial statements and budgets are presented, honorary memberships conferred, reports presented and adopted (e.g., minutes, the president's address, the annual report, council and committee reports) and presentations made by keynote speakers. Aside from resolutions made from the floor brought by branch delegates standing in line behind microphones, much of the agenda of such an assembly is by necessity organized by provincial executives.

Resolutions that delegates to the general assembly make from the floor reflect the broad mandate that they hold for their union officials and can be categorized under at least six headings: curriculum, teacher education and certification, education of children with special needs, collective bargaining, pensions and governance. Occasionally, administrative directives instruct the provincial executive to take particular courses of action. Provincial executives also present their own resolutions to the assemblies. Resolutions must be debated and voted upon before they are accorded the status of association policy and subsequent action to implement them is the responsibility of the provincial executive. In 1998, at general assemblies, the Nova Scotia Teachers' Union heard and debated 75 resolutions, the Saskatchewan Teachers' Federation 90 resolutions, and the Alberta Teachers' Association 190 resolutions! In part, this flurry of activity reflects their interest in political and economic issues during a period of considerable controversy.

The general secretary or executive director is a non-voting member of the executive who is employed by the association on a contract basis. This individual manages the secretariat or permanent staff of the association and handles daily business as directed by the provincial executive. Typical duties include recording minutes, keeping records, carrying out instructions of the provincial executive, handling and depositing monies, and receiving written complaints of a breach of association constitution, by-laws, policies or procedures. General secretaries are often chosen from the ranks of former elected provincial executives. A board of governors, chosen from the ranks of the provincial executive and union activists from across the province, oversees the general governance of teacher associations.

The council of presidents or its equivalent is an important body in association governance. It consists of all local unit presidents or their designates and the elected members of the provincial executive who are voting members. Also on the council as non-voting members may be chairpersons of standing committees, work groups, networks and the principals' council, where applicable. Such councils share decision-making capacity in conjunction with the provincial executive between general meetings or conventions. They have a range of policy-related duties, including supervision of the implementation of policy and formulation of interim policies. They also define and supervise the budget and matters of financial import, receive reports of other governance bodies, prepare the agenda for the general meeting, authorize provincial meetings, ratify or reject collective agreements, scrutinize projects, approve secretariat contracts, and establish units and their boundaries.

Numerous provincial standing committees, work groups and networks deal with a range of topics: awards, collective bargaining, communications and public relations, educational aid, equal opportunity and anti-racism, religion (where applicable), finance, health and safety, legislation, occasional teachers, personnel, political advisory, professional development, secondary schools and teacher education. Special-interest councils, also a feature of teacher associations, are established by a specified minimum number of teachers who have an interest in an established subject area, type of service, interdisciplinary project or in a particular area approved by the provincial executive. Often, these relate to particular curricular or professional development initiatives sought to advance teachers' work at the school-level.

Each association may also have district levels composed of a number of branch units, each with its own executive, council and district committees paralleling those in the provincial organization. The key element in the association's hierarchy starts at the bottom with members who are organized into association units consisting of branch affiliates, or combinations of branch affiliates, and the members of an occasional-teacher local, if one exists. The council of presidents (or equivalent) grant unit status; unit by-laws must be consistent with provincial constitutions and unit by laws must be approved by the provincial executive. Each unit elects its own set of elected officers (i.e., president, vice-president, treasurer and secretary) who work to promote the interests of the association. They report to the general secretary any alleged breach of association constitution and policy, and report on alleged unfairness on the part of a school board/district and on any professional difficulties between members of a unit. Units send delegates to general meetings and provincial conferences, approve and levy local fees, establish local budgets and disburse funds in accordance with members' directives. A public accountant must carry out regular audits of local budgets. Records of unit activities and finances are kept by the secretary and forwarded to the provincial executive upon request.

In consultation with members, local executives set priorities for negotiating collective agreements, but they are also required to keep the provincial office informed of progress in this matter, and to ensure that initial proposals are consistent with overall association policies. Units must consult the provincial office before proceeding to any of the following: fact-finding, mediation, arbitration, final-offer selection, strike and communicating with any governmental agency concerning negotiations. A branch may request assistance from the provincial office for negotiations or may request that the provincial executive negotiate on its behalf. Provincial negotiating teams may consist of one secretariat member, one provincial executive member, and one representative of the branch affiliate.

All but one of the provincial and territorial associations are affiliated with the Canadian Teachers' Federation, which was founded in 1919 (see table 2.3). The members of the CTF are the organizations, not individual teachers. The CTF's policies and activities are determined by an annual general meeting and administered by a board of directors to which member organizations appoint one or more representatives, depending on the size of the organization. The objectives of the CTF are
1. to advance the cause of education and the status of the teaching profession;
2. to serve the interests of members by:
    a. acting as the collective voice of teachers at the interprovincial, federal and international levels;
    b. facilitating the sharing of ideas, knowledge and skills;
    c. providing assistance on request, within limits of CTF policy;
    d. fostering research;

e. co-ordinating and conducting international assistance; and
3. to co-operate with other organizations, in Canada and elsewhere, sharing similar goals.

The Money Side

The main source of income for teacher federations is the revenue from the fees charged to members, prorated if the individual is employed less than full-time. A secondary source is revenue from investments and services or products sold to members or to school districts, such as curriculum units or professional development services. Annual fees vary on a provincial basis and are set by the provincial executive after approval at the general meeting, with a national average fee of $700 in 1997/1998 (1.40% of an average salary of $50 000). Fees may also include contributions to contingency funds that are used for political and strike purposes, and these contributions are not usually described as part of the "basic fee." Nevertheless, annual contributions, usually in the form of a percentage of salary, to the contingency fund are a regular part of what each member is required to pay to the provincial association in exchange for membership. The British Columbia Teachers' Federation is the only association that bases fees on a percentage of salary while others levy a flat rate. For 1997/1998, table 4.1 reports annual membership fees for full-time teachers, based on an average salary of $50 000 per annum, in descending order.

Teachers' associations rely on paid staffers who attend to the day-to-day business of bargaining, professional-relations services, professional development, finances, research and administrative support. Not surprisingly, the size of this bureaucracy is directly correlated to association membership and revenues. The Nova Scotia Teachers' Union lists nine executive staff, two intermediate staff and five support staff. The Federation of Women Teachers' Association of Ontario, before its merger with the Ontario Public School Teachers' Federation, had 24 executive assistants, two assistant secretaries, four administrative assistants and three organizers. The secretariat and support staff of the Ontario English Catholic Teachers' Association numbers 25. The Saskatchewan Teachers' Federation has 13 administrative staff at the executive-assistant level or higher and 47 general support staff. The Alberta Teachers' Association has 27 administrative staff and 94 general support staff. The British Columbia Teachers' Federation has 40 administrative staff and 100 general support staff, and the Manitoba Teachers' Society has 29 administrative staff and 33 general support staff.

**Table 4.1
Annual Membership Fees for Teachers' Unions**

- British Columbia Teachers' Federation: $1535 plus local fees between $250 and $600.
- Saskatchewan Teachers' Federation: $1017.
- Ontario Public School Teachers' Federation: $825.
- Association des enseignantes et des enseignants franco-ontariens: $750.00 plus additional local fees between $25 and $200.
- Manitoba Teachers' Society: $724.
- Ontario English Catholic Teachers' Association: $710.
- Federation of Women Teachers' Associations of Ontario: $650.
- Northwest Territories Teachers' Association: $650.
- Prince Edward Island Teachers' Federation: $650.
- Provincial Association of Protestant Teachers of Quebec: $613 plus local fees averaging $315.
- Alberta Teachers' Association: $597.
- Ontario Secondary School Teachers' Federation: $590.
- Association des enseignantes et des enseignants francophones du Nouveau-Brunswick: $568.
- Yukon Teachers' Association: $550.
- New Brunswick Teachers' Federation: $519.
- Newfoundland and Labrador Teachers' Association: $500.
- Nova Scotia Teachers' Union: $500.

In 1997 the Alberta Teachers' Association disbursed approximately $6 500 000 in salaries and benefits for its executive, program and support staff. The Saskatchewan Teachers' Federation expended about $3 541 900 in staff salaries and benefits; the Manitoba Teachers' Association paid out $2 500 000 for governance that included staff, presidents' council, and committees and various meetings. The Nova Scotia Teachers' Union budgeted approximately $1 500 000 for professional and office staff and $300 000 for employee benefits.

Publicly accessible information on the remuneration of provincial executives is not consistently available for all associations. For the few associations that do provide such information, and from anecdotal evidence, we do know that several presidents and vice-presidents receive a compensation and benefits package on a par with superintendents or directors of education in their respective provinces. For the president's salary, several associations employ a formula, setting the salary at 1.6 times the salary of a teacher at the maximum on the teacher pay scale. In the 1996/1997 budget of the Ontario Public School Teachers' Federation, salary and benefits for the president were $132 000, with an additional $31 000 for expenses and miscellaneous, and $43 400 for relocation costs for a total of $206 400. The first vice-president received $120 069 in salary and benefits, with $28 017 for expenses and miscellaneous, and $39 224 for relocation for a total of $187 310. In the same year the Alberta Teachers' Association listed an expenditure of $117 079 (with no breakdown of salary/benefits) for its president and an expenditure of $834 753 for its executive. The president of the Saskatchewan Teachers' Federation was paid $86 000 plus $15 000 for expenses for a total of $101 000, and Nova Scotia Teachers' Union budgeted for its president $93 000 in salary and $33 000 in expenses.

The revenue available to teacher associations is expended in four budget areas, including 1) transfer payments, 2) governance, 3) programs and services and 4) property. Transfer payments include rebates to locals which average about 15 to 20 percent of fees, membership fees to the Canadian Teachers' Federation, which were $19.30 per teacher for 1998, and payments to the CTF in support of initiatives by Canadian teachers for projects in developing countries. Expenditures on governance represent the costs of conducting general meetings, meetings of the provincial executive, and maintaining full-time elected executives such as the president and in some cases the first vice-president. Programs and services expenditures are used to provide administrative support to continue activities including direct services to members, communications and public relations, and the costs associated with staffing the organization with professional, intermediate and support staff. Of services to members, teacher welfare includes such items as committees, legal assistance and advice, collective bargaining, teachers' dental and vision plans, group life insurance, income protection and retirement programs. Property expenses refer to those costs associated with maintaining the office building including taxes, maintenance and insurance.

The following thumb-nail sketch of the 1996/1997 budgets of two teacher unions – one small, the Nova Scotia Teachers' Union, and one large, the Alberta Teachers' Association – helps to illustrate where the money comes from and where it goes on a yearly basis.

The revenue according to the audited actuals of the fiscal year ending February 29, 1997, of the Nova Scotia Teachers' Union are provided in table 4.2, along with expenditures. The deficit noted at bottom was the third in a row for the NSTU and was eliminated by dipping into the reserve fund. Table 4.3 presents a simplified version of revenues versus expenditures for the Alberta Teachers'

Association for the fiscal year ending August 31, 1997. In that year the ATA had 25 469 full-time members and 4142 part-time and 3311 substitute teachers, the latter two groups paying pro-rated fees.

The resources of the ATA are greater than this accounting suggests. Like other teacher unions, over the years the ATA has accumulated a special emergency or contingency fund, sometimes called a "war chest," from which they withdraw funds to wage strikes, support striking members and to mobilize public opinion. This fund is supplemented each year by a percentage of member fees, but the bulk of its revenue derives from investment income. In 1997, the balance of ATA's war chest was $12 653 488, after spending $701 125 to finance several activities:

1. founding of the Public Education Action Centre to protest educational spending cuts initiated by the Klein government;
2. supporting a public rally;
3. providing a contribution to the CTF for teachers in Ontario striking over Bill 160; and
4. supporting two jobs actions in Alberta.

Table 4.2
1996/1997 Budget for Nova Scotia Teachers' Union

Revenue	
Membership fees	$5 344 592
Investment income	$81 255
Administrative expense recovery	$68 750
Sundry income	$2973
Total Revenue	$5 497 570
Deduct Total Transfer Payments	$1 262 409
Revenue after Transfers	$4 235 161
Expenditures	
Total Governance Council and Executive	$475 988
Total Programs & Services	$3 500 319
Property Expense	$292 830
Total Expenditures	$4 269 137
Deficit	$33 976

Table 4.3
1996/1997 Budget for Alberta Teachers' Association

Revenue	
ATA fees	$13 476 190
Other revenue	$3 279 504
Withdrawal from special emergency fund	$1 864 038
Total revenue	$16 755 694
Expenditures	
Governance	$3 453 685
Member services	$2 526 692
Professional development	$2 116 813
Teacher welfare	$1 472 688
Building	$1 256 287
Office operations	$1 279 768
Nondepartmental including CTF fees and strike support	$2 344 668
Cafeteria	$241 562
Central word services	$1 342 660
Miscellaneous	$27 669
Total Expenditures	$16 062 497
Excess of revenue over expenditure for the year before allocations	$693 202

The contingency fund of the Saskatchewan Teachers' Federation in 1997 was $11 568 815. The STF carried over cumulative surplus of $4 570 701 to the fund after several years of annual surpluses. In 1997 its surplus was $525 422, reflecting revenues of $6 769 935 and expenditures of $6 244 493.

Conclusion

Teachers' unions are substantial organizations that exhibit many of the characteristics of all formal organizations: hierarchical structures, technical and support staff, middle management and clients. In this case, the organization, as with a cooperative or mutual insurance company, is owned by those whom it serves. Some of the services it provides are direct: professional development; information about the union, profession and their environment; and the management of grievances. Other key services, including collective bargaining for salaries, benefits and working conditions are indirect, but crucial to their fulfilling their mission.

Teachers who decide on a union career can aspire to the same economic rewards available within school administration, although the number of more highly-paid posts are fewer. Teachers can rise through elective offices or through appointments to committees or positions that provide opportunities to serve members and the union.

One indirect service that unions provide teachers is quite visible to the public: political action directed at perceived threats to publicly financed and governed education. These initiatives are the subject of the next chapter.

References

Manners, E. (March 14, 1998). President's Remarks to the Annual Meeting of the Provincial Assembly of the Ontario Secondary School Teachers' Federation.

5

Contesting the Neo-Conservative Agenda

Many people today uncritically accept that government debt and deficits jeopardize our children's future. We challenge this view.

BCTF Education Funding Brief, 1998.

While mission and principle statements of teachers' unions are framed to be general and to serve as guideposts over long periods of time, statements of objectives and priorities and resolutions from annual general meetings provide specific examples of current concerns and the present thrust of union agendas. From contemporaneous sources, one discovers the following concerns: 1) educational funding and the neo-conservative strategy; 2) contract-stripping; 3) restriction of public choice; 4) restriction of access to employment and control of the certification process; 5) political campaigns to influence public opinion, to sway governmental policy-making and to determine the outcomes of provincial elections; and 6) curriculum, assessment and governance.

Funding and the Neo-conservative Strategy

In several provinces teacher associations have initiated public relations campaigns and political lobbying to fight real or threatened cuts in funding for public education. Funding cuts to education mean potential loss in terms of compensation and jobs; as such, they are a threat to union potency. Unions respond by promoting the idea that any cuts to funding or policies for increasing efficiency are part of a neo-conservative strategy to undermine a public good. They argue that the rights of children and youth for a fully funded public education will suffer. The purposes of this neo-conservative strategy, in their view, are to substantially reduce public debt, to reduce the role of government in the lives of citizens, to reduce levels of corporate and individual taxation, and to open public spheres of activity for private exploitation. They reject the argument that public indebtedness is itself a threat to the country's well being, including the welfare of children.

Because public education is highly labor intensive, cuts of any magnitude in funding have a number of implications. With actual or pending cuts, salary and benefits to presently employed teachers will not rise and are likely to remain frozen for sustained periods.

Sustained cuts also mean a reduction of programs and services at board/district levels and at school levels. Layoffs ensue, not only for administrators, consultants and professional support staff, but also for teachers, teacher assistants, custodial staff and support staff. Unions argue that instead of contracting in size, new programs and smaller class-sizes are required to meet the challenge of growing enrolments, students with special needs, and English-as-a-second language and aboriginal students. Loss of membership, of course, threatens teachers' unions income and power. What teachers' unions feel about funding cuts is evident in their statements.

> *Too often, governments succumb to political arguments of economic imperative without examining the long-term consequences. Many people today uncritically accept that government debt and deficits jeopardize our children's future. We challenge this view, asking instead: What future will children have if they are denied access to an adequate education? How will they ever participate equally in society and the economy? We must see our [British Columbia] education system as a means of escaping from the debt. If we simply cut, we will end up being worse off than we were when we started* (BCTF Education Funding Brief, *January 1998, p. 3*).

> *That there is insufficient new money [in Alberta] is a problem – the total number of dollars being* reinvested *is no more than an exercise in public relations. After cutting through the smoke and mirrors of the announcement that $379 million dollars will be reinvested in education, the Association calculates that the new money only amounts to $155 million over three years. The 1999/2000 budget is not carved in stone – now is the time to start working on improving that budget.* (Reinvesting in education: What do the numbers really tell? The ATA News, Vol. 32, February, 3, 1998.)

> *This [Ontario Harris] government hates unions. It hates the dues that support these unions as much as it hates taxes for the rich. We will not make ourselves weak just because the government does everything it can ensure that we are weak. . . . Our goal must be to guarantee that our response to the new reality, in fact, makes us stronger. Doing more with less, the phoney rallying cry of this government for Bills 104, 136, and 160, is not an option we will choose. There is no room in this union for the business analogy of retrenchment.* (Earl Manners, [OSSTF] President's Remarks to the Annual Meeting of the Provincial Assembly, March 14, 1998).

> *[Manitoba] [t]eachers disappointed in tightwad Tory announcement on 1998/99 funding level for public schools – Minister locks many divisions into last year's misery. The Manitoba government – flush with a healthy provincial treasury, a $577 million rainy day fund, and three years of budget surpluses – has chosen not to substantially reinvest in public schools with last week's 1998/1999 public schools funding announcement. . . . "[Manitoba Minister of Education] Linda McIntosh's announcement of a*

2.2 per cent increase in funding for the next school year will do nothing to ease deteriorating learning conditions in Manitoba classrooms," said [Manitoba Teachers' Society President] Diane Beresford (News Release, MTS, January 19, 1998).

Be it resolved that this [Nova Scotia Teachers' Union Annual] Council put on record its disgust and contempt for the present government's continued dismantling of Nova Scotia's educational system by deliberate underfunding (Resolution 97-36 of the 1997 NSTU's Annual Council, adopted and contained in a letter sent to the Minister of Education and Culture. NSTU, 1998 Annual Council Workbook).

Contract Stripping

Teachers' unions also make the argument that school boards/districts subjected to reduced funding are being forced by provincial governments to do more with less. Contract stripping means changing the rules of the collective bargaining process to ensure that management has the upper hand in setting who is allowed to be employed in schools, working conditions, staffing ratios, remuneration and benefits. Such stripping is seen as eliminating most of the gains made in union influence on educational policy-making during 1970s and as restricting the number of negotiable items in a contract.

Section 126(2) [of Bill 72, an Act to Amend the Manitoba Public Schools Act] . . . creates a significant impediment to the achievement of professional rights through collective bargaining. It was clearly designed to limit the scope of teacher collective agreements by excluding the following matters from consideration by an interest arbitrator: 1. selection, appointment, assignment and transfer of teachers and principals; 2. method for evaluating teachers and principals; 3. class size; 4. scheduling of recesses and the mid-day break. . . . Section 129 (3) of the PSA [Public Schools Act] now imposes a duty upon an arbitrator to consider a number of criteria including a school division's so-called ability to pay. . . . In reality, this is nothing more than the division's willingness-to-pay, a concept previously rejected by almost every interest arbitrator. . . . [T]eachers have to fight to get [the right to bargain] back. (Tom Paci, MTS's economic analyst, The Manitoba Teacher, May 1998, p. 3.)

[Ontario's] Bill 160 would allow school boards to strip their own collective agreements where the freeze expires before December 31, 1997. This would take place even though teachers would be forced to end a lawful job action on December 31, 1997, whether a settlement has been reached or not. OECTA has grave concerns over the termination of interest arbitrations not settled by January 1, 1998, as well as the termination of strikes on December 31, 1997. This is an unnecessary fettering of free collective bargaining rights. (OECTA reacts to Bill 160, December 1997.)

Restriction of Public Choice

Part of the neo-conservative strategy, teachers' unions assert, is to undermine public education by introducing public choice mechanisms into education that would alter traditional modes of providing educational services. They fear that the union monopoly for negotiating on behalf of teachers in the production of these services would be eliminated by such policies, which include educational vouchers, charter schools and the allocation of public funds to private schools. The British Columbia Teachers' Federation, the Ontario teachers' unions, and the Alberta Teachers' Association, the last in a province with a handful of recently established charter schools, are the more vocal opponents of public choice for schooling in Canada.

Charter schools represent the application of free market principles to education, the Trojan horse of those who would privatize education. Privately run but publicly funded, they are administered by committees of parents and teachers outside the jurisdiction of the elected school board. Most have a special focus – academic, music, arts, or the method of teaching – but adhere to established curriculum and testing methods. Most exist outside the terms of collective agreements; although the majority have a formal open-door policy, many are able to pick their students (Ontario Secondary School Teachers' Federation. Web Site on OSSTF Issues: Charter Schools/Privatization, 1998).

It is unacceptable for a government to starve public schools – which take in and provide services for all *students, including those with special needs – while providing public tax dollars to private schools, which often reject them. The BCTF is opposed to using taxpayer dollars to fund private schools. (BCTF Education Funding Brief, January 1998).*

Restriction of Access to Employment

Teachers' associations reject the employment of individuals within school systems that do no meet association standards for certification. In the context of educational support staff such as custodians, associations reject proposals to "contract out" jobs that are covered by union contracts. Unions also oppose the hiring of non-certified personnel such as individuals who may be specialized in a subject area (such as computers, arts or science) but who do not have formal teacher education and credentials. Unions also oppose the hiring of less formally qualified individuals for certain positions, such as the use of community-college educated early childhood educational specialists for kindergarten or early childhood programs.

Differentiated staffing = unqualified staffing. Differentiated staffing means replacing individuals trained and certified as professional teachers with individuals who do not have the training required to be a teacher in Ontario's public schools. Advocates of this say it will allow certified teachers to concentrate on classroom instruction instead of wasting time on 'administrivia'. However, the real reason for implementing differentiated staffing is to employ less qualified and therefore less expensive people in offering a lower quality of education . . . [in areas such as] physical education, health education, career counselling, cooperative education, technical education, business education, art programs, and music programs . . . (OECTA Web Site, March 1997).

Be it resolved, that The Alberta Teachers' Association urge the Government of Alberta to amend the School Act so that all those employed as counsellors in schools require an Alberta teaching certificate (Resolution 124/98 ATA Annual Representative Assembly, 1998).

Political Campaigns

To influence public opinion, to sway governmental policy-making, and to determine the outcomes of provincial elections, teachers' unions have refined their capacity to think and act as lobbying organizations, public relations powerhouses, extra-parliamentary opposition parties and government-makers. Their efforts are similar to those of any industrial-promotion activity that unions and business often sponsor jointly, although the political element probably is more visible. An accounting of these activities is highlighted in teacher unions' annual reports. The tone often used to describe this activity is laced with frustration and sometimes anger because of perceived insensitivity to union agendas and social visions.

None compare to the plans that Ontario teachers' unions have hatched to defeat the Harris Progressive Conservative government at the polls in the next election after the Bill 160 debacle in the fall of 1997. Consider the $1 000 000 special political action fund the OSSTF set up to mobilize its membership for "election readiness" – to join political parties, to train election activists and to lobby political parties. One goal has been to activate members to participate in Ontario Federation of Labour's coordinated Days of Action and a recently cancelled province-wide Day of Protest against Harris's labor and funding policies. Ontario's opposition parties, the Liberals and the New Democratic Party, have responded warmly to the political agendas of Ontario's teacher unions, and promise if they are elected they will nullify much of Bill 160 and restore the system of educational governance, funding and labor policies that predated that legislation. While the Tory governments of 1943 and 1975 responded to teachers' unions hopes and expectations by conferring upon them both exclusive jurisdiction and collective bargaining, the current one has set the gears in reverse. It is now for the other parties to woo the teachers.

Teacher unions' political activity concerns not only "union issues" but also addresses a wider social activist agenda, in tandem with other organized labor organizations, to fight policies aimed at further global integration of Canada's economy. Teachers' unions, the Canadian Labour Congress and other groups have fought against agreements such as the North American Free Trade Agreement (NAFTA) and the yet-to-be-born Multiple Agreement on Investment (MAI). At its 1997 AGM, the British Columbia Teachers' Federation invited Council of Canadians spokesperson Maude Barlow as their keynote speaker. She expressed her "growing concern [raised by the MAI] over the loss of democracy in Canada and throughout the world as power and control are massively transferred from governments to the private sector in a process that is accelerating every day."

The CTF is leading a national campaign to persuade members of teachers' unions, the general public and the federal government that globalization exposes Canada to tremendous risks. Canadians need to understand the impact of globalization, asserts CTF President Jan Eastman: "With the virtual barrage of daily news on the subservience of labour to economic growth, the unfettered movement of capital and the need to compete on a global scale, it sometimes seems that we have stepped back in history to the days when kings ruled by divine right, except that today, we talk about the divine right of the marketplace and of free enterprise" (President's Address to CTF Annual Meeting, July 30, 1998).

In late 1998, several media reports credited the "underground" campaign against the MAI led by the Council of Canadians, which CTF helps to support, with influencing the governing federal Liberal Party to temporarily shelve its support for the MAI. When France withdrew from scaled-down talks about MAI over concerns about culture, environmental and labor standards, social programs and extraterritoriality, Maude Barlow and other anti-globalization activists "celebrated with champagne" (Scoffield, 1998). Canada has allied itself with France over these concerns, much to the consternation of its primary trading partner, the United States. Teacher association newsletters regularly carry articles highly critical of globalization, of corporate involvement in helping to frame the goals of public education, and of corporate sponsorships and partnerships with schools.

Several teachers' unions recently initiated campaigns to increase public support for their conception of what public education should be and are making a concerted effort to articulate these beliefs beyond the boundaries of their membership. Now "is the time to push hard," declares CTF President Jan Eastman, "especially since public opinion consistently supports increased funding to elementary and secondary schools, and because some governments have begun to put more money into education." The CTF for its part regularly lobbies the federal government on issues such as the "children's agenda, the seniors' pension benefits, reinvestment in social programs and increases in transfer payments" (CTF Annual Meeting, July 30, 1998). The Alberta Teachers' Association funds a provincial and local media campaign which focuses on "high profile" business people voicing their support for public education, i.e., decrying funding cuts and the public funding of charter schools. In conjunction with the Alberta Home and School Councils Association, the ATA is organizing a petition campaign, centred in shopping malls across the province, against the Alberta government's practice of funding private schools. The Manitoba Teachers' Society launched its "Growing Minds" campaign which aims to enhance the image of teachers, build political leverage for Manitoba teachers, position the MTS for the next provincial election, and to engage the public and "less politically oriented teachers." This campaign is supported by radio, print and outdoor advertising. The Saskatchewan Teachers' Federation and the Prince Edward Island Teachers' Federation have launched similar campaigns.

Sometimes when the more socially activist teachers' unions try to promote their version of public education to the wider public, they find a large gap between their own values and those of the public. Recently, The British Columbia Teachers' Federation highlighted the need to "recapture" citizenship education as a central purpose of public education. For the BCTF, citizenship education includes removing all texts from classrooms and school libraries its own watchdogs consider "sexist," "racist" and "homophobic." BCTF encountered a public and media backlash in response to a campaign to counter what it terms "heterosexism" in school policies, in the curriculum and school texts, and in school libraries. The BCTF's webpage (www.bctf.bc.ca) provides the following definitions: "Homophobia is both the individual and collective fear of gays and lesbians, and the hatred, disgust, and prejudice that that fear brings. Heterosexism is the promotion of the superiority of heterosexuality and the assumption that everyone is heterosexual and that being heterosexual is inherently better than being gay, lesbian or bisexual." Recently, the BCTF supported a successful case in the British Columbia Supreme Court, *Chamberlain v. Surrey School District No. 36*, that "overturned the [Surrey] school board's ban on three children's books that mention same-sex parents, because [Justice Mary Saunders] ... said the trustees had violated the *School Act* by making their decision on religious grounds" (*Vancouver Sun*, n.d; Benson & Miller, 1999).

Curriculum, Assessment and Governance

The Canadian Teachers' Federation is very active on the public education front in areas that are of direct concern to public education (available on the Web at www.ctf-fce.ca). In September 1997 the provincial/territorial members identified eight issues on which the CTF and member organizations intend to focus a national public education and lobbying campaign. Several of these issues were touched upon above, including: the erosion of confidence in our public schools (CTF, 1996); less adequate and equitable education funding; and privatization, including charter schools, private schools, vouchers and contracting out.

Other issues identified by the CTF are: the diminishing quality of life of children and young adults; the narrowing of curriculum and standardized testing; the diminishing quality of life of teachers; "agenda-driven" governance (the CTF's phrase) such as increased parental control, site-based management, and the decline in the number and power of school boards; and the declining societal commitment to equity. Below we comment further on issues relating to curriculum and assessment as well as governance.

The narrowing of curriculum usually refers to the trend in recent provincial curriculum design throughout the 1990s to focus more on a core of "new basics" such as literacy, numeracy, and information technology, which are being offered as a compulsory "common curriculum" at the secondary school level, and/or "streamed" according to ability levels. The "new basics" approach has been adopted by several provincial authorities to counter growing public criticism that too many high school graduates do not possess the basic knowledge and skills that are needed for success in post-secondary education and/or that are valued by the marketplace. The "new basics" approach is seen by its critics, especially in teachers' union ranks, as an affront not only to the traditional liberal arts notion of schooling that stresses breadth of knowledge in several domains, but also as an infringement on student choice. It is also viewed as an attack on a social-activist oriented curriculum favored by many teacher federations whose central purpose is to educate students to be critical thinkers and questioners of the status quo. Less student choice and fewer teaching subjects also mean that fewer teachers are needed to staff schools.

The 1990s accountability movement in public education brought to the fore a greater governmental and public interest in provincial and even national student assessment mechanisms for reading and writing, science and mathematics, the latter developed by the Council of Ministers of Education, Canada, in conjunction with provincial ministries (CMEC, 1996). One type of assessment is the "standardized" variety and usually consists of large numbers of students in a particular grade and subject area across the province answering a set of questions designed by a testing agency or ministry specialists. Standardized assessments are designed to answer questions about students' curriculum-based knowledge and skill levels and are appraised in terms of the number of standard deviations from the mean that a school or system falls. Students perform these "pencil and paper" tests with classmates on a strictly individual basis for a predetermined length of time after receiving standardized information about test procedures from the teacher.

The other trend in assessment is quite different and is termed by its adherents as "authentic" assessment. Authentic assessment starts with the premise that the proper assessment of what each student knows about a topic is based on his or her own knowledge-base that is rooted in the social context of a specific classroom rather than with an externally-generated set of specific questions answered in an impersonalized atmosphere. The individual pencil-and-paper approach measured in minutes that are designed and marked by external bodies are discarded in favor of procedures that emphasize how students demonstrate their knowledge of topics through individual and group projects undertaken over long period of time using written, oral, pictorial and acted "portfolios" that are evaluated not just by the teacher but also by the student and his/her peers. While standardized assessments readily conform to a concept of student evaluation that is transmission-oriented and traditional, the roots of authentic assessment are in cognitive psychology and constructivist understandings of the teaching and learning processes most readily identified with the progressive, learner-centred model.

Standardized assessments are favored by ministries of education and by advocates of greater accountability in public education over authentic assessment for a number of reasons. First of all are cost and efficiency concerns. Once a stable curriculum is in place for a particular grade and subject area, a standard test can be administered to large numbers of students for a number of years and modified as changes are introduced to the curriculum. In terms of quality control and information packaging, data generated gives a relatively clear picture of achievement levels of students aggregated at the class, school, district and provincial levels. Such information is necessary to assess whether students, schools and districts are performing as well as they should or whether changes should be made to curriculum design and standards or teaching methods. With participation in CMEC and international assessments, provincial ministries can compare provincial results and even national results to those of other countries. Authentic assessments, on the other hand, do not package student achievement information in bundles that are easily consumable or usable for educational decision-makers precisely because they are unstandardized – geared to specific learning contexts that vary from class to class. For standardized assessments, the reliability and validity of the instruments are the main criteria to judge their merits; in authentic assessments individual teachers are considered the most valued assessment instruments. While standardized assessments are useful for centralized monitoring and control, authentic assessments support a wide definition of professional job autonomy.

Teachers' unions in several provinces and the CTF have resisted standardized student assessment for years and instead have championed authentic assessment. Part of their resistance is related to power issues. As defenders of teachers' professional autonomy, teachers' unions reject assessment mechanisms that can be used for the purpose of teacher evaluation; they also reject the trend towards "high-stakes." Just as teachers' unions have claimed a large stake in the professional development of teachers, they also want to be arbiters in student assessment. As Earl Manners, President of the Ontario Secondary School Teachers' Federation framed the issue for his members:

> *While standardized testing is a valuable tool for assessing individual student's skills and needs, it is not a substitute for broad-based evaluation of student progress or an appropriate methodology for curriculum review. Moreover, we must show our communities that there are numerous strategies to assess student achievement. OSSTF will develop our own comprehensive policies on assessment of student progress. We will collect and catalogue the great variety of valid instruments for assessing literacy in our grade nine students that our members are currently using in their professional practice (President's Address to the OSSTF AGM, March 14, 1998).*

Union critics of standardized testing are also fearful of the use that may be made of data that may be reported in the media, including pitting schools against schools, in evaluating teachers and in stigmatizing students who attend a "low-performing" schools. For example, the BCTF took grave exception to a week-long series of articles, beginning March 2, 1998, in *The Vancouver Province* reporting school performance on the previous June's Grade 12 provincial exams. Using analysis provided by The Fraser Institute, a neo-conservative think-tank that promotes charter schools and vouchers, the paper ranked 256 secondary schools in the province on a scale of 1 to 10 on the basis of provincial exam averages, differences between school marks and provincial exam marks, and graduation rates. A similar fear prompted a Saskatchewan Teachers' Federation local to write a resolution at the 1998 STF annual general meeting criticizing that province's collaboration with CMEC on national assessment. Until recently Saskatchewan was the only province not to join with other provincial ministries in this endeavor. Ontario teachers' unions have criticized the recent "imposition" of provincial quasi-standardized testing in the last two years on similar grounds of the uses of such assessment, as well as levelling the charge that such assessments are inappropriate on ethno-cultural/racial grounds because of the large number of children and youth in urban areas of recent immigrant or refugee backgrounds. The present assessment system is an experimental hybrid of standardized and authentic assessment that has proven costly in time and money, but may represent a type of delicate balance between the preferences of teachers and the need to satisfy demands for political accountability.

The CTF-cited issue of "agenda-driven" governance refers to trends in educational governance that are altering traditional decision-making systems. With the aim of giving parents a greater say in their children's education, advisory or decision-making bodies are assuming influence at the expense of the traditional power brokers, including district-level administrators and trustees, teachers' union representatives and individual teachers. The use of the phrase "agenda-driven" by the CTF aptly describes their belief that any views that conflict with those of teachers' union positions are not in the interest of the public good and are therefore indicative of narrow "special interests." On the other hand, to many provincial governments and to conservative critics across Canada, teachers' unions are "special interests" with their own "agendas." While ministers of education may justify governance changes in terms of championing parent power and increasing efficiency with more resources targeted for the classroom, teachers' unions see them as undermining the local community's role in public education. They believe that they introduce centralized means to emasculate any institutionalized opposition to the policy directives of the centre, particularly those related to cost-cutting measures.

References

Alberta Teachers' Association. (February 3, 1998). Reinvesting in education: What do the numbers really tell? *The ATA News*, Vol. 32.

Benson, I. T. & Miller, B. (January 11, 1999). Court misunderstands the meaning of "secular." *Lex View* No. 25, Ottawa: Centre for Renewal of Public Policy.

British Columbia Teachers' Federation. (January 1998). *BCTF education funding brief*. Vancouver: BCTF.

British Columbia Teachers' Federation. (February 1996). *Inventing crisis: The erosion of confidence in Canadian public education*. Prepared for the Canadian Teachers' Federation. Vancouver: BCTF.

British Columbia Teachers' Federation. World Wide Web site: www.bctf.bc.ca

Canadian Teachers' Federation. World Wide Web site: www.ctf-fce.ca

Council of Ministers of Education, Canada. (1996). *Report of Canada*. Toronto: CMEC.

Manners, E. (March 14, 1998). President's Remarks to the Annual Meeting of the Provincial Assembly of the Ontario Secondary School Teachers' Federation.

Manitoba Teachers' Society. (January 19, 1998). News Release.

Nova Scotia Teachers' Union. (1998). *NSTU1998 Annual Council Workbook*.

Ontario English Catholic Teachers' Association. (December 1997). *OECTA Reacts to Bill 160*.

Paci, T. (May 1998). *The Manitoba Teacher*, p. 3.

Scoffield, H. (October 15, 1998). France pulls out of MAI talks. *The Globe and Mail*, pp. B1 & 6.

Vancouver Sun (n.d.). Surrey board misses deadline to appeal gay books ruling. In *Edvisor*, January 25, 1999: www3.sk.sympatico.ca/edvisor/

6

Province-wide Bargaining in British Columbia

> *The public interest would be well served if government, management and the teachers . . . [assumed] responsibility for improvements in the bargaining system. [It] may require leadership of government to inspire the parties to achieve appropriate solutions.*
>
> Korbin Commission, 1993

The strategies that governments adopt in order to address political, social and economic issues generally reflect, implicitly or explicitly, a set of assumptions about the proper relationship of government to individuals and to interest groups in society. The Korbin Commission's invitation in 1993 to educational interest groups, quoted above, reflects an assumption that economic agents, rather than individuals, are the primary parties for making political decisions and taking social action. This approach is rooted in a corporatist view of society, although it is also a strategy that may be adopted out of political expediency rather than social philosophy. Whether the reasons for its recommendation and adoption in British Columbia were philosophical or pragmatic probably does not matter in terms of the consequences, which are probably the same regardless of motive.

A sense of the outcome of a corporatist approach is suggested by Simpson's (1998) view of the Air France pilots' strike days before Soccer's World Cup:

> *The strike underlined the temperament of French public-sector unions. . . . The Air France pilots make much more . . . than their counterparts at British Airways. . . . That gap should have produced bliss; instead it produced an instant mobilization to defend previously secured gains, regardless of Air France's competitive position.*

Corporatism as a Form of Government

A *corporatist* government is one in which nationwide syndicates or trusts of all employers in a given industry negotiate with industry-wide unions of employees under the government's tutelage. Both France and Germany follow this approach, which provides major political and economic influence to unions. One result is that both nations also have rigid labor markets, a consequence of which has been high rates of unemployment, particularly among youth.

In France, overall unemployment in 1997 affected 13 percent of the labor force versus 9 percent in Canada, 7.5 percent in the United Kingdom, and just 5 percent in the United States, which has one of the world's least centralized and unionized work forces.

Japan and Sweden, like France, have followed a corporatist path, perhaps with more success. However, after 20 years of success in the 1970s and 1980s, Japan is now mired in a recession and seems unable to develop a set of policies that, at one time, both move the nation ahead and satisfy key interest groups. Sweden confronts economic problems in part through extensive training and retraining programs that incidentally keep many individuals off the unemployment rolls. As a small nation, it seems more facile tactically than larger nations, but has not avoided the ups and downs of economic swings: in the mid-1990s its unemployment rate exceeded 9 percent and averaged about 6 percent for 1998 (Assarsson & Jansson, 1996; Statistics Sweden: www.scb.se/snabb/akueng.htm).

These contemporary examples of corporatism are generally termed *neo-corporatist* and emulate a form governance that has long been promoted by Canadian-American economist John Kenneth Galbraith (e.g., 1967) for both Canada and the United States. He emphasizes its benefits in terms of the economic equity such arrangements produce. With their more equal income distributions, neo-corporatist nations do not exhibit the extreme wealth and poverty evident under more competitive, free-market arrangements.

The decision of British Columbia's government to move toward province-wide collective bargaining with elementary and secondary teachers is consistent with adopting a neo-corporatist approach to provincial political, social and economic issues. The government may have been motivated to "minimize the kinds of disruptions experienced by students in . . . previous bargaining rounds" (Korbin, p. F27) but created a central roundtable reminiscent of Quebec's province-wide sectoral system of bargaining (table 3.1) or Bob Rae's "Social Contract" than, say, the administratively centralized state being created in Ontario under Mike Harris (chapter 7). Although different, both are quite distinct from the highly decentralized political and economic regime in most states of the United States.

A Look Back at Bargaining

British Columbia came late to providing full collective bargaining rights to teachers, having granted these rights only in 1987 with passage of the *Teaching Profession Act* (R.S.B.C. 1996, c. 449).[1] Furthermore, a government formed by the Social Credit party, known for its pro-business orientation, rather than a labor-oriented government as one might expect, made this decision. Apparently, the government of the day felt that a two-pronged approach would reduce the influence of the British Columbia Teachers' Federation (BCTF) and its locals. First, the government would separate the professional roles of teachers' associations (e.g., standards, ethics, etc.) from their economic roles (e.g., bargaining for wages). Second, it would allow teachers in each school district to vote in favor of forming either a union or a professional association. As one labor expert commented, their plan backfired (Burnham & O'Neill, 1991).

The Social Credit government's legislation created the British Columbia College of Teachers and called for a majority of the seats on its governing body to be elected by the province's teachers. Legislation also removed mandatory membership in BCTF and allowed teachers to organize on a voluntary basis. The BCTF treated the new legislation as an opportunity and responded with a strong and active campaign to encourage teachers to unionize and to select to BCTF's affiliates as their bargaining agents. The Federation was successful: not only did teachers' groups in all school districts vote to unionize, BCTF also gained control of the governing council of the fledgling College of Teachers.

With BCTF members effectively in control of the College, it has not developed into the autonomous force originally envisioned by the government of the day. For example, after almost a decade, the College of Teachers has yet to adopt a code of ethics for teachers, stating that to do so would be redundant since the BCTF already has a code of ethics (Geisert & Chandler, 1991). At the same time, the BCTF has amended its code to include a clause that reads, "The teacher acts in a manner not prejudicial to job actions or other collective strategies of his/her professional union" (BCTF, *Policies and Procedures*, n.d.). The appropriate penalty for violations of this clause, such as crossing a picket line during a strike, is "a fine equivalent to gross pay received from the employer for days upon which said picket line is crossed." The BCTF's influence is also evident in its success in persuading the subsequent New Democratic Party government to transfer responsibility for professional development from the College to the BCTF. Hence, the union now has direct control of two key professional functions that the Social Credit government had intentionally removed from the union and given over to the new professional body.

When teachers in British Columbia's school districts voted for unionization, provincial legislation provided for either an "agency" or "closed" shop if the bargaining unit chose unionization over professional association. Gunderson and Riddel (1993) explain these terms and describe the critical role they play in ensuring union security:

> Craft unions generally have sought to raise the wage of their members by controlling entry into their craft through the apprenticeship system..., high union dues, and such devices as the closed shop (the worker has to be a member of the union before being hired...) Needless to say the craft union will try to control the whole trade; otherwise the benefits of the supply restriction [i.e., higher wages] also go to nonunion craft workers. Hence the importance to the union of apprenticeship licensing, the closed shop, the union shop (the worker has to join the union after a probationary period of employment) or the agency shop (the worker must pay union dues but need not be a member of the union) (pp. 375-376).

In most cases where British Columbia teachers did not wish to become union members, they received notices of dismissal even if they were tenured teachers because their school boards acceded to union demands for closed shops instead of agency shops, which would have allowed dues or fees to be paid without actual union membership. Teachers in School District #23, Central Okanagan, received the following missive:

> Any of the above-named [44] individuals who do not become and remain members of the Central Okanagan Teachers' Association and the British Columbia Teachers' Federation by June 30, 1990, shall be deemed to have resigned from their employment with School District #23, by giving notice of resignation as of May 31, 1990, to be effective June 30, 1990 (Letter of Understanding, April 7, 1989).

One can only imagine the fight that a teachers' union would wage if a school board attempted to dismiss 44 tenured teachers for failure to do a satisfactory job. Bridges (1984) noted that in the United States, "From 1939-1982 only eighty-six cases involving the dismissal of tenured teachers for incompetence were reported in the annual issues of *The Teacher's Day in Court* and the *School Law Reporter*" (p. 6). It is evident that the primary motive of the BCTF was union power and control, not just quality of teaching or the welfare of the profession. Otherwise, it could have achieved its economic goals without forcing membership upon those who did not desire, for whatever reason, to become members.

Although some teachers fought to gain an open shop or even an agency shop, wealth and commitment of the BCTF and the Canadian Labour Congress, which lent support to the BCTF in defending its position, ultimately intimidated opponents into dropping a court challenge. The case was put forward on the basis of the

Canadian Charter of Rights and Freedoms, which guarantees the following fundamental freedoms for all citizens:

> *(a) freedom of conscience and religion; (b) freedom of thought, belief, opinion and expression, including freedom of the press and other media communication; (c) freedom of peaceful assembly; and (d) freedom of association.*

Some who did become members of union locals fought compulsory membership in province-wide BCTF as a condition of employment, arguing that this requirement, too, violated the guarantee of freedom of association. That is, they argued that freedom of association has no meaning unless one can choose to join or choose not to join. In this case, it was the right not to join that was the issue. They pointed out that less than a quarter of labor agreements in Canada require union or closed shops. A counter-argument in defense of compulsory membership holds that for unions to function democratically, all voices, including those in opposition to current leadership and policies, need to be included in what forms, in essence, a body politic.

Ultimately, only a handful of school boards did not sign closed shop agreements. By December 1996, the test case opposing BCTF had been dropped. *The Reader's Digest* carried the following report:

> *A British Columbia teacher had to drop a legal challenge to the province's labour laws because the court rules threatened her with bankruptcy. Norma Janzen had taught for 24 years when she was "deemed to have resigned" from a B.C. school as a result of her refusal to join the teachers' union, as a provincial law required. A dedicated professional, she had refused because it would have prevented her from crossing a picket line to teach. And that, she believed, violated her right to freedom of association.*
>
> *"As a result [of the hundreds of thousands of dollars in potential court costs should she lose and have to pay the costs of the intervenors such as the Canadian Labour Congress, she said] the rights and freedoms guaranteed by the charter are of little real use since no one, except governments, big unions and big business, will be able to afford to use it in court."*

Under the new legislation, local collective bargaining in British Columbia was to be carried out in all school districts at the same time, with school boards negotiating three-year contracts with the teachers' local bargaining units. Orchestrating the management side of negotiations was the British Columbia School Boards' Association (BCSBA), a voluntary association of school district boards of trustees. Not all districts were members of BCSBA since some preferred to act as autonomous employers. On the employees' side, the BCTF coordinated bargaining to play one school board against another. According to one critic, "The apparent BCTF strategy was to focus first on sympathetic, left-leaning districts, to gain all the concessions they could, and then use these as a whipsaw to force other boards to do the same. By the time mediators are called in, it's too late to change the pattern" (Burnham & O'Neill, 1991, p. 39).

One factor that amplified the effects was a new *Education Act* (R.S.B.C. 1996, c. 412) in 1989 that gave school boards more scope in managing their own affairs, which included the authority to bargain workload, class size and the like. That is, trustees gained the right, if they so chose, to yield, in negotiations, their authority to make independent decisions about the nature of education in their districts. To complicate the matter still further, in 1990 the province assumed control over 100 percent of the funding of education and a problem that plagues the system to this day was created. If school trustees agreed at the bargaining table to lower class size below the level which the province funded, it now found it could not raise taxes to meet the obligation. That is, the variation among contracts in school districts was not matched by variation in provincial grants. Although school districts were permitted to hold referenda for over-ride taxes, which might have helped solved the problem, few were held and even fewer passed. As special elections, referenda are notoriously expensive to mount and they provide voters a rare opportunity to indicate their desire or willingness to pay higher taxes.

In some school districts, generous clauses were granted on key financial and management issues such as class size. Some class size provisions were so restrictive that a school must remove a student from a class if the number of students enrolled exceeded a limit, even if it meant sending the child by taxi to another school. In other contracts, hours-of-work clauses dictated the times during which classroom instruction could be assigned. As a result, schools could not offer extended-day schedules that would help to utilize the school plant more fully. This type of restriction had a particularly negative impact on a number of fast-growing districts where schools were bursting at the seams. Many of the portable classroom buildings in their paved playgrounds could be eliminated if schools could use the main facility an extra hour or two per day. One official commented, "We're not servicing the students, we're servicing the contract!"

Pressures for Change

Over three rounds of bargaining that took place under the 1987 legislation, about 30 teachers' strikes disrupted schools. In March of 1991, Burnham and O'Neill reported that, "Last week teachers in Nanaimo and Fernie were on full-out strike; for Nanaimo it was the second week. Saanich teachers were conducting a rotating strike and contemplating a full one. Six other districts had taken strike votes. Strikes had been inflicted upon Vancouver and Victoria, and a month-long lockout upon South Okanagan." There was fairly widespread dissatisfaction with the collective bargaining system from politicians of all stripes. One trustee commented, ". . . the BCTF was doing province-wide bargaining and we were acting like hicks."

To end the strikes, teachers typically were ordered back to work, with the issues being sent to arbitration. Arbitrators tended to look at prevailing practices in adjacent communities where settlements made without strikes were likely to be generous, so the outcome usually favored employees. According to one estimate, costs escalated by 37 percent between 1988 and 1992.

In 1993, *The Report of the Commission of Inquiry into the Public Service and Public Sector* (usually called the "Korbin report" after its chair, Judi Korbin) recommended province-wide bargaining for all public employees with those employed in a given service (e.g., health, social services, education, etc.) being treated as a separate "sector." This recommendation was made at a time that Ontario's New Democratic Party government under Premier Bob Rae was trying to implement the "Social Contract" in order to increase provincial control over public employees and to temporarily reduce public-sector wages. Both initiatives reflected neo-corporatist solutions to problems of governance and management.

In both provinces, teachers' unions were adamantly opposed to province-wide bargaining. They strongly preferred the existing arrangement for themselves: they had province-wide perspective and considerable sophistication, while school district trustees had a weak central organization and suffered from naiveté. As well, the teachers' unions may have been aware of the potential risks of having a province-wide negotiator on the other side of the table, a situation which would create what economists term a monopsony: a market of goods or services limited to one buyer. Monopsony is similar to a monopoly in business except it is on the buyer's rather than the seller's side. While a single seller often tries to extract "monopoly rents" by setting prices above what they would be in a free competitive market, a monopsonist is tempted to hold prices down in order to save on input costs. While Rae's Social Contract was temporary, the British Columbia legislation was meant to be permanent.

Legislated Action

British Columbia adopted several key acts of legislation in 1994 in hopes of taming the public sector employment relations turmoil, including Bill 52: *Public Education Labour Relations Act* (PELRA) (RSBC 1996, c. 382) and Bill 78: *Public Sector Employers Act* (RSBC 1996, c. 384). These *Acts* provide the framework for centralized bargaining in which employers bargain through their agent, the British Columbia Public School Employers' Association, to which all school districts and the French Education Authority (FEA) must belong.[2] This approach to centralized bargaining contrasts with the centralized bargaining that has taken place in New Brunswick for a many years in which the province (usually through the office of the treasurer) bargains directly with teachers' unions. In many ways the scheme is similar to those used in Saskatchewan and Nova Scotia, which use teams representing both trustees and government (see table 3.1). The British Columbia Teachers' Federation (BCTF) represents the teachers' side in British Columbia. The BCPSEA home page (www.bcpsea.bc.ca) describes the its own structure and role:

Representatives from the 59 school boards and FEA elect nine school trustees to the Board of Directors including the Chair and Vice-Chair; they are joined by four government representatives and a non-voting representative from the B.C. School Superintendents' Association and the B. C. School District Secretary-Treasurers' Association.

As the employers' association, we have responsibility for:

1. Negotiating provincially with the British Columbia Teachers' Federation (the teachers' union) for a provincial teachers contract covering all 59 school boards and the FEA ...

2. Acting as the accredited bargaining agent for all 59 school boards for their support staff employees ...

3. Coordinating compensation for employees who are not subject to collective agreements ...

4. Promoting beneficial and cooperative human resources practices ...

5. Determining collective bargaining objectives for the public education sector.

As a way of facilitating these responsibilities, the B. C. Public School Employers' Association (along with the other employers' associations in the public sector) is a member of the Public Sector Employers' Council, established by the provincial government to provide a link between the government and public sector bodies on compensation and human resource management issues.

If a neo-corporatist state is one in which jurisdiction-wide "syndicates or trusts of all employers in a given industry negotiate with industry-wide unions of employees under the government's tutelage" then this legislation moved British Columbia well along the neo-corporatist path.[3]

The First Round

The first round of province-wide collective bargaining did not go particularly smoothly. After 18 months, only four or five of over 100 clauses that had been proposed had been agreed upon. Part of the problem, is has been argued, were radically different approaches to bargaining chosen by the two sides. The BCTF, for the teachers, used "positional bargaining" in which they proposed a master contract that was composed of the "best" clauses from all of the existing collective agreements found in the province. The BCPSEA, for its part, used "interest bargaining," in which it shared the key desires and needs of school trustees, in the expectation that the other side would do the same. Interest bargaining works best in mature relationships where trust exists between the parties. This was not a mature relationship.

One problem, beyond the newness, is that BCPSEA was not the ultimate paymaster; the province was. BCPSEA entered bargaining with the understanding from the provincial government that there was no more money for schools than that which had already been allocated by the government for schools. Though socialist, the governing NDP was also trying to bring in a balanced budget as it moved toward an election in the immediate future. Time was running out for the government; it wanted the matter settled. Ultimately, the provincial government intervened with some off-table bargaining and proffered a two-percent increase in salaries. The BCTF accepted, knowing that an election was in the air and that it would be more advantageous to teachers for the NDP to be reelected since the opposing parties were less inclined to accommodate teachers' desires.

An alternative interpretation of the BCTF's actions at the bargaining is that it has been unable to accommodate competing internal interests in order to develop a bargaining stance that involved trade-offs among member locals. Like the Air France pilots, each local was anxious to preserve its past successes at all costs and was not willing to make modest sacrifices so that some less fortunate bargaining unit might gain. As a result, according to this argument, the only position BCTF could table was one which demanded the best benefits for all – and which therefore also reflected internal discord and incapacity for political compromise.

Formally, all school boards voted on the agreement the province had negotiated. The proposed three-year Transitional Collective Agreement included a handful of uniform clauses, the pay increase – which on top of salary grid increments made the total cost about 4.5 percent over three years – and a roll-over of remaining local agreements. A majority of school boards voted in favor. All other school districts had to accept the results, even if they had a local collective agreement that could not be funded by the provincial grants that they were being provided. The government, claiming a balanced budget, was re-elected, albeit with a new leader who had assumed his position before the election. Only later did it become evident the government had not reported financial updates that indicated a shortfall of hundreds of millions of dollars in the provincial budget. That news was made public only after their election victory.

The Second Round

In many ways, the second round of bargaining was a re-run of the first. Bargaining proposals were exchanged on September 16, 1997, beginning a process that had a deadline of June 30, 1998, when the existing agreement expired. The BCPSEA focussed on four main issues: teacher workload, the posting and filling of positions, teacher evaluation and the extended day, the last relating to their desire to make better use of existing facilities. Progress was not rapid and the Public Sector Employers' Council requested that the two parties enter an expedited bargaining process with a narrowed focus. Again, little or no progress was made.

BCPSEA then accepted an earlier government offer for the latter to "facilitate" negotiations by moving between the two parties in order to develop a framework for negotiations. In the end, the government entered directly into negotiations with BCTF without BCPSEA present. According to BCPSEA,

Government saw this as a way to achieve its corporate agenda of a 0-0-2 compensation settlement which they were then able to use as a pattern to achieve similar settlements throughout the public sector. In addition, the agreement reflected government's priority of strengthening funding for public education. Government provided an additional $150 million in funding over the 3 years of the proposed agreement in order to provide additional non-enrolling and K-3 teachers (BCPSEA, 1998).

On April 17, 1998, a tentative three-year agreement was reached which the BCTF Executive endorsed, acting to override the position of its own bargaining team. Teachers voted 75 percent in favor of the agreement. On the recommendation of the BCPSEA, individual school boards rejected the agreement by an 87 percent margin due to concerns relating to equity among school districts and decreased flexibility in their ability to manage their schools. On June 25, 1998, the government introduced legislation in the form of the *Public Collective Agreement Act* to require school districts to implement the agreement it had negotiated with BCTF; the legislation was enacted on July 30, 1998.

The agreement (if it can be so designated, given that the employers did not agree) included no across-the-board salary increase until April 1, 2000, when there would be a 2 percent increase. In the meantime, teachers would be eligible for annual increments and increments associated with movement to higher salary categories. As well, funding was set for 145 librarians, 79 counsellors, 145 learning assistance teachers, 79 special education resource teachers and 79 ESL teachers. Referred to as non-enrolling teachers, these teachers play roles that, as noted in chapter 7, are being negotiated away by teacher union locals in Ontario. As well, an additional 700 classroom teachers were funded to reduce class size in the primary grades to 20 in kindergarten and 22 in grades 1 to 3, a modest early-retirement scheme was introduced, and funding was promised for 200 new classrooms per year for five years. As before, all other clauses were rolled over, including those that exceeded these new provincial standards.

The BCTF engaged in an active campaign to sell the agreement to the public before the legislation was introduced, sending an "open letter" to parents in the province, regretting that both BCPSEA and the British Columbia Confederation of Parent Advisory Councils campaigned against the agreement. No mention was made to the declining economic fortunes of the province whose forestry, mining and tourism industries were suffering from economic turmoil in Asia. The province once again entered into recession and deficit spending. In short, the province could not afford the agreement it negotiated and the agreement reduced still further the ability of trustees, superintendents and principals to manage their districts. Their full-time job has become one of implementing the handiwork of the government and teachers' unions without encountering an excessive number of grievances. One bright spot is that both the BCTF and arbitrators agreed that school districts did not have to spend more than the provincial government gave them.

Changed Roles

The roles of many individuals and groups in British Columbia have been substantially affected by the move to province-wide collective bargaining. Local school boards, some feel, now "play with trains while others run the railroad." A similar dislocation is happening with the union locals, where union leaders have been accustomed to full release time. The question now has been raised as to whether local officials need any time off now that only a handful of minor issues are bargained locally.

Trustees still feel they broker provincial policies and set the climate for their school district. They view themselves as the last pillar of local democracy and one of few powers that can hold the province accountable for its actions. Who else, they ask, can challenge a social-activist tendency that is promoted by both government and teachers' unions? One example that has caused considerable debate and conflict, including a case that has gone to the British Columbia Supreme Court (Benson & Miller, 1999), has been over how the province's family life curriculum portrays families with same-sex parents. School boards elected in communities whose members hold traditional religious and cultural values have exercised their mandate to review and approve curriculum resource materials to ensure they are in keeping with local mores. Also, who else but a school board can initiate programs that may not be blessed by the central government, such as schools that are based upon traditional models of direct instruction?

Nevertheless, the *Public Education Labour Relations Act* must be viewed as a failure. In both rounds of bargaining to date, the province has undercut the employers' negotiating body by taking over bargaining and reaching a settlement. In the first instance, it provided funds that it previously had indicated were not available. In the second, it effectively joined with the leadership of the teachers' unions to implement a government policy that would have appeared quite modest in its direct benefit to teachers currently in the system but which set the provincial benchmark for salary settlements that the government desired. The government, for its part, could be accused of exercising its status as the single buyer of teachers' services to hold wages in check and use most new moneys for additional teaching positions rather than for pay increases. That the final agreement proved too generous given subsequent economic problems was just bad luck.

Concerns about Corporatist Trends

The corporatist tendencies of the British Columbia government are also reflected in policies adopted in many other provinces. Examples include the abolition of school boards in New Brunswick, the elimination of boards linked to religion in Quebec and Newfoundland, the amalgamation of school districts in Nova Scotia, Quebec, Ontario, Alberta and British Columbia, and the centralization of school finance in all but three provinces. Taken together, this innovative rearrangement of provincial governments in Canada concentrates tremendous power in the provincial capitals. A simultaneous decline in power in the federal government, beset by financial woes and constant threats of separation from Quebec, leaves these principal powers relatively unchecked from above.

Labor unions in Canada have tended to oppose these trends which, in a sense, is surprising in that social democratic governments in Europe have favored this form of social and economic policy making. Their skepticism in Canada may reflect a lack of appreciation of this tradition, a gut-level instinct that the hand that gives may also take away, or the view that in most cases management has a stronger hand at the table than labor.

In any case, the trend has received little debate except in the work of John Ralston Saul, whose *Voltaire's Bastards* (1992) criticizes the over-rationalization and corporate bureaucratization that is invading many aspects of Canadian society. He echoes the faint cries of school trustees who argue that making local democratic decisions, holding public discussions and being engaged in voluntary associations reflect key values of Western democracies. He believes these values and practices are being uprooted by the corporatist approach to social, economic and political management. In this view, province-wide bargaining is more than an attempt to gain efficiency by streamlining government, it is also a significant step toward corporatist government. In his writings, Saul is particularly concerned about the power of corporate business interests, which he sees as supreme today. While this may be so in the private sector, in the public sector more power often lies with labor rather than management, as the British Columbia experience demonstrates.

Without overstating the case, corporatist governments, particularly if they fall into the hands of charismatic demagogues, confer incredible power on a small group of individuals who represent groups in society rather than individuals or regions. These persons are likely to advocate group rights that favor the majority, such as mandatory membership in unions, rather than individual or minority rights. As well, they may take positions that do not represent, in a democratic sense, the interests of their members. A 1992 survey of BCTF members, for example, determined that 73 percent of the members viewed themselves as passive members of BCTF and only 12 percent as active members. Overall, 22 percent were very satisfied with BCTF, 59 percent somewhat satisfied, and 16 percent somewhat or very dissatisfied. Further, although they believed BCTF represented them well in protecting their rights and improving their professional lives and conditions in schools, a "major source of criticism... is that it is overly involved in political or what members perceive as issues unrelated to education (the abortion issue being the most common specific example cited)" (McIntyre & Mustel, 1992).[4] When the executive of the BCTF recommended the union join the Canadian Labour Congress, the membership voted the motion down.

What is termed the "iron law of oligarchy" holds that leadership in organizations tends to become concentrated in the hands of a few. This phenomenon may explain the divergence in views between the members of the BCTF and their leaders. As well, it can have disconcerting effects when a province or nation acts as if it were a corporate body – after all, the root word of "corporation" is "corpus" which means body in Latin – then the "needs" of the state, as perceived by those at the top, are given preference over the needs of individuals and minorities.

With centralization and a trend toward corporatist government, individuals and local agencies such as school boards are becoming little more than spectators while others decide how society and schools will be run. While it may be alarmist to suggest concentrated power will ultimately harm the social and economic welfare of individual citizens, there is evidence that this may be an outcome. Whether one considers higher rates of unemployment, the elimination of constitutional rights to religious schools in Newfoundland and Quebec, or mandatory union membership in British Columbia, one finds the state using its authority, directly or indirectly, to remove something that was precious to many individuals. In times of national emergency, such sacrifices are willingly made for the common good. Whether the times justify the strong actions that have been taken, or whether it would have been better to have left traditional structures and processes in place to work things out at a local level, are questions that it is probably too late to answer unless evident failures engender a reaction against centralized provincial control.

For teachers' unions, a drift toward neo-corporatist government presents a challenge. As a partner in government, unions in both the public and private sectors may be tempted to push their own agendas and to exert control over government or may be cajoled into putting aside their members' interests for the "benefit of the common good." Or, they may find themselves a junior partner subject to neglect by senior partners in government and business. Whatever the strategy they take, there are risks well beyond those normally faced in local negotiations simply because the stakes are much higher.

References

Assarsson, B. & Jansson, P. (1996). Unemployment persistence: The case of Sweden. FIEF (Trade Union Institute for Economic Research) Working Paper No. 40: www.fief.se

Benson, I. T. & Miller, B. (January 11, 1999). Court misunderstands the meaning of "secular." *Lex View* No. 25, Ottawa: Centre for Renewal of Public Policy.

Bridges, Edwin M. (1983). *Managing the incompetent teacher*. Eugene, OR: ERIC Clearinghouse on Educational Management.

British Columbia Public School Employers' Association (BCPSEA). (1997/98). *Annual Report*. Vancouver: BCPSEA.

British Columbia Public School Employers' Association (BCPSEA). (1997/98). www.bcpsea.bc.ca Vancouver: BCPSEA

British Columbia Teachers' Federation. (1998). www.bctf.bc.ca: Vancouver: BCTF.

Burnham, R. & O'Neill, T. (March 18, 1991). *British Columbia Report*, 37-39.

Galbraith, John Kenneth. (1967). *The new industrial state*. Boston: Houghton Mifflin.

Geisert, G. & Chandler, C. (Spring 1991). Learning the ABC's the hard way: Teacher unionism in the 1990s. *Government Union Review* 12(?), 1-21.

Gunderson, M. & Riddell, W. C. (1993). *Labour market economics*. (3rd ed.). Toronto: McGraw-Hill Ryerson.

Korbin, J. (1993). *The Report of the Commission of Inquiry into the Public Service and Public Sector. Volume 2. Final Report. The public sector in British Columbia*. Victoria: The Province of British Columbia.

McIntyre & Mustel Research Associates Ltd. (November 24, 1992). British Columbia Teachers' Federation Membership Survey. Presented to the British Columbia Teachers' Federation, Vancouver, B.C.

Reader's Digest (December 1996). Flexing union muscle, p. 24.

Saul, J. R. (1992). *Voltaire's bastards: The dictatorship of reason in the west*. New York: Viking.

Simpson, J. (July 3, 1998). The French may be a pain, but they're key to European integration. *The Globe and Mail*, p. A12.

Statistics Sweden (1998) *Unemployment (Labour Force Surveys)*: www.scb.se/snabb/akueng.htm

Notes

1. Helen Raham, Executive Director of the Society for the Advancement of Excellence in Education, collected much of the original material on which this chapter is based and generously made the files available for research purposes. The use made of these materials and inferences drawn from them are those of the first author.
2. Abbreviated BCPSEA, the employers' association is locally referred to in speech as "BCPC", the last "C" being the SEA in BCPSEA.
3. During 1997 and 1998 the New Democratic government worked to formulate a similar model of labor relations for the private sector but significant opposition from business and non-unionized labor stalled these plans.
4. The decision of BCTF leadership to poll its members on their opinions is a positive approach to formulating policy. It assists members in registering dissent without concern of retribution.

7

The Battle over Ontario's Bill 160

We need to invent a crisis.

John Snobelen, Minister of Education and Training

In Ontario's battle over Bill 160, the *Education Quality Improvement Act* (S.O. 1997, c. 31) a Biblical sense of righteousness motivated two organizational Goliaths as they girded their loins for the fight to the finish.[1] During the fall of 1997, on one side was the Progressive Conservative government of Premier Mike Harris and two Ministers of Education and Training, John Snobelen and his successor, Dave Johnson. Their equally bellicose opponents were the executives of the five teacher unions and their umbrella organization that collectively spoke for 126 000 educators in public, separate and francophone components of the publicly-funded education system. This system directly serves more than two million children and youth in Kindergarten to the end of secondary school as well as their parents and guardians, a public enterprise that in 1997 cost in excess of $14 billion, including government contributions to the teachers' pension fund.

The Harris government's rhetoric in support of Bill 160 reflected a neo-conservative spin on efficiency and accountability, the need to restore management rights, provider capture – the tendency for those providing a public service to capture the benefits of public funds for themselves – and on the legitimate authority of a democratically-elected government. Key features of the bill included a reduction in the scope of collective bargaining to exclude both preparation time and pupil teacher ratios (i.e., working conditions); a provincial takeover of school finance; and the replacement of special legislation for teacher collective bargaining with the province's *Labour Relations Act*. On the other side, the teacher union heads appealed for the maintenance of equity and the protection of a public good, for the exercise of democratic rights in consensual policy-making, and for a respect for professional autonomy. In the absence of any compelling vision of education from either the government's or the unions' side to galvanize the public imagination, such claims and counter-claims were reflected through the media as war-cries and chanted slogans dimly heard, and less understood, in the tumult of a public sector war.

Most of the front-page and lead-story media attention to Bill 160 was focused on the unfolding of the two-week "illegal strike," the government's description, or the "political protest," the teacher unions' label, that was called by union executives to protest the imminent imposition of the Bill. The strike over Bill 160 was larger than any teachers' strike in North American history, with more lost teaching days than the 1975 teachers' strike in New York City.

The Rules of Engagement

The battle over Bill 160 raises several issues that are of interest to public policy-makers on a national scale. One of these is the role of provincial governments and their agencies in labor relations, specifically for the public sector. In private sector negotiations, government is usually a disinterested party and may act as an intermediary in collective bargaining between corporations and unionized workers. This neutral role is more difficult, if not impossible, to maintain with public sector bargaining. In this case, it is sometimes said that there is a "ghost at the table" during negotiations: the spectre of the provincial government. Either directly or indirectly, the fact is that the government is the employer. Over the past two decades both the federal government and provincial governments have found it difficult to maintain their distance during collective negotiations, even when they occur at the local level, and have become directly involved, often with legislation to decide public sector disputes (Belman, Gunderson & Hyatt, 1996).

The rules of collective bargaining for teachers, moreover, differ because they often are guided by various teaching profession or education acts as opposed to provincial labor relations acts that govern most private and public collective bargaining. In effect, provinces and school boards now contract with unions, not teachers, to provide educational services to most schools across Canada. For publicly funded education, the vast majority of schools operate under a union contract that helps define, among other things, working conditions, staffing and staffing ratios, and the length of the working day. Legislation in most provinces grants the right to strike to teachers who provide a necessary service to the public, fostering an environment in which even provincial governments have been afraid to say "no" to their well-financed and politically powerful unions. In the critics' view, teachers' unions are frequently accused of having a hidden agenda. They suggest that, under the guise of achieving professional status for their members, teachers' unions have, over the past two decades, usurped control from management over many aspects of the public education system, including finances, curriculum, teaching methods, and professional development of teachers and administrators. According to critics, the potency of teachers' unions and the high degree of professional autonomy granted to teachers have contributed to a growing public concern about "provider capture," that teachers, union bureaucrats and school trustees are the primary beneficiaries of public funding to education, not students in schools.

For critics of the educational status quo, the telltale signs of provider capture were found in a variety of phenomena such as "Taj Mahal" school board offices presided over by scores of "educrats" whose salaries were often in the range of $100 000 or more per annum; trustees whose first concern of business seemed to be voting themselves pay raises and who seemed unwilling to restrain ever-rising spending and taxation; better salaries and earlier pensions for teachers whose compensation package differed little within one province, regardless of wide variations in the costs of living (especially housing) and in the ability of different districts to pay for such packages; Cadillac costs for Edsel results in student achievement, judging by recent national and international assessments; the consistent shrinking of the percentage of funds used for in-class resources such as books and materials; and the steady increase in students per classroom. An alternative view, voiced by opposition parties and the teachers' unions, was that the government was creating a deficit in order to pay for a reduction in the province's income tax rate, and forcing teachers, other public sector workers and beneficiaries of government transfer payments to carry the burden.

Bill 160 attracted considerable public heat for a number of reasons. Relative to the Bill's size (two hundred plus pages) and complexity, the government allowed only about four weeks for its discussion, either in the Legislature or in committee – with a few amendments inserted along the way. The haste attending to the evolution and discussion of the Bill, similar to the handling of other far-reaching pieces of legislation coming from the Harris government, sparked criticism that this government had deviated from the consensus-building approach to public policy that had been a fixture of Ontario politics since the 1960s. The present approach, some said, was an affront to the notion of natural justice. Often such a major piece of legislation is preceded by a white or green paper that outline the issues and options and invites public discussion. Bill 160 was preceded by no such papers, and its public discussion was truncated.

The Grievance: Bill 160

The commitment of the Harris government to Bill 160 was nevertheless unshakeable: it conformed to the efficiency and cost-cutting vision of the Progressive Conservatives' election platform, *The Common Sense Revolution*. Bill 160 had emerged as a central piece in the government's overall strategy of restructuring public services and downsizing budgets as well as downloading provincial responsibility for welfare, public housing, and policy in tandem with the amalgamation of a number of municipalities, including the Metropolitan Toronto Area, on January 1, 1998. Simultaneously, the Minister of Health was restructuring the publicly-funded health care system by merging and closing hospitals. To make all this possible, the province needed to assume a larger share of educational funding out of its general revenue in order to provide tax room on the property tax base for municipalities. Effectively, the property tax for education was being cut in half and school boards were to be barred from access to it to raise funds. For this "tax swap" to occur, Bill 160 – or at least key parts of Bill 160 – had to be passed.

The depth of government commitment to Bill 160 was probably not understood initially by the federations' spokespersons who hailed the dumping of Minister Snobelen on the eve of the walk-out as an indication of a weakening of governmental knees. After all, the union reasoning went, the government had earlier caved into the medical profession's fee-related demands, so what not the teaching profession's? But Snobelen's successor in the portfolio, Dave Johnson, proved no less determined to push the Bill through, with a few amendments along the way, in a forceful but controlled manner. He left no illusions that Bill 160 received the full blessing of the Premier and key members of the Cabinet, although a few Progressive Conservative backbenchers ventured to voice their public doubts about the government's intentions.

While Ontario school boards are technically the employers of educators, the Harris government had no faith in trustees' ability and desire to rein in the escalating costs and attendant property and commercial taxes required to underwrite them. It would thus fall to the government's side to publicly champion the rights of management to define the parameters of the bargaining process. Management in this context meant the Ministry of Education and Training and educational administrators and trustees at school board levels, but the battle for Bill 160 also stretched that role to include, unequivocally, principals and vice-principals at the school level. The scope of teacher contracts from other provinces was used to justify a renorming of management rights. According to the Harris government, the "working conditions" that were negotiable in Ontario teacher contracts, such as the length of the school day and teacher preparation time, were too favorable to teachers and did not make efficient use of either teacher time or numbers. Bill 160 was fashioned to address these issues.

Bill 160 also replaced Bill 100, *The School Boards and Teachers Collective Negotiations Act*, passed in 1975, that had defined collective bargaining between school boards and teacher federations on behalf of teachers. Scrapping Bill 100 was one of 14 recommendations of the 1996 review of collective bargaining in education by Windsor lawyer Leon Paroian (1996). Paroian found that in Ontario over the past two decades, teachers' unions had with regularity used their collective muscle and professional negotiating expertise, with implicit or explicit threats of working-to-rule and strikes, to exact favorable contracts from local trustees. He recommended revising the definition of a teacher's working day to include extra-curricular activities, adopting a regional model of collective bargaining, excluding principals and vice-principals from bargaining units, providing conciliation and mediation services under the *Labour Relations Act*, eliminating the Education Relations Commission, constraining the right to strike or lock-out, and using mandatory arbitration to settle disputes.

While Paroian's report clearly had a seminal influence on the shape of Bill 160 (Shilton & Pask, 1997), few commentators in the media made this connection and his report met with bitter denunciations from teacher union heads. Paroian, a labor lawyer, had for years acted on behalf of teacher unions in negotiations with school boards, but had come to the conclusion that Bill 100 had stacked the deck in favor of teachers and their unions to the clear detriment of the interests of students, parents and taxpayers.

Some clauses of Bill 160 drew upon the recommendations from the first report of the Education Improvement Commission (EIC) headed by former NDP Minister of Education Dave Cooke and former chair of the Metropolitan Toronto School Board, Ann Vanstone. The EIC recommended increasing learning time by extending the work day and the school year and the use of differentiated staffing, or allowing non-certified individuals to assist in teaching specific subjects such as computer science and physical education.

Prior to reports from Paroian and the EIC, Ontario's Royal Commission on Learning (RCOL, 1994) had raised concerns about the conflicting roles assumed by teachers' unions, concluding that while success in negotiating contracts had allowed teachers within a single professional lifetime to advance from being members of the lower-middle class to becoming members of the upper-middle class – and the best compensated teaching force in all ten provinces – teachers' unions had accomplished this by making collective bargaining the central focus of their agendas. Professional concerns of teachers, RCOL believed, had received insufficient attention. This recognition prompted the Commissioners to recommend the creation of The Ontario College of Teachers to assume a governance role over professional issues such as teacher accreditation and discipline (*The Ontario College of Teachers Act, 1996*). The need for such a body had in the 1980s received support from Progressive Conservative Minister of Education Bette Stephenson, but the idea was withdrawn because of fierce opposition from teachers' unions, who portrayed it as an encroachment upon the collective bargaining process. NDP Minister Dave Cooke, however, agreed with the Royal Commission and pushed through the legislation creating the College in 1995, the second in Canada after British Columbia.

As introduced for its first reading to the Ontario Legislature by Minister of Education and Training John Snobelen on September 23, 1997, Bill 160 would allow the Ontario government and the Ministry of Education and Training to: set limits on class size; cut teacher preparation time for the secondary panel by as much as fifty percent; increase the number of days students and teachers spend in class each year; have teachers come back to work the last week of August to prepare for the school year, thus removing five professional days that were inserted in the school year that required students not to have classes on those days; expand the use of non-certified instructors in specialty programs such as counselling, computers or guidance; take over the setting of educational property tax rates from school boards; fund students equally whether they are in public or separate schools; and establish advisory school councils for every school in the province to get more parental involvement in education.

For their part, teachers' federations, who formed the core opposition to Bill 160, countered with the following demands: retain the negotiation of preparation time and pupil teacher ratios; no layoffs of teachers; no non-certified staff replacing teachers; and school boards to maintain control of property tax rates.

In the complicated topography of Ontario educational politics, the fractured nature of federation memberships reflected a number of factors related to panel (elementary or secondary), gender, secularity and religion, and language that were paved over, at least temporarily, through the formation of a united front against Bill

160: Ontario Teachers' Federation (OTF), the umbrella organization, 126 000 teachers; Ontario Secondary School Teachers' Federation (OSSTF), 35 000 educators in the secondary panel, public system; Association des enseignantes et des enseignants franco-ontariens (AEFO), 6500 educators at elementary and secondary levels; Ontario Public School Teachers' Federation (OPSTF), 13 000 male educators at the elementary level, public system; Ontario English Catholic Teachers' Association (OECTA), 31 500 educators at elementary and secondary levels in the separate (English-speaking Roman Catholic) component; and the Federation of Women Teachers' Associations of Ontario (FWTAO), 40 000 female educators at the elementary, public level.

OSSTF has been also the most politically militant of the federations, with a long history of supporting social democratic principles of the provincial New Democratic party. OSSTF shared with OECTA the distinction of joining the Ontario Federation of Labour; their presidents publicly proclaimed their pride in all the connotations that the word "union" suggests while their counterparts were more comfortable with the label of "professional association" which has distinctly other professional and public connotations. The OSSTF executive, along with those of other public unions, had led the criticism of the former NDP government's imposition of the Social Contract in 1993 that not only cut public sector salaries for over three years but also downsized the public sector. Some public sector unions executives viewed Premier Rae's Social Contract as a betrayal of social democratic principles and urged their members to withhold their support for the NDP in the election of June 8, 1995. Instead they promoted a strategy whereby public sector unions would initiate direct political action on behalf of their own members. In this scenario the public sector unions were carving a role for themselves as an extra-parliamentary opposition, and this mindset was operationalized when the results of that election brought to power the Progressive Conservatives led by Mike Harris. For their part, public sector union executives, including teacher unions, were in no mood to cooperate with a new government whose prescription for renewing fiscal health to Ontario was considered even more repugnant than the previous government's perceived betrayal. For them, direct political action and confrontation would be their answer to Harris's agenda.

Bill 160 threatened the five teacher unions differently. All of them would be of less value to their members if the list of negotiable items in a contract was reduced. All unions would lose an undetermined number of their members under Bill 160, but those representing public secondary school teachers would be the hardest hit, since some specific clauses were aimed only at the secondary panel. OSSTF, which represents public secondary teachers exclusively, was the most directly affected since reductions in preparation time, elimination of examination days, the elimination of the Ontario Academic Credit year, previously Grade 13, are primarily that panel's concerns. OECTA, which bargains for all Catholic educators, also had a healthy secondary contingent, as did the much smaller AEFO. Reducing preparation time for secondary school teachers would not only change their working conditions but would also reduce the numbers of teachers needed to cover all classes, although hard numbers as to magnitude were not forthcoming from either side. The elimination of the OAC year would also cost jobs and induce considerable "bumping" based on seniority, although protections for incumbent teachers were included in the *Act* (s. 177.13(3)).

The Battle

The strike called to protest Bill 160 lasted a total of ten teaching days, from Monday, October 27 to Friday, November 7, 1997. On and off again negotiations between teachers' federations and the government ended on November 5 when teachers withdrew from negotiations. In between, a judge refused a government-sought injunction to end the strike. Members of all five federations went on strike collectively, and more than 60 000 unionized custodians, secretaries and other non-teaching personnel honored their picket lines. The decision by unions to return to work, however, was not collectively reached but was triggered when elementary school teachers' spokespersons (FWTAO, OPSTF and AEFO) decided to throw in the towel, thus forcing their more aggrieved counterparts in OSSTF and OECTA to follow suit.

During the strike, parents, students, trustees were largely on the side-lines, although some parents and students chose an active role in mushrooming protest groups, several of which had close ties to opposition parties in the Legislature, to express solidarity with educators. Some activists were ejected from the visitors' gallery at the Legislature as this sentiment became demonstrative, and several teachers staged a sit-in of several days' duration at the Ministry of Education and Training. Within the Legislature, the opposition Liberals and New Democrats took their cue from one parent group's "apple green" ribbon campaign to protest Bill 160 and donned articles of green clothing in sittings over a couple of weeks, lending the proceedings the surreal flair of a St. Patrick's Day celebration. For many activists Bill 160 was the lightning rod that crystallized a growing sense of public uneasiness about the wider Harris agenda, in which every public sector was simultaneously being subjected to large-scale restructuring and retrenchment.

The relative passivity of school board trustees during the strike was partially motivated by the decision of the government to amalgamate boards and to cut the number of trustees. Powers of elected school trustees had already been reduced by the recently adopted *Fewer School Boards Act* (S.O. 1997, c. 3) which merged Ontario's 169 school districts into 68 that are divided along religious (public and Roman Catholic) and linguistic (English, French) lines. Most sitting trustees did not run for office in elections on November 10 since the *Fewer School Boards Act* reduced their numbers by two-thirds and limited their salaries to $5000; formerly trustees in large cities were paid as much as $50 000 per year. School boards, as employers, might have requested a hearing before the Labour Relations Board in order to obtain a back-to-work order since they were the affected parties; i.e., it was their contracts that were being violated. Instead, school boards' associations, after nine days without teachers, tried to act as peace makers, suggesting that the most contentious parts of the legislation be put on hold while the funding arrangements were altered in preparation for school district mergers under a new Ontario regulation, *Establishment, Areas of Jurisdiction, and Names of District School Boards*.

This restructuring was due to come into effect in a few weeks after the passage of Bill 160, also on January 1, 1998, and school board officials and staff had more than enough on their organizational plates to ready themselves for this change, without being dragged into another fight not of their making. Bill 160 posed an additional impediment to school board cohesion and solidarity as the proposed new funding formula promised to rectify a long-standing complaint by separate school trustees that the existing funding formula penalized one-third of all publicly-funded students. This fact not only separated the ranks of public and separate trustees but also prompted the spokespersons of the Ontario Separate School Trustees' Association to distance themselves from the anti-government posturing of their OECTA counterparts. The OSSTA refused to join OECTA in a legal challenge to the Bill that claimed that, because Bill 160 stripped Roman Catholic school boards of the right to levy their own taxes, it violated Section 93 of the *Constitution Act*'s provisions guaranteeing the denominational rights of Roman Catholics in Ontario. The Catholic trustees' association was willing to exchange separate school boards' tax levying powers for a uniform funding model that would put their per capita funding on a par with the public component, a change that would increase funding across-the-board for students in Catholic schools. OECTA, on the other hand, was willing to make no such concessions, contending that the OSSTA did not have a right to bargain away constitutionally entrenched rights.

Public opinion during the strike began to swing more favorably towards the educators when a leaked performance contract of the deputy minister indicated that the government indeed had some hard numbers to suggest that a further cost-cutting was a priority of their agenda. Around $670 million was anticipated in the next round of cuts, a revelation that enforced the claim of the government's critics who contended all along that beneath the smoke and mirrors, Bill 160 was about "gutting public education" to finance an overly ambitious tax cut. The general uncertainty about the magnitude of the change was heightened because the new funding model that would specify per pupil and program funding would not be in place until March 1998, several months *after* Bill 160 had been passed in the Legislature.

After the dust had settled upon the battlefield with the collapse of the strike, the government claimed victory, having used its hefty majority to push Bill 160 to third reading over the raucous denunciations of opposition party members in the Legislature. The federations' spokespersons cited polls to proclaim that teacher organizations had won the battle for public opinion. While teachers probably earned a public relations victory thanks to perceived government skullduggery on the hidden part of the cost-cutting agenda, they were able to coax few substantial changes from the government, which introduced a number of amendments to the Bill after it was first introduced in the Legislature.

To quell accusations that cabinet would have too much power over staffing levels, the government introduced amendments to specify average class sizes (22 secondary and 25 elementary) and reductions in preparation time for secondary teachers (a one-third reduction rather than the one-half reduction initially proposed). However, the government expressed its dismay at seeing principals leaving schools along with teachers for the picket lines by adding an amendment that would remove principals and vice principals from teacher federations. This action alone could cost the unions around 10 percent of their members and revenue. The government also quickly passed legislation, after Bill 160 received third reading, granting affected parents $40 a day for child care for each school child 13 years-old-and-under for up to ten days. Also, a clause was attached that would protect teachers who crossed the picket line from union reprisals, evoking howls of derision from the Legislature's opposition during first reading on November 17, 1997.

While the editors of the *Toronto Star* took an increasingly critical tone about the government's agenda around Bill 160, their counterparts at the *Globe and Mail* and the *Sun* were much more positively inclined. Both the government and the unions in the war for public opinion had used print and television to explain their arguments and to deride their opponent's motivation. Some of the propaganda on both sides was of questionable taste or veracity. After the strike, the OTF and five affiliated unions launched a libel suit over the government's portrayal in the media of their positions, claiming that the ads, in the words of OTF head Eileen Lennon, "deliberately misrepresented our positions." OECTA also commenced litigation to clarify the legal status of principals and vice-principals who also teach because the removal of principals from bargaining units would leave these individuals filling positions designated for members of teachers' unions.

The Aftermath

In March 1998, at its annual general meeting, the OSSTF executive announced its plans to influence the outcome of the next provincial election, and OECTA agreed to join in the effort. The associations plan to identify 25 to 40 key ridings where the Tories are vulnerable, to provide special training to members and make them available to candidates, and to lobby and possibly publicly boycott corporations that have contributed $1000 or more to Conservative re-election coffers. Spokespeople for the other teacher federations were less enthusiastic for this type of electioneering, although in 1998 the newly formed Elementary Teachers' Federation of Ontario (ETFO) adopted a supplemental levy of $25 per member to fund political action committee election initiatives. With 70 000 members, ETFO became the largest teachers' union in Ontario on July 1, 1998, with the merger of FWTAO and OPSTF. At OSSTF's general meeting in March 1998, its president, Earl Manners, also proposed merging all teacher unions and support staff unions into one big union to "give us one strong voice for the public schools." Other teacher union heads, however, publicly distanced themselves from Manners' merger plan.

Also in March 1998, the Johnson Ministry announced the details of its long-awaited and overdue funding formula for schools and the budget for the 1998/1999 school year. The government's objective with this model is threefold:

1. to provide adequate and uniform funding to meet the needs of all students regardless of which component of the system they find themselves in;
2. to increase the amount of spending that goes directly to the classroom and at the same time reduce non-classroom spending, especially central office administrative costs; and
3. to stabilize class sizes.

According to the government, the good news of this budget for all school boards was that no substantial cuts of the type imposed in the previous two years were included for total educational spending, which was set at the same level through the year 2001; namely, $13 billion, with $1.4 billion in additional funding for teacher pension contributions and restructuring costs associated with the amalgamation of school systems. Roman Catholic separate boards were pleased because the new uniformity in provincial funding on a student per capita basis ended decades of what they viewed as inequitable funding. Although some were surprised to find that the new funding model offered little or no additional funds; for public boards, especially big city boards, the budget imposed a decrease in per student funding. One separate school official ironically noted, "When we said we wanted equity, we meant we wanted to move up to the public board level, not bring them down to ours."

The bad news for all types of school boards, aside from no longer being able to tap the local tax base, is that new funding was placed in specific envelopes such as the classroom foundation, special education, early learning and central administration. Boards would no longer have discretion to move funds from one envelope to another, although dispensations to this rule began to flow during frustrating contract negotiations in the fall of 1998. In the eyes of teachers' unions and many school trustees, the budget was anything but generous. They insisted that the new funding model accompanying the budget entailed substantial cuts to funding because the model did not take into account increased enrolments and inflation.

If the Harris government thought that the passage of Bill 160 would stabilize educational politics it was in for a rude awakening. On the legal front, OECTA's constitutional challenge was addressed at the provincial level in July 1998. In *Ontario English Catholic Teachers' Association et al. v. Ontario*, the Ontario Court's General Division ruled a section of the Bill unconstitutional because it violated the rights of Roman Catholics to have their own school boards with tax levying powers as guaranteed by s. 93(1) of the *Constitution Act*, 1867. Justice Cumming also criticized the Bill on the basis that it was hastily put together and discussed, and suffered from a lack of sufficient prior analysis. The same ruling shocked public school trustees because the Court maintained that public school boards did not possess the same rights to levy taxes as separate boards because the former's authority in this regard was not constitutionally entrenched. The judge's ruling seemed to ignore judicial precedents in Alberta and Quebec, as well as other Anglo-democracies, where full state funding has been found compatible with minority rights. The Catholic trustees' association and the government scrambled to construct an *ad hoc* arrangement that would allow the funding model to continue, the government decided to appeal the General Court's decision on the constitutional issue. The Ontario Public School Boards' Association also launched an appeal, aiming to overturn the decision that nullified public boards tax-levying powers.

Nor on the labor front was lasting peace forthcoming in the wake of Bill 160, one provision of which made all existing negotiated contracts null and void after August 31, 1998. Both public and Roman Catholic teacher unions used this opportunity to signal that they would strike to support their demands. Compensation issues were not often cited as motivating factors. Rather, still smoldering fury at Bill 160, particularly the section that increased secondary school teachers' instructional time and threatened thousands of jobs, galvanized renewed militancy. Some school boards were seen as being opportunistic, mandating more time for classroom instruction than the legislatively imposed 1250 minutes, suggesting that "contract stripping" was the order of the day.

This time, though, no general strike was in the offing. Rather OECTA encouraged members to refuse to take on an additional class. Faced with having one-seventh of their classes uncovered, a number of separate boards, including the massive Toronto Separate School District, locked-out their teachers, although teachers did strike in several separate school districts. In public schools, the dominant strategy was to teach additional classes as assigned, but to refuse all "voluntary" activities such as coaching sports, conducting concerts and accompanying field trips. Some instructional days were lost through rotating strikes called by OSSTF and the Elementary Teachers' Federation of Ontario. At the same time, with a new funding formula that penalized excess classroom capacity, as defined by the Ministry, school boards throughout Ontario began to plan for the closure of up to 600 schools – about 10 per cent of all schools – prompting angry reactions from many trustees, parents and teachers' unions.

By the end of September 1998, the government felt pressured to end this disruption as parents became increasingly disgruntled. A number of polls suggested that neither the government nor the teachers' unions escaped the public's blame for this impasse. Acting quickly, the government decided to bypass normal procedures that required the Education Relations Commission to declare the school year "in jeopardy" before the government considered back-to-work legislation. Instead, on September 28, 1998, the government introduced Bill 62 to force the teachers back to work. Bowing to a threat from opposition parties to tie up the passage of this legislation through procedural wrangling, Minister Johnson agreed to "split the bill in half" and to deal with the contentious issue of defining instructional time for a later date. With that concession, the Bill passed in one day. Within one or two days all students were back in the classroom, almost one month after the official school year commenced.

While school boards began to plan how the missed days would be made up, teachers' unions instructed their returning members to withdraw their services in all "voluntary" areas, and extracurricular activities were not supervised by teachers until contracts were settled. In short, the bitterness engendered by Bill 160 remained and at least two main issues the definition of instructional time and the constitutionality of sections of the Bill itself await further resolution on year after the Bill's passage.

The Meaning of It All

In assigning some meaning to the evolution of Bill 160 and its possible implications for the future of teacher collective bargaining in Ontario, we begin with a quote from University of Toronto political scientist Ronald Manzer (1994, p. 18) who noted that,

Institutional arrangements for public decision-making thus incorporate the influences of both public philosophy and partisan doctrines, and their structure and functioning over time reflect changes in both public philosophy and partisan doctrines.

The fight over Bill 160, and the content of the legislation itself, as well as recent related legislation, can be seen in this light as a partial restructuring of the decision-making process within the Ontario educational system. In this perspective, Bill 160 is about party and partisan politics, about contested authority and the exercise of power by various institutional actors possessing differing resources to further their particular agendas, whether they are the Harris government and the Ministry of Education and Training, or trustee associations, or teachers' unions. But this was also a fight about public values and about how public decisions are made in the educational community. Of particular interest in this discussion are three differing conceptions of the relationship of central and local educational authorities, to which are related models of teacher collective bargaining.

Early within the radical liberal tradition two different positions were developed to prescribe the mutual relationship of a central government to a local form of government or agency. One position, "administrative agency," is associated with Jeremy Bentham, who was influenced by Napoleonic reforms of government. This position posits that maximizing utility – the greatest good for the greatest number of citizens – requires a systematic hierarchy of legislative and executive agencies, over which the central legislative assembly is supreme. Thus the proper role of local governments, in the Benthamite scheme, is as a subordinate agency of the centre to ensure accountability and efficiency, through regulation enforcement and uniform service delivery. School boards in this scenario are faithful executors of centrally defined mandates.

Another radical liberal position, associated with John Stuart Mill and the movement for local democracy, is called "policy tutelage," whereby the centre decides uniform policy goals and sets guidelines and standards for policy implementation. In this scenario, school boards would be allowed discretion over administration, and should be allowed sufficient slack to adapt central policies to fit local circumstances. A corollary of this Millian view is subsidiarity, that while the centre should define principles, the power to deal with details should be matched by the agency most competent to deal with it (Manzer, 1994, pp. 24-25). But just as the term "tutelage" implies, the centre also plays a key role in educating local decision-making units about their responsibilities and their limitations.

A third understanding of central-local relations is that of policy interdependence in which central and local authorities are separate institutions that share power to make public policy. Unlike administrative agency and tutelage, however, where the centre remains the key policy-making unit, interdependence means that policy evolves out of dialogue and bargaining. In this conception school boards are not subordinate units of the Ministry, but rather partners who encourage the involvement of other stakeholders in the decision-making process.

In terms of the distribution of power within the educational policy community, the Harris government's changes – in collective bargaining, in school board amalgamations, in a new funding model and in curriculum development and assessment – all point to a degree of centralization that puts the government and the Ministry of Education and Training back in the driver's seat of publicly-funded education. The Benthamite logic of this centralization seems to suggest that uniformity and standardization are the main criteria by which the Harris government assesses its policy initiatives. Some of these initiatives were a recent legacy of the former government and all of them reflect national trends in governance in which school boards' discretion has been steadily eroded. Of all the provinces, Ontario has had the most ground to cover in implementing an agenda of centralization because, since the late 1960s, its educational system had evolved to be the most decentralized in Canada. This situation allowed particularly large city public boards to operate in a relatively autonomous fashion *vis à vis* the Ministry, using their privileged access to commercial and property taxation as the foundation. The accountability movement of the 1990s, pushing and pulling from the outside until governments got the message, demanded clearer provincial educational standards, better quality assurance, and controlling the costs of education and the taxes levied to finance them. Seen in this light, educational governance in Ontario is being moved rather abruptly away from a model of policy interdependence that had dominated centre-local relationships since the late 1960s and is being pulled by the Harris government towards the Benthamite administrative agency model. How well this model fits with the reality of collective bargaining is problematic.

Presently, as described in chapter 3, models of teacher collective bargaining differ across Canada. Newfoundland, Prince Edward Island, New Brunswick and Quebec have provincial bargaining; Nova Scotia, Saskatchewan and British Columbia have shared provincial and local bargaining; and Ontario, Manitoba and Alberta employ local bargaining. Each model has its strengths and weaknesses. More centralized systems lead toward more uniform practices, reflect economic and political priorities of provincial governments, and may engender either a province-wide teacher identity or yield more distant ties between teachers' and their unions, depending on circumstances. More localized bargaining emphasizes relationships between local teacher groups and trustees, and reflects local political and economic priorities. Often, local bargaining is paired with province-wide activities coordinated by provincial teachers' federations, trustees' associations, and sometimes agencies of the provincial government.

Decentralized arrangements for education, including local taxation and bargaining, seemed to disappoint fiscally conservative provincial governments in the past decade. Putting aside educational matters – what students are taught and how well they are learning – about which concern has also been raised, it is not apparent that local economic control has led to efficiency, as predicted by the Millian theory of subsidiarity. Local decisions often led to tax and expenditure increases at a time when other levels of government had committed themselves to deficit reduction and reduced program spending. One could argue that, with the Millian approach to local educational governance in a number of provinces, it was the provincial government's responsibility to offer strong tutelage as to the fiscal parameters within which school boards needed to operate, given provincial and federal priorities. Perhaps provincial governments believed that they had made such efforts and that they had failed to convince school boards whose immediate concern was to maintain labor peace at any cost. At one point, Ontario had even offered financial bonuses to school boards that set their tax rates within provincially set guidelines. Few school boards collected. In any case, in Ontario, centralized direction and regulation have now replaced policy interdependence and tutelage.

The dynamics of collective bargaining invariably play a major role in directing regulatory change. In Ontario, the existing framework was developed in the mid-1970s when Bill 100 was adopted, conferring upon teachers the right to strike as well as creating a complex process of information collection and dissemination, mediation and fact-finding. This legislation resolved a crisis that had involved *de facto* strikes by teachers' federations in the form of mass resignations and a march on Queen's Park, as described in chapter 2. Subsequently, it became evident that the two sides in bargaining – trustees and teachers' federations – were not equally matched. Local teachers' unions drew upon the resources of provincial offices staffed by seasoned experts, practicing "pattern" bargaining in which the provincial officials would draft the contract clauses, and fought by whipsawing school boards so that each school board felt compelled to match the clauses won by teachers in neighboring boards. When, on occasion, little was to be had in terms of wages, job security in the form of better staffing ratios were sought. The net result was that total compensation costs often outstripped any increases in provincial funding, thereby necessitating local tax increases.

Trustees, for their part, had to run for election every three years; their provincial organizations often fought among themselves over issues such as the financing of Roman Catholic schools. The trustees' province-wide coordinating organization collapsed over conflict about the extension of funding to Catholic high schools beyond Grade 10. Also, trustee associations lacked the tens of millions of dollars in dues enjoyed by teachers' unions. At one point, the Ontario government extended to trustees the right to set their own compensation in the expectation that more confident and capable trustees would be elected. It hoped that they would be able to rise to the challenge. In the Conservative government's view, they did not and Bill 160 stripped them of this privilege. Trustees' honoraria are now limited to $5000 per year or less.

The new regime in Ontario certainly rectifies many of these problems, but not by providing increased tutelage. In terms of finance, the province has assumed responsibility for 100 percent of educational funding and restricted how much school districts will be able to spend in each of a number of areas. While under Bill 160 collective bargaining will still be at the local level, there will be significant differences. Key parameters affecting the numbers of teachers will now be set provincially, not locally through the negotiation of working conditions.

The net result is a very restricted arena in which collective bargaining can take place. The province, with its controls the amount school boards spend on education and approximately how many teachers are employed, now essentially determines the compensation budget for teachers. Locally, the primary matters to be negotiated are how these funds will be allocated between salary and benefits, and how funds are distributed on the salary grid. The narrowed scope for bargaining compensation may direct the bargaining process to focus increasingly on "non-financial" matters that invariably have financial implications. Among these will be issues such as grievance procedures, the authority of principals, and the structure of schools and school programs. Ultimately, bargaining on such issues can result in a diminution of management rights. A pattern of settlement spreading across the province for secondary schools reduces management's authority to allocate staff within schools:

> Of the 1250 minutes, a minimum of 125 minutes of instructional time [each week] will be assigned to other timetabled instructional duties, including: library and media instruction; guidance and counselling; scheduled student evaluation and assessment time; assigned on-call classroom instruction, including special education and remedial classes; tutorial and remediation instructing including special education resource; teacher advisory group/mentoring, or assigned time in other provincially mandated programs (Public District School Board).

Other clauses also constrict the ability of management, including principals, to develop innovative organizational structures. One agreement include the statement that all "school-based positions of added responsibility, including Head and Associate Head, shall be subject/curriculum based and set the number of such heads and associate heads." Requirements that each teacher shall be given 40 minute lunch and 50 minutes of preparation time are typical, as is the creation of a staffing advisory committees. In one board, such a committee is "composed of three (3) members appointed by the Board and three (3) members appointed by the bargaining unit" to oversee the implementation and operation of the staffing clauses, an approach that comes very close to co-management. It is doubtful that such a departure from traditional governance ought to be adopted without widespread discussion in a public forum.

Ontario's Benthamite solutions to its political and administrative problems may provide the grip on the educational system the government seeks. Yet, while this approach may serve to temporarily bolster management rights with this current government, a future government could just as easily use the same approach to undermine them. A Benthamite centralization may allow a government with unabashed sympathies for public sector unions an unfettered opportunity to express that solidarity in political and monetary terms because school boards no longer have any substantial countervailing powers. That is, the Benthamite solution is by no means a sure remedy to what ails centre-local relationships and teacher collective bargaining in Ontario, and its application in this context in the next few years merits close scrutiny.

References

Belman, D., Gunderson, M. & Hyatt, D. (Eds.). (1996). *Public sector employment in a time of transition*. Madison, WI: Industrial Relations Research Association.

Bentham, J. (1962). The constitutional code. In J. Bowering, (Ed.), *The collected works of Jeremy Bentham, Vol. 9, Book 2*. New York: Russell and Russell.

Council of Ministers of Education, Canada. (1996) *The Development of Education: Report of Canada*. Toronto: CMEC.

Education Improvement Commission. (1997). *The road ahead: A report on learning time, class size and staffing*. Toronto: Ontario Ministry of Education and Training.

Education Quality Improvement Act. S.O. 1997, c. 31.

Establishment, Areas of Jurisdiction, and Names of District School Boards. Regulation 186/97 as amended O. Reg 278/97, O. Reg. 80/98.

Ibbitson, J. (1997). *Promised land: Inside the Mike Harris revolution*. Scarborough, ON: Prentice Hall Canada.

Lawton, S. (August 1997). Pressure for change: Bargaining in British Columbia. *School Business Affairs*, 63(8), pp. 21-24.

Manzer, R. (1994). *Public schools and political ideas: Canadian educational policy in historical perspective*. Toronto: University of Toronto Press.

Mill, J.S. (1912). Considerations on representative government. In John Stuart Mill, *On liberty, representative government, the subjection of women: Three essays*. London: Oxford University Press.

The Ontario College of Teachers Act, 1996. S.O. 1996, c. 12 as amended. 1997, c. 31, s. 161.

Paroian, L. (1996). *Review of the school boards'/teachers' collective negotiations process in Ontario*. Toronto: Ministry of Education and Training.

Public District School Board. (October 1998). *Memorandum of Settlement between the Public District School Board and the Ontario Secondary School Teachers' Federation*.

Royal Commission on Learning. (1994). *For the Love of Learning*. Toronto: RCOL.

Shilton, E.J. & Pask, A. (1997). Collective bargaining in an era of fiscal restraint: More regulation or deregulation? In W.F. Foster & W.J. Smith (Eds.). *Navigating change in education: The law as a beacon*, Montreal: CAPSLE, pp. 142-144.

Snobelen, J. (1996) Quoted in *Inventing crisis: The erosion of confidence in Canadian public education*. Ottawa: Canadian Teachers' Federation, p. 4.

Notes

1. A portion of this chapter was first published under the title, "The battle over Ontario's Bill 160 and the shape of collective bargaining," *Policy Options*, 19(6), 49-54.

8

Teachers' Unions in Anglo-Democracies

Pennsylvania Governor Tom Ridge [treats] all public education groups, not just the teachers' unions, with suspicion and ... disdain.

Boyd, Plank and Sykes, 1998

The emergence of central authority as a barrier or opponent to the realization of teacher unions' aspirations is not limited to Canada. In the United States, the United Kingdom, Australia and New Zealand confrontations have occurred as governments adopted policies to bring about changes, often opposed by teachers' unions, to their schools. A brief survey of their experiences may be useful on several counts: first, to understand that the tensions between governments and teachers' unions exist elsewhere; second, to place our own experiences in context – our images of events here may appear less extreme in comparison; and third, to discover alternative approaches to employer-teacher relations that may have merit or ought to be avoided.

United States

About two-thirds of the states of the United States have labor relations legislation permitting collective bargaining (Bascia, 1997); in other states, school districts may engage in discussions with teachers' associations. These discussions are usually voluntary and may be one-sided or amount to collective negotiations, in which case the parties may agree to be bound by the resulting contracts. Most U.S. teacher unions and associations are linked with either the National Education Association (NEA), which converted to a union model in the early 1970s, or the American Federation of Teachers (AFT), which has followed the union model since its founding early in the 20th century. Teachers in states allowing collective bargaining permit teachers to vote upon the organization that will represent them; some allow agency shops, while others do not. That is, U.S. states do not adhere to the predominant Canadian model in which legislation defines teachers' bargaining units and bargaining agents and forgoes the issues of organization, jurisdiction, dues check-off and the like. As a result, teachers' unions in the United States, where they exist, have less in the way of union security than is typical in Canada.

In spite of the weaker regulatory structures at the state level, U.S. teachers' associations have proven to be powerful influences on the national and state levels, in part because of the relatively uniform character of education across the country. As well, the significant role in education that the U.S. federal government has come to play no doubt acts as a unifying factor. The NEA and AFT can and do lobby the U.S. Congress for direct aid to education, as reflected in the "teacher friendly" budget adopted for 1999 which includes partial funding for 100 000 additional teachers. In Canada, divergent educational structures in the provinces, Quebec's defense of its autonomy, and the sovereigntist orientation of its largest French-language teachers' union, have limited the extent of federal actions supporting education in Canada. One cannot imagine Prime Minister Chrétien announcing federal funds for new teachers across Canada, or the Canadian Teachers' Federation lobbying for such a program.

During the 1990s, educational politics and policies in two Great Lakes states, Michigan and Pennsylvania, echo many of the themes evident in the events experienced in Canada. These states are similar in size and economic diversity to Quebec and Ontario and, like them, have experienced a wrenching conversion from smokestack industries of the 1980s "rust belt" to the knowledge and information based industries of the future.

Boyd, Plank and Sykes (1998) write that, "In the 1970s and 1980s, the teachers unions in Michigan and Pennsylvania were among the most powerful and strike-prone in the United States. They won rapid and substantial gains for their members, and played a dominant role in school politics and state politics more generally. . . . The Michigan Education Association [MEA] (an affiliate of the NEA) assumed 'Godzilla-like' preeminence within the state Democratic party. . . . ." This dominant role in their state educational systems, however, has declined since the election of "activist Republican Governors in the 1990s" (pp. 1 & 3).

In Michigan, Governor John Engler's first educational initiative was to put forward a proposal to reduce property taxes and to redistribute wealth to benefit poorer rural areas. Opposed by the MEA, the initiative was defeated, but in the aftermath,

a Democratic legislator, positioning herself for a gubernatorial campaign, proposed that property taxes simply be eliminated as a funding source for public schools. Recognizing an extraordinary political opportunity, the Republican caucus supported the bill, and Governor Engler signed it. At the end of a protracted political struggle Michigan voters approved . . . [shifting] the main responsibility for funding schools from local school districts to the state (p. 6).

With this change, unions lost their ability to engage in pattern bargaining, whipsawing one school district against another to increase salaries and benefits. "Emboldened by their victory ... Republicans in the Michigan Legislature ... took advantage of their temporary majority in the House to push through a bill which directly challenged the power of teachers' unions" (p. 7). The bill, known as PA 112, narrowed the scope of bargaining to exclude matters such as the composition of site-based planning bodies, the creation of charter schools, contracting out support services or the use of volunteers. As well, it gave school boards the right to impose their "last best offer" in the event of an impasse in negotiations, and "imposed severe penalties on teachers who strike, fining them a day's pay for each instructional day they are out of the classroom. The bill also imposed stiff fines on the unions to which striking teachers belong" (p. 8).

In the view of some, Michigan is now one of the most "voucher-ready" states in the U.S. Meanwhile, teachers' unions struggle to "keep up with inflation, and keep their benefits" (p. 11), prompting one union leader to acknowledge, "If [the members] knew how little the union can do in return for their [annual dues] they would be leaving the union in droves" (p. 13).

In Pennsylvania, Governor Tom Ridge "could be called an 'equal opportunity' opponent of the status quo in public education . . . consistently push[ing] for vouchers and charter schools, and treat[ing] all public education groups, not just the teachers' unions, with suspicion and, at times, disdain" (p. 14). A major source of political backlash against unions was the "trend toward the use of 'selective strikes' . . . that maximized disruption by being announced unpredictably, at the last minute, and involved only selected schools within a district" (p. 16). Act 88, adopted by the outgoing Democratic administration in 1992, "established mandatory timelines for bargaining, new impasse procedures, a requirement of a 48-hour notice before strikes, and measures allowing substitutes to be used during strikes" (p. 16).

Part of Governor Ridge's strategy has been to make an "end-run around the legislature and the education interest groups, through the appointment of an Academic Standards Commission" that has only one teacher on it. The Commission conducted "radical surgery" on curriculum standards proposed by task forces of professional educators to yield a "traditionalistic standard that had been reviewed and revised by conservative curriculum consultants from out of the state" (p. 18). Perhaps the primary battle ahead will be over Philadelphia's schools, where teachers are members of an AFT affiliate. After the Philadelphia school board threatened to close the schools unless the state gave it more money, the legislature adopted a bill that would allow the state to take over the district and convert its schools to charter schools. "A new coalition is emerging between traditionally Democratic African-Americans and the Republican Party. Both share a conviction that the unions will never make the changes necessary to rescue urban education" (p. 21).

Boyd *et al.* suggests that there are two streams of reform in Michigan and Pennsylvania, one focusing on firmer curriculum and student assessment and the other on school choice. They suggest that teachers' unions would find it easier to embrace the former, in the name of professional expertise, than the latter, which would create near impossible organizational challenges. They note that many of Michigan's charter schools have actually contracted out management responsibilities to private companies that employ teachers on annual contracts that have not been very attractive to teachers. Some states where charter school laws that are more "union-friendly" – requiring, for example, that all teachers hold state certificates and that all charters be granted by local school boards – have not experienced this problem, perhaps because teacher security is greater. However, the authors suggest that both trends could have de-professionalizing effects if teachers are treated like day-laborers and simply told to implement a standard curriculum using prescribed methods. The question is, can complex reforms that require capable teachers who commit themselves to innovative programs succeed under such a regime?

Australia

As in the United States, Australia's federal government plays a significant role in education, including the direct funding of private schools across the country and the management of the nation's wage settlement tribunals. Still, in all three federal nations – Canada, the United States and Australia – education is primarily a state/provincial responsibility and the real foundation of teacher unions has been with the state/provincial associations.

Australian state governments, like that of Governor Ridge's Pennsylvania, have been "equal opportunity" opponents of the *status quo* in public education, although they began with public systems that looked much like New Brunswick's does today. The Australian state departments of education ran the schools, which had school advisory committees with no real authority. Economic challenges and the impact of federal grants to private schools introduced in the late 1970s led the Australian states to adopt a program of "devolution" which increased the authority of those in schools, particularly principals and elected school councils (Queensland Teachers' Union, 1999). Chadbourne (1966) comments that, "Devolution has been adopted in the UK as local management of schools (LMS), in part of the USA as site-based management and across Australia in the form of self-managing schools" (p. 100).[1] Some Australian states began the devolution process "during the late 1970s and early 1980s . . . [and it] has been associated more recently with a series of prominent reports. . . . Ideologically, devolution in its various guises has received political support from the Left and the Right. The Left favours a social democratic view of devolution . . . [favoring local democracy and corporate managerial models]. The Right leans more toward . . . [corporate management and] market models" (p. 101).

In Western Australia the second wave of reforms in 1995 attempted to introduce a controversial set of reforms that would "1) prohibit unions from entering workplaces if they had no members or members who did not want to be identified; allow employers to stop unions checking time and wage records; forbid unions from using central union funds to make political donations and fine officials who break this rule up to $25 000; [and] require union members to vote in secret ballot" (p. 104). In the ensuing struggle, the Secondary School Teachers' Union of Western Australia (SSTUWA) fought for the loyalty of secondary school principals, most of whom were union members. The principals were also being wooed by the Western Australia Education Department with a collective workplace agreement that provided better benefits than were likely under an enterprise agreement negotiated by the SSTUWA. One principal explained that the principals went with the department's offer in part because, "the union did not demonstrate interest and commitment to the needs of special groups [such as secondary principals who] saw the workload implications of further devolution. . . . The last differentiation for principals – a 10 per cent pay rise – was initiated by the department, not the union. . . . [The union] wanted WASPA [Western Australia Secondary Principals' Association] to work the within union structure, to elect reps to union committees. . ." (pp. 103-104).

Surveys of Western Australian principals indicated that they felt that early devolution had not gone far enough. They believed they needed more authority at the site level. In their agreement, the principals agreed to: "manage utilities; support a revised staffing formula based upon differential resourcing; implement reporting and accountability practices . . .; carry out local selection of school staff; manage school-based staffing profiles; implement site tenure; manage the performance of staff they supervise; monitor the professional development of . . . classroom teachers; support the phased implementation of an enhanced school grant with allocations for professional development, relief staff, supplies, services, utilities and contract payments . . . and costs associated with the local selection of staff" (p. 113). As part of this agreement, they received a 20 percent pay increase vs. a 15 percent increase negotiated by SSTUWA for teachers that was approved by the Australian Industrial Relations Commission. Chadbourne wonders if principals will place their "loyalty to the department above loyalty to the teaching profession" when disputes arise over educational and management policy.

Australian reforms tend to reflect both a heavy dose of managerialism and a desire to emulate in public education the perceived benefits that autonomy and initiative bring in private education. Federal grants for the latter have increased competition for public institutions, but a history of centralization in both schooling and wage settlement processes create strong supports for existing arrangements.

New Zealand

New Zealand's educational devolution legislation was adopted in 1988 and implemented beginning in 1989. Elementary school boards were abolished and both elementary and secondary schools gained elected boards of governors who became the employers of teachers and principals. As well, each governing board was required to work with its community to develop a charter that had to include a number of clauses specified by law and which had to be approved by the department of education (Lawton, 1996). The government planned to allocate funding directly to schools on a "bulk" (i.e., lump sum or block grant) basis, with the boards taking on the responsibility for negotiating salaries, but this was not implemented. Opposition to bulk funding from teachers' unions was strong and there were technical problems caused by the difficulty of dealing with staff of varying seniority and salary levels. Nevertheless, an experiment was begun and about 50 schools are receiving bulk funding.

In late 1998, collective negotiations were underway, with the government having made an opening offer for the Collective Employment Contract to the New Zealand Post Primary Teachers' Association, which includes secondary and some post-secondary teaching personnel. The PPTA rejected "in the strongest possible way" a proposed "opt-out" clause because of its "opposition to site contracts, and its links to bulk funding." It also rejected "all other anti-union aspects of the Government's offer, including the abolition of paid union meetings, and paid Presidential leave."

PPTA has proposed a Teaching/Qualification Improvement plan in response to the government's proposal to abolish the service increment. The TQI is designed "to encourage and reward teachers to 'upskill and upgrade' in terms of either teaching technologies or curriculum knowledge." They have "re-tabled the claim for hours of work; i.e., a maximum of 450 student contact hours per week, a maximum of 20 hours [1200 minutes] student contact time per week, and average maximum class size of 20."

Also, the PPTA proposes a starting salary of $34 000 and a maximum to $51 500; the government has proposed a maximum for the basic scale rate of $50 000.[2] Finally, they wish to maintain existing arrangements for "Pay Progression/Professional Standards," arguing the performance appraisal system developed after the previous 1996 agreement is being effectively applied and is "maintaining and enhancing professional quality within secondary teaching" (PPTA On-line web page, September 1998).

New Zealand is roughly the size and population of British Columbia and the economies of both jurisdictions are heavily dependent upon natural resources and tourism. While one may decry centralization as excessively rigid – the fact New Zealand has never moved completely to bulk funding is evidence of this – the appeal of settling all issues at one table for the whole nation is beguiling. Yet, having moved beyond all other Anglo-democracies in its efforts to localize day-to-day governance and operations of schools in the late 1980s, it has found further decentralization a formidable task.

England and Wales

"The Tories won power in 1979 believing that reducing trade-union power held the key to reviving Britain's economic fortunes. In a series of labor laws enacted since 1980, unions were made liable for the actions of their members and became easier to sue for damages when strikes were called illegally. Secondary picketing . . . and the closed shop . . . were outlawed. Corporations won the right to withdraw recognition of a union," writes *The Economist* (1996). Teachers' unions were no exception. The "*Teachers' Pay and Conditions Act* abolished teachers' negotiating rights and gave the Secretary of State for Education power to impose a settlement" in 1987 (Barber, 1992, p. 69). Before 1987, the levels of teachers' pay and salary structure were nationally negotiated in the Burnham Committee and its agreements had statutory force (Barber, p. 113).

Today the unions engage in "collective begging" before the government.

The National Union of Teachers (NUT), Britain's largest teachers' union with 192 000 members, is currently in "negotiations" with the Labour government of Tony Blair. For its part, the government has promised 1 billion pounds to fund a salary increase for teachers in England and Wales (plus 100 million pounds in Scotland), a gain that would average between 3 and 4 percent. It has also put forth a Green Paper which recommends larger increments for teachers who are assessed as meeting given standards of performance – what NUT terms "payment by results," which the union rejects. Even then, NUT argues, if just 60 percent of the 260 000 teachers were successful, the actual cost would be at least one-third more than the government has budgeted.

Although the Prime Minister is supportive of teachers, "It is not just a job for many of you, it is a vocation.... Helping a five-year-old to read . . . is fulfilling in a way that money cannot be." He also warned that "he would not tolerate failure in the public sector, saying where services failed he would call in others, including private companies, to take over" (*Times Education Supplement*, January 29, 1998). As it stands, "some grant-maintained schools . . . have moved in the direction of not only individual contracts but also non-recognition of teacher unions" (Barber, p. 114) and Local Education Authorities have "lost some powers – particularly resource allocation and personnel power – to schools.... They are no longer able to ... require schools to accept redeployed teachers" (Barber, p. 114).

For the present, teachers' salaries range from 13 362 pounds per year to 35 787 pounds in 34 half-steps, even though "The Union is opposed to the introduction of half-points." Supplementary salary incentives up to the 2000 pound range are available in high-cost areas, such as London, and for positions in more remote areas and hard-to-fill positions. The current pay scale was recommended by the Schoolteachers' Review Body, one of the government review bodies that administers public sector wages in the post-Thatcher era, and accepted by the Secretary of State for Education and Employment (National Union of Teachers, www.teachers.org.uk, 1999). Recently, NUT commissioned Coopers and Lybrand to prepare a report, *Review of Teachers Salaries*, to support NUT's case for salary increases in face of a what it believes is a growing shortage of teachers.

In his 1992 assessment of teacher unionism in England and Wales, Barber (pp. 126-132), a long time employee of NUT, advised five foci for the future:
1. **Accountability and the community.** Unions should put the quality of education at the heart of their mission. This would assist in enhancing the relation with the public and hence extend influence over the policy-making process, thus leading to improved salaries and conditions of service for members.
2. **Responsiveness to members.** It is important that the full-time union staff of the Union understand, and are in touch with, the demands and needs of members in schools.
3. **The strength to say "no."** Bloody-mindedness becomes a positive asset at times.
4. **Unity and collaboration.** Work together with other teacher unions as a common force when needed and collaborate to pursue shared objectives.
5. **Teacher unions and democracy.** Given the relative weakness of all the other actors in the drama, it falls to teachers to limit government interference.

Conclusion

This sampling of events in four jurisdictions that share a political, social and economic heritage illustrates the dramatic realignments in relations between governments and teachers' unions over the past decade. In all cases there is evidence, as there is in Canada, of a trend toward greater control by management over educational systems and their employees, including teachers. Evident in these accounts are the multiple dimensions that characterize educational reforms.

If one focuses on labor relations, specifically, it would seem that Canadian teachers have done no worse, and in fact probably somewhat better, than their sister organizations elsewhere in maintaining the collective bargaining processes and systems of compensation that had been developed over the preceding decades of this century. In the jurisdictions described, changes in labor relations legislation curtailed the scope of bargaining, enhanced management rights, altered impasse resolution processes in order to reduce the number of strikes and to improved the likelihood of reasonable salary settlements, as judged by school board and government officials. In no case, however, were unions abolished, although policies to encourage "opting out" of the state school system may have this effect on a school-by-school basis.

A second theme is the introduction of quality assurance mechanisms, including standard testing, school profiles and, at least in

Britain's case, school inspection. The push for effectiveness is based on an assumption that education is a technically rational service that can produce pre-conceived standards. This assumption is doubted by many teachers and all teachers' unions, but until a better model on which to base school reforms is developed, this notion is likely to be a recurring feature of labor disputes, particularly if tied to remuneration.

A final theme is school choice, which is based on the notion of altering educational systems to foster competition in the delivery of services. In the New Zealand model, a strong element of democratic localism inspired the conversion of all schools to self-managing institutions with community and government approved charters. The U.S. approach has fostered competition through publicly-funded charter schools and initiatives to provide vouchers in private as well as public schools. Australia's federal government initiated grants to independent institutions several decades ago and public schools' management has been trying to emulate independent schools' perceived success ever since. In Britain, the current Labour government has continued previous Tory reforms, including those that allow schools operated by Local Education Authorities to opt out and become "grant-maintained schools."

The final theme apparent is that of the corporate managerial model, to use the Australian terminology. Reflected in provincial initiatives to develop more explicit curriculum, to improve assessment systems, to amalgamate school districts and to close inefficient schools, this philosophy places paramount importance on efficiency, measurement and effectiveness. Its production-function rationality is an irritant to humanistic educators who view it as the antithesis of the liberal values that are a foundation to contemporary education. Philosophically, managerialism is hollow at the core; yet, it is functional in addressing financial problems and forcing choices in values when not all aspirations can be satisfied.

References

Barber, M. (1992). *Education and the teacher unions*. London: Cassell.

Bascia, N. (1997). Teacher unions and teacher professionalism in the U.S.: Reconsidering a familiar dichotomy. *The international handbook of teachers and teaching*. Amsterdam: Kluwer Academic Publishers.

Boyd, W. L., Plank, D. N. & Sykes, G. (1998). Swimming against the current: Teachers' unions in hard times. Paper prepared for the conference on "Teacher Unions and Educational Reform," Kennedy School of Government, Harvard University, Cambridge, MA, September 24-25, 1998.

Caldwell, B. J. & Spinks, J. M. (1988). *The self-managing school*. New York: The Falmer Press.

Chadbourne, R. (Winter 1996). Educational vision or self-interest? The response of Western Australian principals to further devolution. *Leading and Managing*, 2(2): 100-117.

The Economist. (1996). Life with more agreeable unions. Reprinted in *The Globe and Mail*, October 19, 1996, p. D4.

Lawton, S. B. (1996). *Busting bureaucracy to reclaim our schools.* Ottawa: Renouf.

National Union of Teachers (U.K) (1999): www.teachers.org.uk

Queensland Teachers' Union (Australia). (1999): www.qtu.asn.au

Times Education Supplement. (U.K). (January 29, 1998): www.tes.co.uk

Notes

1. For his doctoral dissertation at the University of Alberta, Brian Caldwell, an Australian who worked in Canada, studied the school-based management system introduced by Superintendent Mike Strembitsky in Edmonton during the 1970s and 1980s. On return to Australia, he published on the topic of the "self-managing school" and conducted training sessions on the topic across Australia and New Zealand (Caldwell & Spinks, 1988). Although Strembitsky has retired, Edmonton is considered one of the more choice-oriented public school boards in Canada. Caldwell is now Dean of Education at the University of Melbourne.

2. In early 1999, the exchange rate for one New Zealand dollar is approximately $.821 Canadian (*Globe and Mail*, February 13, 1999, p. B25), so that proposed starting and maximum salaries have exchange rate values of $27 914 and $42 282 respectively. However, the purchasing power parity of the Canadian dollar is approximately equal to $1.06 New Zealand, meaning that one Canadian dollar will purchase 6% more in goods and services in New Zealand than it will in Canada (*The Globe and Mail*, October 19, 1998, p. B1). Therefore the purchasing power of the minimum and maximum salaries would be equal to $29 589 and $44 818.

3. On February 13, 1999, the exchange rate for one British pound was $2.4347 Canadian. Hence, the teacher pay range for England and Wales would be approximately $32 532 to $87 131. However, in terms of purchasing power parity, a Canadian dollar would purchase only $.71 worth of goods and services in the U.K., so the purchasing power of the minimum and maximum salaries, expressed in terms of Canadian dollars, are $23 098 and $61 863.

9

Teachers' Unions, Salaries and the Cost of Education

Knowledge is the only instrument of production that is not subject to diminishing returns.

J. M. Clark

Unionized employees earn more than those who are not unionized. This truism is widely assumed by both labor and management. Why else would employees form associations and seek certification as bargaining units other than to assert demands for greater salaries, benefits and better working conditions?

Yet, for several reasons this truism is very difficult to demonstrate unequivocally for current Canadian teachers. First, during the 1990s the real expenditures per pupil for education have actually declined in constant dollar terms (i.e., after taking inflation into account). As demonstrated in table 9.1, between 1994/95 and 1995/96, the average expenditure per student declined by 2.9 percent. Second, a methodological problem is created by the simple fact that all teachers in publicly financed and operated schools in Canada are unionized. Typical studies of the impact of unions on enterprises use comparative methods with unionized enterprises compared with non-unionized enterprises. This approach is still feasible in the United States since unionized school districts can be compared with non-unionized districts in terms of their employees' compensation and working conditions, controlling for the effects of other relevant variables such as the size, wealth and location of the district. A third problem is the difficulty of controlling for some variables that are external to the school district such as the overall supply and demand for teachers, the availability of government revenue that can be allocated to public services, and the characteristics of teachers and programs involved.

To approach the issue systematically, the impact of unionization on teachers' salaries and benefits and on educational expenditures is addressed through three questions: What is the nature of the teacher labor market? What mechanisms do employees in an occupational group use in order to raise their incomes? And, how can the appropriateness of compensation for an occupation be assessed?

Table 9.1
Expenditures per Pupil by Province in Constant 1986 Dollars, 1991-1996

Province	95/96	94/95	93/94	92/93	91/92
British Columbia	5125	5025	5017	5233	5221
Alberta	4343	4638	4869	4874	4764
Saskatchewan	4281	4369	4226	4474	4430
Manitoba	5252	5258	5281	5326	5352
Ontario	5384	5623	5662	5667	5747
Quebec	5595	5691	5442	5620	5430
New Brunswick	4471	4488	4636	4642	4418
Nova Scotia	4183	4442	4472	4182	3959
Prince Edward Island	3750	4081	4217	4122	4251
Newfoundland	4273	4447	4559	4493	5022
Unweighted Average	4666	4806	4838	4863	4859
Percentage Change	-2.9%	-0.7%	-0.5%	0.1%	
Standard Deviation	619	559	504	570	585
Coeff. of Variation	13.3%	11.6%	10.4%	11.7%	12.0%
Weighted Average	5139	5291	5281		
Percentage Change	-2.9%	0.2%			

Source: *Lawton, Menzies, and Ryall (1996).*

Notes: One 1986 dollar was worth $1.335 in 1996. Therefore in current 1996 dollars the weighted average expenditure (weighting by number of students in each province) was $6862 in 1995/96.

The coefficient of variation equals the standard deviation divided by the mean, expressed as a percentage.

Teacher Labor Markets

Teacher labor markets have many special characteristics. To a degree, the supply and demand of teachers, and the salaries offered and accepted, behave as they do for any other good or service being traded in a competitive market. In other ways, due to social, political and regulatory factors, teachers and their unions occupy a unique niche in contemporary society. This section first provides a theoretical foundation for considering the topic and then applies these ideas to explain policy options used to manage and respond to changes in teacher labor markets as the need for teachers and needs of teachers change.

A Theoretical Perspective

A theoretical analysis of labor markets uses as its benchmark the same type of competitive free market analysis used to study the prices of any commodity, good or service. Figure 9.1 provides the classic diagram demonstrating the tradeoffs between supply, demand and price. The following discussion is heuristic rather than technically complete and is based on analyses in Stager (1978, pp. 2-8), Samuelson (1967, pp. 536-538) and Gunderson and Riddell (1993, pp. 187-214). In figure 9.1, demand for teachers is represented by a downward sloping line, D_1, with the vertical axis representing teachers' wages (or price) W, and the horizontal axis representing the number of teachers employed, N. If price increases ($W_1 \rightarrow W_2$), then the demand for a good or service will tend to decrease ($N_1 \rightarrow N_2$), all other things being equal, so fewer teachers will find employment. On the demand curve, this corresponds to a movement of the point at which demand for and the amount of service provided are in balance from point F to point G.

Typically, though, all things are not equal. In practice, an increase in wages causes the supply of potential employees to increase, a phenomenon represented by an upward move on a supply curve, represented by upward sloping line S_1. The forces of supply and demand balance out at a point of equilibrium indicated by point H where the supply curve intersects the demand curve. At that point supply will balance demand and W_0 will be the so-called "market-clearing price." That is, at that price all of the supply of the good or service will be sold and all of the demand of the market will be met. A higher price would be too high for some potential purchasers and, therefore, some demand would remain unfulfilled. A lower price would create additional demand that could not be met by the existing supply, so again there would be unfilled demand. Conversely, if the price were set higher, then supply would outpace demand, resulting in a surplus.

We would typically call W_0 the fair market price for the good or service, which in this case is the market price for teachers as represented by the wages being offered. The term "fair" in this case simply means that no other forces are at work to drive the prices or wages higher or lower. It does not mean the price will seem "fair" in terms of social norms. The fair market price could be less than the amount it cost to produce the good or service – a phenomenon that produces a loss for the producer – which hardly seems fair. Or, the market price may be more than purchasers can afford, which may not seem fair to them. Either the producer or purchaser in these situations may argue in support of some other mechanism to set

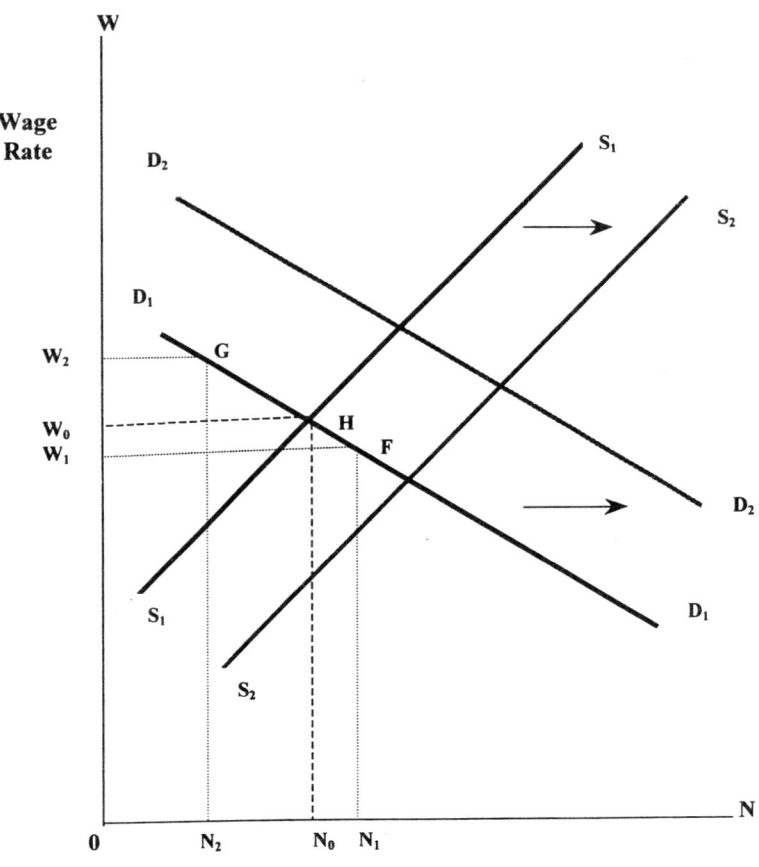

**Figure 9.1
The Labor Market for Teachers**

Number of Teachers Employed

prices that seems to satisfy their normative sense of what is a proper price. In terms of the teacher labor market, employing school systems may wish to offer lower salaries than teachers desire or teachers may prefer wages higher than those that are offered. Both parties may try to intervene in the labor market through legislation and regulation in order to achieve their objectives.

Two situations certainly make an alternative price mechanism possible. If a group holds a *monopoly*, it can set a higher price than would be set in a competitive free market. Economists refer to this as collecting *monopoly rents*. Or, a group may be the only one in a position to make a purchase and choose to offer a price that is lower than the market-clearing price. If those seeking employment have no place else to turn, they may find this an offer they cannot refuse. Economists refer to this situation as *monopsony*. In either case, the situation deviates greatly from the free-market model and the prices would be unfair in an economic sense. Whether the prices in question were unfair in normative sense probably would depend on whether one is the beneficiary or victim.

Supply and demand curves in a competitive free market can change. A supply curve may change with the development of new technology that, in terms of figure 9.1, would move the supply curve to the right from S_1 to S_2. This event means that more of a good or service can be produced at a given price; conversely, because of increasing scarcity of resources, the supply curve may move to the left, meaning that a higher price is needed for the supply to continue. Also, the supply curve for a higher *quality* of good or service will be to the left of S_1. As a result, the supply and demand curves will intersect at a point associated with a lower demand. This phenomenon reflects the common sense notion that luxury goods have smaller markets than do middle and lower priced goods. In terms of the teacher labor market, a shift in the supply curve to the right could be brought about be a decline in alternative employment opportunities; conversely, if other opportunities open up at higher wages, the supply curve for teachers may shift to the left.

An increase or decrease in demand is also associated with a shift in the location of the demand curve. The primary purpose of advertising is to increase demand; that is, to move the demand curve to the right. If demand increases, and there is no change in the supply curve, then the demand will only be met at a higher price; e.g., higher wages for teachers would be needed to attract more persons in to the occupation, thereby raising the cost of education. However, if people grow tired of a good or a service, then demand may fall; in this situation, consumption levels will only be maintained if there is a decrease in price. One activity of educators, their associations and educational institutions is promotion of education as a valuable activity in terms of its investment value, individually and collectively, and as a worthwhile and prestigious pastime. We are used to seeing industry associations promote consumption of their goods or services, be they milk, eggs or tourism. Thinking of the actions of educational groups in this way is a bit crass, but this does not mean that the perspective does not have merit; even intrinsically good activities need publicity to enhance public awareness.

In addition to advertising, increasing family income is a major factor that tends to shift the demand curve to the right. All other things being equal, an increase in a family's income will be associated with greater demand for all goods and services, including education. Families do not have to increase the share of their income devoted to education, purchased privately or through the tax system, in order to increase demand. Even a declining share of income may be associated with increasing support for education if income is growing fast enough. During the postwar years, substantial increases in income have been a critical factor in increasing demand for education. The bigger pie, so to speak, benefited all providers of goods and services, including educational systems. Conversely, the flattening and even decline of income during the 1990s can account for a drop in demand and the call for more "value for money"; i.e., a lower price. This demand for accountability is understandable regardless of any actions by educators and their associations since the real after-tax income for most Canadians is less today than a decade ago. We may place too much emphasis on political and social causes of changing preferences and overlook economic factors and theories that can explain popular discontent.

It must be noted that the "law of supply and demand" is an abstract expression of relationships that may or may not fit reality. It has been accepted, for the most part, as a "natural law" since its validity has been demonstrated on a regular basis, all other things being equal. More properly, though, we might term it the "theory of supply and demand" to emphasize that it is a very much a scientific model developed to predict human behavior in the economic sphere. As such, it is apparent that it is not a moral statement about what should occur. Its formulators did not mean to imply that the world ought to work this way or that it was "good" in a transcendent sense if it did so. It is meant to express simply how free economic markets work in practice.

Managing Supply and Demand

What do theories of supply and demand have to do with teachers' salaries and the cost (or more properly the price) of education?[1] If we are interested in the behavior of the price (i.e., wages) of a beginning teacher, figure 9.1 suggests that when demand for schooling suddenly increases, as happened in the 1950s and 1960s with the baby boom, then beginning salaries will increase in order for demand to be fulfilled. An alternative scenario exists, however. Sometimes when prices rise, purchasers seek a less expensive substitute. That is, increasing demand might tempt school districts and departments of education to approve the appointment of individuals with fewer qualifications than normal in order to meet the increased demand at the current price levels. In fact, during the peak hiring period of the baby boom, this is exactly what transpired with alternative certification routes being made available. In terms of figure 9.1, these policies shifted the supply curve to the right so that supply would increase at existing prices. This type of "deregulation" also has been proposed for specialist teachers in the sciences, mathematics and technology in order to "solve" the problem of short supply. How such changes would affect the quality of teachers, as measured by the instructor's classroom performance, student achievement, or career longevity, is a separate issue.

A very different supply/demand context occurred in the 1970s when school enrolments began to decline after two decades of growth. With teacher education institutions still graduating peak numbers of certified teachers, a surplus of teachers-in-waiting was created. According to figure 9.1, free market forces would result in a drop in the price of teachers until a new equilibrium was established. In part to prevent this occurrence, certification regulations were changed, as reported in table 2.1, to increase the number of years of education required for new teachers. No longer were elementary teachers hired with one year of normal school training after high school. As well, faculties of education reduced enrolment during the 1970s in order to restrict the size of the growing surplus. The trend toward higher qualifications has continued into the 1990s, where deans of education – without the support of teachers' unions – have become strong advocates of a two-year post baccalaureate program for new teachers.

It is evident that the teacher labor market is not an unregulated free market in which supply, demand and price find their own levels. Nevertheless, the free market model is useful in accounting for the intended impact of regulations on the supply in order to achieve policy objectives. The supply of teachers at a given level of salary will increase if regulations are reduced, moving the supply curve to the right. Or, if there is a fall in demand for teachers, salaries will be maintained if regulations increase standards, thereby shifting the supply curve to the left.

Characteristics of Unionized Labor Markets[2]

Collective bargaining creates a dramatic departure from the competitive market model because the employer now has a "duty" to bargain – something that simply does not exist in the purely competitive model. First, not only must the employer bargain, but must do so with a collective entity that has, in most instances, superior bargaining power to that possessed by individuals. As well, collective sanctions such as organization-wide strikes simply do not exist at the individual level. For example, if a private individual withdraws from work, he or she has effectively quit and the employment relationship ends with no further employer obligation to the employee – not even severance pay.

Second, because an employer may face severe economic harm if productive labor is withdrawn by virtue of a strike, the bargaining power of the union means that it can obtain a better settlement typically valued at between 10 and 15 percent above the competitive market.

Third, the rights arbitration process and collective bargaining legislation place restrictions on the ability of an employer on discharge an employee. A non-union employer can terminate an employee even without cause, assuming notice is given in lieu of severance pay. The unionized employer cannot unilaterally do so because of the contractual right of reinstatement that is unique to the unionized labor force. Non-union employees only have a right to reinstatement if it established by statute such as human rights legislation. Otherwise, their only remedy for a without-cause dismissal is a financial settlement, which is available only if proper notice of termination was not given. If a unionized employer wishes to terminate employees without cause it must first negotiate the terms and conditions of such termination with the union. In most cases, the *quid pro quo* will be seniority-based termination, which means that the highest paid employees are the least likely to be terminated. Thus, termination is a less than satisfactory avenue to reduce labor costs. As a result, the employer is not as free as is a non-union employer would be to invest in capital equipment to replace labor, even though the labor costs are higher than at a non-union firm. To substitute capital for labor, a unionized firm must first negotiate the terms of such an arrangement with the union.

Finally, through collective negotiations unions will seek to increase labor demand at the level of the firm and through political lobbying to increase employment at the provincial or national level. Better working conditions which may involved reduced workload may translate in to more positions, as may legislation requiring health and safety personnel to ensure a safe workplace.

In the case of teachers, unionization, particularly when it is combined with provincial funding of schools, creates a distinctive setting for employer-employee relations. First, the employer is a *de facto* monopsonist acting as the only purchaser of teaching services, since private schools enrol fewer than five percent of all elementary and secondary students in Canada. Second, the prime beneficiary of the public school system, parents of children who attend public schools, are unable to find a substitute for public education, at least in the short term. In contemporary society, in which both parents often work or there is only one parent in the home, an interruption in their children's schooling is a significant inconvenience, to say the least. Third, education is a labor-intensive industry and the ability of employers to substitute capital for labor is low, particularly in the lower grades. Fourth, existing school plants, with classrooms designed for 25 or 30 students, place an upper limit on class size. Finally, employed teachers form a stable and mature workforce with a commitment to teaching and an inability to leave for alternative opportunities. While in a sense this makes them captives of the system, it also means that, without other options to choose from, they will be willing to invest considerable energy in protecting their interests.

What does all this mean for teacher negotiations? Because the employer is a monopsonist, one would think it had the upper hand. However, this may not be the case. Employers will avoid locking teachers out because of the potentially high political costs, particularly where province-wide negotiations were concerned. Long strikes are equally damaging to governments' and school trustees' political futures. As the case studies of both British Columbia and Ontario demonstrate, well-organized unionized teachers form a potent force that engage in lobbying at both the local and provincial levels, launch full and partial strike actions, and run effective advertising campaigns aimed at the public. When accommodation, if not agreement, is reached, it is on terms that are more generous than a competitive model would predict.

Evolution of Teacher Labor Markets

The current status of teacher labor markets evolved over a century. Teacher certification standards were the first and perhaps most critical element in moving the teacher labor market away from the unregulated free market of the early 19th century. The primary rationale for setting and increasing standards of teacher certification was to improve the quality of teaching, not to restrict the supply of teachers in order to drive wages up. There are questions about this equation that link training standards with quality, to which we shall return to later. For the time being, it is enough to accept that governments can affect the supply curve in that they control, directly or indirectly, the regulations for the certification of teachers, including the number of years of training and the kinds of training required. Legislation and regulations can also determine the demand for education – the student "labor" market, so to speak – by setting the age at which children begin school and the number of years of compulsory schooling.

For private schools, in contrast to public and separate schools, the supply curve evolved in a less regulated labor market. In general, the private school teacher supply curve is to the right of that for public schools, meaning that private schools can satisfy their demand for teachers while offering lower wages than public schools. Private schools may choose to pay higher salaries in order to obtain more highly trained teachers or may be required to do so by provincial legislation, a common practice if the schools receive public subsidy. If there is a surplus of certified teachers, it may be possible for private schools to purchase their services at wages lower than that paid in the unionized public sector. In effect, these private schools receive any added benefits of the additional training for free. However, they may also find that they will lose teachers to the public sector unless teachers enjoy other benefits such as smaller classes or more motivated students in the private-school setting that compensates for the lower pay.

An additional characteristic of teacher labor markets is their division along linguistic lines (French, English and, to a degree, Native languages) in all provinces and along religious lines in Ontario, Saskatchewan and Alberta (and formerly Newfoundland and Quebec). The impact of this segmentation is difficult to unravel. Francophone Roman Catholic teachers can be employed, in Ontario, in any one of four systems (French public and French Roman Catholic in regular programs and English public or Roman Catholic in French-immersion programs); Roman Catholics anglophones are limited to two systems; non-Catholic anglophones are largely restricted to the English public system. The situation for administrative positions is yet more difficult. Roman Catholic boards will rarely hire or promote non-Catholics to positions of authority. Also, most systems prefer appointing women and racial-minorities as administrators in order to increase the diversity of their administrative staff. This web of regulations creates asymmetrical career opportunities related to gender and ethnocultural background that may discourage some individuals from entering teaching. Loney (1998) deals with some aspects of this matter.

Currently, regulations concerning tenure, collective agreements, and pensions combine to reduce teacher turnover to low levels.

Tenure means that it is difficult for school districts to dismiss teachers without the existence of substantive and thorough documentation. It is essentially impossible to dismiss senior, highly-paid teachers in order to replace them with with lower-salaried teachers, a practice that apparently had been a commonplace in pre-tenure days. As well, tenured teachers are protected from dismissal for reasons of political activity, including actions directed at the employer or of personal lifestyle. For teachers, then, tenure is a critical security guarantee that creates a sound foundation for an independent and sometimes pugnacious professionalism.

Pensions also ensure a high degree of employment continuity, since the economic interests of departing teachers suffer. Leaving employment after one's pension has been vested can be an expensive option for an individual. Although pension benefits are maintained if a teacher moves within a province (assuming a move does not result in a lower salary), inter-provincial relocation is more difficult, even though exchange agreements exist that allow the transfer of pension funds.

Collective agreements also ensure stability in the workforce, possibly reducing turnover from the relatively high levels that occurred in earlier periods. Agreements provide for predictable salaries and benefits, reward seniority and provide for a systematic approach to resolve grievances. Evidence suggests that in some industries, unionization is associated with overall higher productivity compared to non-union firms, although this is by no means a universal effect. Seniority clauses preserve jobs for the most experienced in case of downsizing and provide salary increments for up to 10 or 12 years of experience. As well, salary grids provide increments for increased professional training including masters' degrees, specialist certificates and the like and class size, pupil-teacher ratios, and other workload clauses, termed "working conditions," ensure a certain level of staffing and therefore reduce redundancies.

Table 9.2 reproduces a typical salary grid, this example taken from an urban school district in British Columbia. From the table it can be seen that each year an teacher not at the maximum will have a salary increase due to increased experience. If, as well, the individual has earned additional qualifications, then a category change will also result in an increase in pay. Finally, if an across-the-board salary increase has been negotiated, another increment will be paid.

Table 9.2
Salary Grid for a British Columbia School District,
June 30, 1994

Years of Experience	Category I B.Ed.	Category II B.Ed.+1 yr.	Category III B.Ed.+M.Ed.	Category IV M.Ed.+1 yr.
0	29254	29917	34684	38369
1	30558	33534	36680	40573
2	31862	35151	38676	42777
3	33166	36768	40672	44981
4	34470	38385	42668	47185
5	35774	40002	44664	49389
6	37078	41619	46660	51593
7	38382	43236	48656	53797
8	39686	44853	50652	56001
9	40990	46470	52648	58205
10	42294	48087	54644	60409
11		49704	56640	62613

Newspaper reports usually provide only the size of across-the-board increases, which in 1998 were in the 0 percent to 2 percent range in most provinces; i.e., at or just below the rate of inflation. Yet, the actual cost increase for an entire teaching staff may be on the order of 2 to 6 percent, well above the rate of inflation. A teacher paid on the grid in table 9.2 with seven years of experience and additional training warranting a move from category II to category III will have a salary increase of 17.2 percent, assuming no across-the-board increase. Of this, 3.4 percent is due to the annual increment from $43 236 to $44 853 and 13.4 percent is due to the category change from $44 853 to $50 652. This salary schedule would serve as an incentive to earn additional qualifications. In Winnipeg School Division No. 1, in contrast, annual increments average about 5 percent and category changes 5 to 6 percent. Such a salary grid would tend to reward further academic study experience about equally (Manitoba Education and Training, 1996).

Changing Markets for Teachers

The impact of regulations, collective agreements, professional standards and school district policies has been the elevation of teaching into a rather attractive occupation that has, in fact, drawn increasing numbers of applicants during the late 1980s and early 1990s. Declining enrolment during the 1970s and 1980s was in part offset by the establishment of new programs including special education and the extension of education to include Roman Catholic secondary schools in Ontario and grade 12 in Newfoundland. Faculties of education continued to train more teachers than were immediately required and in some years only one-third of new graduates could find positions. Periodic claims of current or impending teachers shortages have been made, but in fact no real shortage has been documented, although patience may be needed to fill positions with candidates in areas such as French immersion, special education, mathematics, science and technology (Press, 1997).

The decline in enrolments during the "baby bust" generation threatened to reduce the market for teachers and teachers' salaries. As demand dropped, the surplus of certified teachers was exacerbated by the "stickiness" of salaries. Supported by collective agreements, various regulatory controls and a prevailing attitude in both the public and private sector that the negative effects on morale caused by salary reductions made them undesirable, salaries did not drop to achieve a new equilibrium. Indeed, until the early 1990s, when fiscal crises caused most provinces to institute some type of wage rollback, salaries continued to increase. The surplus of teachers that developed can be explained in terms of figure 9.1. The demand for teachers dropped and a new equilibrium should have been established at a lower wage. However, regulatory factors and prevailing practices supported existing salary levels, resulting in posted wages that exceeded the free market conditions. One result, in addition to the obvious benefit to teachers already employed in school districts, was that above-market wages made teacher preparation programs appear to be an attractive option to students in universities. The supply of new teachers, rather than dropping in response to falling wages to create a new balance between supply and demand, was maintained. Lists of supply teachers and job application lists became very long, as a queue formed composed of certified teachers waiting for regular, full-time appointments. This oversupply was particularly acute in large urban areas and less pronounced in northern and rural parts of provinces where many certified teachers are reluctant to move.

Ironically, even though less than half of all new graduates from faculties of education found teaching positions during the late 1970s, 1980s and early 1990s, evidence suggests entering teacher preparation programs remained an economically rational choice for university students (Wolfe, 1980). The wage bonus accruing to those who obtained permanent appointments to teaching was sufficiently great that, on average, teacher trainees earned more than individuals without such training, but who otherwise had comparable backgrounds. Further, their gain was enough to offset the lower salaries experienced by those who were not able to find positions in teaching. Even for these persons, the generic skills learned and practiced in teacher training – organizational, presentation, human relations, etc. – apparently enhanced their employment opportunities in what was becoming an increasingly competitive service-oriented economy.

Achieving Higher Salaries

The preceding analysis considered the nature of teacher labor markets primarily from a free-market perspective, with the suggestion that in recent decades regulatory factors (legislation, collective bargaining, administrative practices and court decisions) have allowed teachers to achieve above-market wages. Indeed, one major purpose of teacher associations has been to advocate legislation, regulations and legal rulings that enhance remuneration by restricting the number of eligible candidates. Included among these were increasing certification requirements, tenure laws that guarantee permanent positions and salary grids that reward longevity and further qualifications.

These types of initiative are well-defined strategies for individuals and occupational groups to achieve higher salaries. In the contemporary knowledge-based economy, the acquisition of higher levels of skills that are in short supply has been one of the most successful strategies. A good argument can be made that the decision by educators' organizations in the first half of the century to increase educational standards for teachers was beneficial to educators and the public in many ways. It followed the path previously developed by doctors, lawyers, ministers, engineers and others. Increasing the skills and education of practitioners increases the quality of a service and creates a justification for charging higher prices for their services.

Certification standards developed and overseen by either government regulators or an occupational body help to ensure that uniform and adequate services are provided to the public while yielding economic benefits to the occupational group. Although they may increase prices, appropriate standards assist those using a service. Without certification of service providers, a buyer must make an independent judgement about the quality of a service, a judgement that may be extremely difficult. The so-called "transaction costs" – the cost of collecting information, analyzing it and making an informed assessment – become greater the more sophisticated the service, such as brain surgery or preparation of a legal brief. In education, it becomes more difficult to judge quality as the level of education increases. Requiring that those offering a service first obtain certain types of training in approved programs managed by experts in a field helps to create a more efficient labor market. To maintain confidence in the arrangements and to prevent abuse of the privileges that have been granted, there must be some form of supervision and public accountability of the training agencies.

Higher salaries for certified personnel who have received sound training are justifiable in economic terms so long as required training programs genuinely improve the quality of services. Individuals devote time, effort and forego income in order to become certified. The capital they invest to earn their certificates warrants a reasonable rate of return that they expect to be reflected in a salary premium. In fact, the higher salary for trained individuals creates the demand for training and certification in the first place. However, in a competitive market with a surplus of certified personnel, the premium may fall below the break-even point and bring about a decline in supply of trained personnel as the costs of entry appear unattractive. Competition from uncertified personnel may also drive down the price of certified personnel if purchasers decide their salary premium is excessive. It is for these reasons that certification bodies (e.g., licensing commissions, governing bodies for professions) may limit the numbers of individuals granted certification and request governments to grant their graduates' unions or associations monopolies for the provision of the services in question.

A recurring problem with occupational self-governance has been a tendency of the occupation's practitioners to resist changes and innovations that may improve the services they deliver because they wish to protect their vested interests in existing procedures and standards. This behavior is rational in economic terms since it slows the depreciation of their human capital and avoids the cost of further training that may not yield higher incomes. One example of this occurred when typographers insisted on using linotypes to set type in lead years after computer-based word processing made the earlier technology obsolete. In this example, the fear of job loss added to the costs of retraining for a new technology. In competitive labor markets, individuals and groups will change in order to compete successfully.

During this century, elevating qualifications for educators paralleled the expansion of the school system, improving literacy rates, increasing retention rates in schools, and higher percentages of youth graduating from secondary school. Throughout this period, the "education industry," including trustees, administrators, architects, desk and book manufacturers, and teacher organizations, educated the public about the value of education and the need for more and better schooling. While economists debate whether the ever-larger and more expensive public education system promoted industrial development or vice versa, from a pragmatic viewpoint the individual student was wise to gain more education. As a result, the existing system developed an image of effectiveness and provided a systematic route to economic success for the economy of the day. The extent to which that system still provides an effective route has become a focus of public debate (e.g., Radwanski, 1988).

Maintaining Standards

Public education is plagued by two difficulties that are common to many organizations serving the public's needs and wants. First, it is very much a mass scale operation, making it difficult to maintain standards both in the selection of new members for the profession and in the oversight of training and delivery systems. Second, it is difficult to demonstrate qualitative differences in the services being offered to the public at large, particularly with a service like education which serves a decreasing share of the population age as fewer adults have children in school. In 1976, school-aged youth accounted for 26 percent of Canada's population; in 1997 it formed only 19 percent of the total (Statistics Canada, 1997). While the "echo" to the baby boom had raised the number of school-aged children from its low of 5.2 million in 1986 to 5.8 million in 1997, the number of children aged 0 to 3 – who represent tomorrow's students – has declined since 1995, suggesting that school-aged youth as a percentage of the total population will soon begin a descent with no bottom in sight.

The entire educational system is dependent upon what Meyer and Scott (1983) refer to as a "logic of confidence" that entails a string of trust relationships from parent to teacher, principal, supervisory officer and minister of education. Trust is based on the assumption that expected outcomes will occur if responsibilities are carried out in a prescribed way, even though the connections between means and ends are uncertain – or even mysterious. These authors do not view the current school system as one that is entirely rational in a technical sense. The actions of teachers, principals and others do not always have positive effects on a school's outcomes. In fact, in their view, attempts to impose technical rationality throughout the system may actually destroy the trust between parties if results fail to demonstrate the validity of the beliefs that justify action. Many decisions taken to reform the educational system in this decade can be seen as attempts to restore trust by creating new institutions, such as colleges of teachers and school councils, and to increase central control over the technology of education, including curriculum, class size and class time. Meyer and Scott's analysis might view these alterations as shaman-like rituals meant to drive out interfering spirits rather than tightly engineered solutions. With human beings, often belief is all that is necessary to achieve desired goals.

In education, the validity of current certification processes is one critical element that has been questioned. Ballou and Podbursky (1998) compare graduates of institutions in the United States holding accreditation from the National Council for Accreditation of Teacher Education (NCATE) with graduates from non-accredited institutions. Data for three states, Massachusetts, Missouri and Pennsylvania, indicated that there were no differences in teacher quality between the two as measured by test scores on standardized elementary teacher examinations. The authors comment for Missouri that, "NCATE schools are to be found at the top, middle, and bottom of the distribution. Indeed, the poorest performing institution in the state, as measured by licensing pass rates, is NCATE-accredited" (p. 13).

Ballou and Podbursky doubt the value of the four point agenda being advocated by educators in the U.S. that includes 1) mandatory accreditation by NCATE, 2) assessment of beginning teachers by instruments from the Interstate New Teacher Assessment and Support Consortium (INTASC), 3) certification of 105 000 "master" teachers by the National Board for Professional Teaching Standards, and 4) "establishment of independent professional boards in all states to set policies regarding teacher education, testing, licensing, and continuing certification" (pp. 3-4). The last point is equivalent to a call for U.S. states to emulate British Columbia and Ontario in creating colleges of teachers.

Their skepticism is based not only on the apparent ineffectiveness of NCATE. "The activities of NCATE and the independent boards – accreditation of teacher education programs and control of teacher licensing – are well-recognized means of restricting the supply of would-be teachers and creating pressures for states and districts to raise salaries in order to recruit enough qualified applicants. . . . [But on] closer analysis . . . there is little reason to expect that professional self-regulation will improve teacher quality" in part because "there are signs that professional self-regulation will be used to restrict teacher supply in ways that impede efforts to recruit better teachers. Among them are costly accreditation standards that make it prohibitively expensive for small liberal arts colleges. . . . [Also] prolonged pre-service training . . . deters too many capable students and . . . excessive credentialism . . . restricts administrative flexibility. . . ." (pp. 26-27).

In effect, Ballou and Podbursky are questioning whether there is any value being added by the professional certification process. The actions of the Ontario College of Teachers in responding to changes proposed by the government of Ontario seem to confirm their suspicions. In an article, "College Stands Firm on Unqualified Teachers," Denys Giguère writes, "The College took a well-publicized stand against sections of Bill 160 which appeared to allow the use of unqualified instructors to replace teachers. The government withdrew those sections on the advice of the College. . . . [T]he College insisted that only teachers are specially trained to teach children and adolescents. Computer technicians, musicians, athletes and people with any other background are not, unless they have successfully completed a teacher education program" (p. 10).

The College, in adopting the term "unqualified" rather than the more precise term "uncertified," made a semantic choice that boosts the prestige of the College and denigrates the expertise of skilled practitioners who could share their knowledge with school children were it not for hurdles imposed without demonstrated justification. The College does not, at this point in of time, assess the quality of current teachers, offer periodic recertification of teachers or have quality control assurance measures that would validate present certification requirements. To ensure the public's confidence, such initiatives, which were part of the College's mandate, are critical. At present, quality assurance relies solely upon a complaint-based system that requires a member of the public advance cases of educational malpractice.

The contradictory positions of the teaching profession on certification standards is particularly evident in the treatment of Ontario teachers who entered the classroom in the 1950s and 1960s with a high school diploma and one year of normal school. Although such individuals would be deemed "unqualified" were they to apply today, they continue to teach with no reassessment of the quality of their work or their need for improvement other than the sporadic evaluations that may be carried out by their principals.[3] Further, in the late 1980s teachers' unions claimed that teachers with these minimal qualifications were being discriminated against because they received less pay but did the same work as teachers who had earned bachelor of education degrees.

Invoking Ontario's pay equity legislation, the unions challenged school boards in *Wentworth County Board of Education v. Wentworth*

Women Teachers' Association and the Ontario Public School Federation, (1. P.E.R.). Ontario's Pay Equity Tribunal found in favor of the teachers not holding bachelor's degrees, finding, in effect, that they should be paid on the same pay scale as university graduates.[4] A key distinction in the case revolved around the question as to whether the seven pay categories (D, C, B for those without bachelor's degrees and A1, A2, A3, and A4 for those with university degrees) were different "job classifications" or different "job classes." If they were simply different classifications of the same job distinguished by differences in quality as measured by level of study, then the fact that there were 6 men and 118 women in categories D through B would be irrelevant. But, if the categories were considered distinct "job classes," then the disproportionate number of women in the lower categories allowed the *Pay Equity Act* (R.S.O. 1990, c. P.7) to be invoked. The teachers' unions took the latter view, even though they admitted that one grade three classroom might have a teacher in the D category while the neighboring grade three classroom might have an A4 category teacher: "[The federations] were opposed to including merit as a basis for compensation . . . [Instead], the federation advocated [pay]. . . . based on qualifications and teaching experience" (p. 154).

The Tribunal found in favor of the teacher unions and, as a result, hundreds of teachers across the province who had not made the effort to attain bachelor's degrees, as many of their peers had done, received substantial pay increases.[5] Apparently, the professional belief in the importance of extensive training for new teachers or in justifying pay increments from one category to another did not extend to this group. The profession's actions implied just the opposite; namely, that fiscal benefits were the first priority and that what counts most in making a good teacher is experience in the classroom, not formal training.

An ironic side to the impact of union bargaining or professional control in driving up most salaries is that they also tend to depress wages for members with highly specialized skills. This phenomenon is probably what accounts for the persistent shortage of new teachers in the physical sciences, mathematics and information technology. It also could account for the situation that Western Australian principals confronted when they chose to leave the teachers' union for a unit of their own, as reported in chapter 8. Individuals in high demand areas, including today the principalship, may find that the income they would forego while completing certification programs is too great to be offset by future salaries paid to them as school teachers. Liberal arts graduates who can find little employment elsewhere and for whom teaching salaries are attractive may not experience this problem. While bargaining agents may, if they choose, emphasize higher salaries for specialists, a practice common in universities with faculties of medicine and law, it is rarely practiced at the elementary and secondary levels. Fortunately, love of teaching and children will motivate some specialists who could earn more elsewhere to enter teaching, but in doing so they may make a financial sacrifice many of their peers do not. Still, many other talented individuals may be lost to the profession.

Ideally, professional bodies do monitor the quality of their members' work, ensure that sound training programs are offered, arrange high quality professional development and discipline members who violate professional standards. Skepticism about alternative motives behind much of the business of teacher preparation, teacher certification and professional upgrading does not prove that successful efforts are not possible. Certification bodies and those involved in the profession ought to be carefully evaluated to ensure that it is the quality of teaching provided children, and not teacher job protection and salaries, that is the primary objective. To do this, one must go beyond the rhetoric and look for evidence that the standards set truly matter and are consistently applied.

Appropriateness of Compensation

How does one decide if the compensation a person receives for a job is appropriate? The economic test of the question is straightforward. If one cannot find an employee to fill a position at the posted wage in a reasonable amount of time, the wage is too low. Conversely, if a queue of qualified individuals forms, individuals who are willing to wait months or even years for a position, then the wage must be too high. When a few adequately qualified individuals are available within a modest period of time, then the wage must be set at the right level since supply and demand are in balance. As for teaching in Canada, a queue of certified candidates existed for most of the past two decades, although this situation is in flux given increasing numbers of retirements and overall improvement in the Canadian economy and labor market. Many teachers have waited years before they have received a permanent appointment.

There is a counter-argument to the position that a queue for jobs implies that that uneconomically high wages are being paid. The "efficiency hypothesis" argues that employers will, in practice, review the applicants and select from among them the best-qualified individuals (Gunderson & Riddell, 1993, pp. 298-301). Therefore, these persons who are hired are actually more highly qualified than is the average member of the queue. Therefore, they deserve the high salary being paid. If this argument is valid then the current situation in Canada with high wages and a surplus of trained teachers may in fact be an economic solution, even if it does not appear to be so at first glance. Press (1998), in his survey of teacher demand in Canada, reports confirmation by employers that they do, in fact, try to find the best available candidate from among those who apply and that they prefer a situation in which they have a good choice of candidates.

The efficiency hypothesis is more difficult to demonstrate for teachers who are high up the salary schedule. Indeed, the primary justification given for early retirement schemes (chapter 10) is that employees in their mid-50s are both costly and past their prime, which implies that seniority-based wage scales become inefficient in the long run. With no simple mechanism to reduce wages to an economically appropriate level and no personnel assessment system that can determine who is or is not "at their prime," employers offer across-the-board early retirement incentives to employees. On the surface, this approach appears to be an efficient solution for the employer, at least in some cases, but whether or not it is an efficient solution for society is more difficult to determine. After early retirement, the individual becomes a recipient of transfer payments from those who are still working via the tax and pension systems. Is this social cost greater than that of paying these individuals above-market wages for a few years? We do not know.

Alternatives to the free market model for assessing whether compensation is appropriate are normatively based and can be applied both within the teacher labor market and between markets for teachers and other occupations. In the first instance, the higher pay for more senior teachers can be understood not as an index of their competence but an index of the costs of remaining with one employer, including loss of mobility and opportunities to earn more elsewhere. Also, they are more likely to be married and have families to support and thus have greater income needs. The salary grid thus may be a trade-off between senior and junior teachers whereby the latter effectively defer some income until a time when they have greater needs.

Normative comparisons across labor groups require that the compensation for one occupational group, such as teachers, be compared with the compensation of those occupying positions that have either similar, higher or lower qualifications and status. That is, prevailing norms for other occupations are considered as a guide rather than abstract economic theory. One would expect, for example, that teachers would receive higher compensation than retail clerks but lesser compensation than doctors, since clerks require less specialized training and doctors considerably more than teachers.

Pagliarello (1995) traced the shifts in employment income for a variety of occupational groups from 1970 to 1990 (table 9.3).[6] Teachers' incomes increased, on the average, from a level 19% above the national average income to 31% above the national average, an increase of approximately 10% relative to the base year. Teachers' gains relative to more highly paid professions were greater; their salaries increased from a level equal to 25% of physicians' and surgeons' to 33%, equivalent to an increase of 32% relative to the base year. The only occupational category that fared better than teachers was police force members. In 1970, teachers' salaries averaged 72% of police wages, but by 1990 had dropped to 69% of the average salary for police.

Income gains fluctuated during the two decades investigated: "Between 1970 and 1990, it was primarily public sector employees (school teachers and police officers) whose average earning rose much more quickly than the CPI [Consumer Price Index], and faster than the average of all occupations" (p. 12). After "removing the effects of inflation as measured by the CPI, average school teachers' earning rose 30% ($7500 in 1990 constant dollars) from 1970 to 1980" (p. 13). Salaries of physicians and surgeons meanwhile dropped by 3.7%; those for lawyers by 16%, although the latter rebounded by 11% in the next decade. To explain the teachers' good salary performance during the 1970s, he quotes a Canadian Teachers' Federation study that states, "in contrast to some of the provincial restraint programs of the 1980s [and later 1990s], annual teacher increments and reclassifications due to formal upgrading of formal qualifications were not subject to review" (p.14).[7] Pagliarello does not explain how police officers did even better than teachers did in spite of very little increase in educational level (table 9.4). He concludes his paper by stating that, "in 1970, school teachers were on average earning about 20% more than the average worker. By 1990, they were earning roughly 30% more ... even with inflation taken into account. ... These increases were not necessarily due to overall salary increases, but rather to school teachers acquiring more education and experience and entering the higher earning categories of their pay scales" (p. 19).

While the methodology in Pagliarello's study is generally sound, his view that salary grid increments do not represent pay increases is puzzling and misleading. He seems to have accepted the arguments and terminology of teachers' unions which view increments that are linked to years of experience and additional training as pay for quality improvements, not increases in pay for the doing the same work at the same level of performance. If there was clear evidence that all experience and qualification payments were linked to increased productivity, then he would have a case since grid increments would reflect quality improvement, not price increases.

Table 9.3
Average Employment Income of School Teachers as a Percentage of Selected Occupations (Constant 1990 Dollars), Age 15 and over

	1970		1980		1985		1990	
Occupation – Profession	$	%	$	%	$	%	$	%
Physicians and surgeons	97585	25	93962	34	97919	32	95728	33
Lawyers and notaries	74256	33	62261	52	63712	49	69121	46
University teachers	48108	51	49950	64	46625	67	48892	68
Police force (government)	34273	72	42858	75	43375	72	46110	69
Economists	40591	61	46116	70	42485	74	40972	78
Accountants and auditors	35738	69	39462	82	37047	85	37382	85
Systems analysts & programmers	32477	76	33928	95	33337	94	34475	90
School teachers (elem. & sec.)	24763	100	32206	100	31394	100	31864	100
All occupations	20781	119	24247	133	23319	135	24329	131
Secretaries and stenographers	15558	159	17920	180	17777	177	19315	165
Janitors and cleaners	13384	185	14294	225	13945	225	14939	213

Source: Pagliarello (1995), Table 1.

Note: Teachers' median salary was 82% of the average income of all employees for 1949/50 and 110% in 1960/61; for female public elementary teachers, respective percentages were 65% and 94%; for male secondary teachers, 145% and 171% (Stager, 1978).

While there is evidence that a teacher's effectiveness does increase during the first five to seven years, counting payments for experience beyond this level as a quality improvement is questionable, as is counting higher levels of education. It also appears Pagliarello was not aware of Ontario teachers unions' contradictory assertions in the pay equity case noted earlier that grid increments are not linked to quality of performance. Given that public sector police unions, whose salaries and benefits are typically settled through arbitration, did even better than teachers, it seems the salary increases for both teachers and police is better explained by the common cause of public sector unionization. Teachers' unions just used the salary grid as a mechanism to acquire automatic salary increases.

Another Statistics Canada study (Gendron with Pagliarello, 1994) analyses the shifts in the cost structure of education in Canada over the same two decades during which elementary and secondary enrolment declined substantially. They project that "if the financing effort [as defined by the amount of spending per student as a percentage of GDP (Gross Domestic Product) per capita] had remained at its 1971 level, the decrease in total spending per GDP would have been much larger than what was observed. In fact, it would have represented 3.9% in 1991 ($26.2 billion instead of $33.6 billion) and Canada would have ranked on the OECD average along with Germany, Ireland and Spain" (p. 20). Demographic declines in the 5-to-19 age group would have lowered expenditures by the equivalent of 2.2% of GDP while increased participation rates in this same age group would had a positive impact of .2% of GDP. Expenditures for increased levels of financing relative to GDP had an upward impact of 1.4% of GDP. As a result, spending on education as a percentage of GDP declined from 5.6% to 5.0% of GDP.

Where did the extra $7.6 billion per year ($33.6 billion minus $26.2 billion) go? The authors indicate, "fixed costs and job security clauses often prevented governments from aligning costs with decreasing demand. Furthermore, the variety of programs was expanded to include French immersion and French as a second language [and special education (p. 18)]. Most importantly the student/educator ratio dropped significantly [from 21 to 15 (p. 17)]. Consequently, curricula were enriched, pupil/education ratios reduced and the general level of education was increased significantly over the two decades" (p. 22). They do not define what they mean by "general level of education" nor provide any evidence that students learned more or left school better prepared in 1990 than they did in 1970. Also, they provide no evidence that students in western Canada and the Atlantic provinces, where spending per pupil was lower, were less well prepared than those in Ontario and Quebec, where expenditures during the period in question were highest. Hence, their conclusions about enrichment and the "level of education" are conjecture unsupported by the data in their paper.

Table 9.4
Percentage of Persons Aged 15 to 65 with a University Degree in Selected Occupations

Occupation – Profession	1970	1990	Difference
Physicians and surgeons	97.5	98.3	0.8
Lawyers and notaries	93.5	93.5	0.0
University teachers	98.0	99.2	1.2
Police force (government)	1.0	10.3	9.3
Economists	63.5	62.7	-0.8
Accountants and auditors	18.8	39.5	20.7
Systems analysts & programmers	34.7	40.4	5.7
School teachers (elem. & sec.)	37.0	80.1	43.1
All occupations	6.7	17.3	10.6
Secretaries and stenographers	2.1	3.4	1.3
Janitors and cleaners	0.6	1.6	1.0

Source: Pagliarello (1995), Table 4.

Another questionable assumption in this paper is that, "During the 20-year period the price of education inputs did not rise disproportionately to other prices in the economy" (p. 14). They make this statement despite the fact that the average salary for educators increased from $10 029 in 1971 to $55 979 in 1991, a 9% average annual increase vs. an average increase in the CPI of 7.1%. Most businesses, we suggest, would view this as a considerable increase in the cost of inputs. Their explanation is that "many educators moved to higher salary categories, thereby increasing the average salary" (p. 15). Again, they naively discount what factually is a salary increase as not being an increase because it reflects the grid structure of salaries for teachers. Recall that a teacher changing on the salary grid in table 9.2 might receive a pay cheque 17.2% greater than the year before. Both the teacher and the employing school district would probably consider this a salary increase. As well, the authors' comment that the 9% annual increase was "not above Canada's capacity to pay as measured by GDP per capita which increased 8.8% annually on average" (p. 16) implies that a fair salary increase is one which relates to the growth in the GDP per capita. Of course, as Pagliarello's 1995 report indicates, teachers were one of only a few groups (notably police) who were able to achieve salaries that paralleled growth in the economy during the 1970s and 1980s. Finally, this statement ignores the growing government debts that increased from 29% to 97% of GDP during years in question. Perhaps it was not within Canada's capacity to pay increasing salaries to members of an occupation where demand was falling and job queues were forming.

A study by Hay Associates Canada Limited for the Committee on the Costs of Education (1976) in the mid-1970s provided a comparison of "salary levels and employee benefit plans for employees of boards of education in Ontario." The Hay approach uses a job analysis to develop a scoring system representing the challenges that a position places on its incumbent. The scale ranges from 100 to 1100 points, the latter reflecting the apex of large private sector corporations. Table 9.5 reports a summary of their findings in terms of "Hay Control Points"; minimum, maximum and average salaries of the day; and a "developed range" suggesting what compensation in school boards would look like if it paralleled the private sector's modal practice. On average, the Hay study implied that educators in Ontario were, at that time, fairly compensated relative to the private sector.[8]

Patterns in remuneration were evident, however. Minimum pay for teachers – particularly elementary teachers who did not have a bachelor's degree – was below that which would be expected in the private sector. On the other hand, maximum salaries were somewhat higher than they would be in the private sector. Also notable is that principals of large elementary and of large secondary schools collected wages that were 10 to 20 percent *below* what a private-sector manager with similar responsibilities would collect. The study reported in other charts that senior administrators, including directors, were paid salaries equal to those in the lowest 15% of private-sector managers holding similar responsibilities.

The Hay study also assessed the benefits of educators relative to the private sector. For pensions, it reported that, "Both the Ontario Teachers' Superannuation Plan . . . provide[s] benefits that are superior to the average practice in industry in the areas of retirement income, widow's benefit, and disability benefit, placing those boards among the top 5% of employers. . . . A teacher may retire on full pension when the sum of his years of service and age total 90 while our industrial comparison indicates that a full pension is seldom provided before age 65" (p. 29). They considered including summer holidays as equivalent to a salary benefit of 15%, but noted that "a majority of teachers appear to devote significant additional time in course preparations and curriculum development beyond the normal working hours during the school term" (p. 30). Thus, they did not address the question as to whether teachers are paid for 10 months rather than 12 months of work. They concluded with the remark that, "The readers . . . may be interested in knowing that our impressions are very favorable. If the people we met are repre-

Table 9.5

Hay Control Points and Salary Range for Ontario Educators, 1972

Position	Hay Control Points	Weighted Average Salary Minimum	Average Salary Range Maximum	Average Salary Range	Developed Range Minimum	Developed Range Midpoint	Developed Range Maximum
Secondary Schools							
Principal (900 to 1900 students)	412	23 270		23 860	18 050	22 560	27 070
Principal (under 900 students)	344	22 950		23 120	15 820	19 780	23 740
Vice-principal II	271	19 710		20 240	13 350	16 690	20 030
Vice-principal I	236	19 710		20 240	12 110	15 140	18 170
Major department head	236	15 730		18 030	12 110	15 140	18 170
Minor department head	199	14 720		17 480	10 960	13 700	16 440
Assistant department head	193	13 850		16 900	10 630	13 290	15 950
Classroom teacher	168	11 850	8 540	16 080	9 890	12 360	14 830
Elementary Schools							
Principal (over 600 students)	334	19 860		20 890	15 490	19 360	23 230
Principal (250 to 600 students)	291	18 200		20 220	14 010	17 510	21 010
Principal (under 250 students)	254	16 040		19 230	12 780	15 970	19 160
Vice-principal II	222	14 120		17 900	11 620	14 520	17 420
Vice-principal I	193	14 120		17 900	10 630	13 290	14 950
Classroom teacher II	168	9 060	8 540	16 080	9 890	12 360	14 830
Classroom teacher I	146	9 060	6 470	16 080	9 060	11 330	13 600

Source: Committee on the Costs of Education, No. 6 (1976). Note: One dollar in 1972 was equivalent to $4.18 in 1997; e.g., $16 080 → $67 214.

sentative of all the people in elementary and secondary education ..., the education of our children is indeed in competent hands" (p. 32).

The data for the Hay study was collected in 1973, near the beginning of the period of time covered by the two studies from Statistics Canada and at the time Ontario teacher federations were moving toward union status.

A national perspective on teachers' salaries is provided in table 9.6 in which average teachers' income for each province is correlated with the average family income in the respective province. The correlation between the two is $r = .80$; since the coefficient of determination is $r^2 = 0.64$, this correlation implies that 64% of the variation in teachers' annual income is accounted for by the wealth of the province as measured by family income. Wealthier provinces pay more; less wealthy provinces pay less.

These data, from Statistics Canada, include incomes for private school teachers and part-time teachers as well as full-time teachers in publicly-financed schools. As a result, they suggest somewhat lower levels of compensation for teachers than do data on public and separate school system full-time teachers. The relationship between family income and teacher compensation, however, is not affected by this conservative measure of teachers' income, since correlations depend upon the relative rather than absolute values of income. Saskatchewan teachers, however, do seem to have anomalous salaries since family income in that province is among the top five provinces while teacher compensation is near the bottom. Fiscal restraint programs in that province under a New Democratic government that inherited an exceptionally large deficit from the previous Conservative government resulted in a larger decrease in real incomes for teachers in that province than in any other (Lawton, Ryall & Menzies, 1995;1997). This point aside, it is evident that the relationship between capacity to pay and teacher salaries suggested by Gendron (1994) is present.

Conclusion

Statistical data on expenditure trends in table 9.1 and salary trends in tables 9.3, 9.4, 9.5 and 9.6, when assessed against both free market economic models and normative standards, yield a surprisingly moderate conclusion, given the sound and fury over teacher unionism. As far as compensation is concerned, the data suggest that over the past quarter century, teachers' unions managed to maintain compensation gains teachers had obtained previously and avoided losses in purchasing power that many other occupations have experienced. Key accomplishments such establishment of a uniform salary grid that recognizes both experience and qualifications applicable to both elementary and secondary teachers, increased certification requirements and excellent pension benefits were actually in place before unionization occurred.

Nevertheless, given the assaults on the Canadian economy of oil price shocks (both up and down), two severe recessions – one in the early 1980s and one in the early 1990s – and phenomenal growth in government indebtedness, simply holding on to the gains of previous decades may be seen as no mean accomplishment. Maintenance of employment, protecting benefits and defending salary schedules is more than many of teachers' private and public sector brethren achieved. If there is one flaw in their effort it is that the foundation of the salary grid – namely the value of experience and additional qualifications – is not backed by a system of professional accountability that demonstrates and assures its value to the educational system and the students that this system serves.

Table 9.6
Average Family Income and Average Teacher Income by Province, 1995

Province	Family Income	Teacher Income	Ratio
Ontario	$59 356	$42 758	.72
British Columbia	$56 925	$38 737	.68
Alberta	$53 361	$36 390	.68
Manitoba	$51 467	$36 296	.71
Saskatchewan	$50 056	$33 059	.66
Quebec	$49 498	$35 094	.70
Prince Edward Island	$45 450	$32 227	.71
Nova Scotia	$44 826	$35 530	.79
New Brunswick	$44 454	$31 771	.71
Newfoundland	$42 328	$35 253	.83
Ratio of high to low:	1.40	1.21	

Correlation between Family Income and Teacher Income: $r = .80$

Source: *Statistics Canada, February 1997; October 1997.*

References

Ballou, D. & Podgursky, M. (August 1998) Teacher unions and education reform: Gaining control of professional licensing and advancement. Paper presented at the conference, "Teacher Unions and Educational Reform" held at the Kennedy School of Government, Harvard University, Cambridge, MA, September 24-25, 1998.

Committee on the Costs of Education. (October 1976). *Salary + Benefits = Compensation. Interim Report Number Six.* (Hay Study) Toronto: The Committee.

Gendron, F. with Pagliarello, C. (1994). Does Canada invest enough in education?: An insight into the cost structure of education in Canada. *Education Quarterly Review, 1*(4), 10-25.

Giguère, D. (June 1988). College stands firm on unqualified teachers. *Professionally Speaking*, pp. 10-11.

Gunderson, M. & Riddell, W. C. (1993). *Labour market economics.* (3rd ed.) Toronto: McGraw-Hill Ryerson.

Hickcox, E. S., Lawton, S. B., Leithwood, K. A. & Musella, D. F. (1988). *Making a difference through performance appraisal.* Toronto: OISE Press.

Lawton, S. (1996). *Financing Canadian education.* Toronto: Canadian Education Association.

Lawton, S., Ryall, M. & Menzies, T. *A Study on Costs.* (August 1996). Background Paper. Toronto: Ministry of Education and Training.

Loney, M. (1998). *The pursuit of division: Race, gender and preferential hiring in Canada.* Montreal & Kingston: McGill-Queen's University Press.

Manitoba Education and Training. (January 1996). *Enhancing accountability, ensuring quality: A discussion document on teacher collective bargaining and compensation.* Winnipeg: MET.

Menzies, T., Ryall, M. & Lawton, S. (Fall 1998). Trends in Canadian educational expenditures: Is the worst over? *Journal of Education Finance, 24*(2), 120-136.

Meyer, J. W. & Scott, W. R. (1983). *Organizational environments: Ritual and rationality.* Beverly Hills, CA: Sage Publications.

Pagliarello, C. (1995). Employment income of elementary and secondary teacher and other selected occupations. *Education Quarterly Review 2*(2), pp. 9-21.

Pay Equity Commission: http://www.gov.on.ca/lab/pec/acte.htm

Press, H. (1998). *National survey of teacher demand in Canada.* Ed.D. Thesis, Department of Theory and Policy Studies in Education, University of Toronto.

Samuelson, P. A. (1967). *Economics: An introductory analysis.* (7th ed.). New York: McGraw-Hill Book Company.

Stager, D. (1978). *Elementary and secondary school teachers' salaries in Ontario, 1900 to 1975.* Working Paper No. 5, Commission on Declining School Enrolments in Ontario (CODE). Toronto: CODE.

Statistics Canada (Summer 1997). Education at a glance. *Education Quarterly Review* 4(2), 77-86.

Wentworth County Board of Education v. Wentworth Women Teachers' Association and the Ontario Public School Federation. (1990) *Pay Equity Reports*, Vol. 1. Toronto: Pay Equity Tribunal, pp. 132-177.

Wolfe, B. (1980). *An analysis of the labour market experiences of recent graduates of Ontario teacher training institutions.* Ph.D. Thesis, University of Toronto.

Notes

1. Although cost and price are often used interchangeably, they have different technical definitions. Cost is the amount paid for a given quantity of a good or service of a given quality; price is fair market price. The two need not be the same for a variety of reasons. For example, two school districts may have similar pay scales (i.e., prices) for teachers yet their educational costs may differ because one has only senior teachers at the top of the pay scale whereas the other has a variety of junior and senior teachers. This example assumes that there is no difference in quality of education delivered by the all-senior or mixed seniority staffs. See Lawton (1996, pp. 139-147) for a more complete discussion.
2. The analysis in this section is based on material provided by Kenneth Wm. Thornicroft, Faculty of Business, University of Victoria, although appropriate use of that material is the first author's responsibility.
3. In the 1980s, when the Ministry of Education attempted to develop a provincial policy for performance appraisal of all educators, teachers' unions blocked its efforts. The first author was part of a team that conducted a major research study funded by the Ministry of Education on performance appraisal (see Hickcox, E. S., Lawton, S. B., Leithwood, K. A. & Musella, D. F. (1988) *Making a difference through performance appraisal.* Toronto: OISE Press.) and observed two union representatives decline approval to Ministry officials, who dared not move without the consent of union representatives, even though the area of staff appraisal is clearly a matter of management rights.
4. A Hay salary study (Committee on the Costs of Education, 1976) provided direct evidence that work actually carried out by teachers without bachelor's degrees would have commanded higher salaries in the private sector. This finding does not contradict the point made here since at issue is the extent to which teacher education provides value-added skills beyond those learned in the classroom as a practice or probationary teacher.
5. When contacted, the Hamilton-Wentworth District School Board, the amalgamated school board that is the successor to both the Hamilton and Wentworth County boards of education, was unable to locate former Wentworth County Board's union agreements or school board minutes for 1990 which would have described the exact settlement. A clerk recalled that a new "category A" was created that extended to 11 and then 12 steps rather than 6, 9 and 10 steps of categories D, C and B. This agreement provided immediate increases to those teachers with seniority over six years who had never earned addition credits beyond high school and one year of teacher's college. To reach step 12, specific courses had to be completed. By 1999, virtually all affected teachers still with the board had earned at least a bachelor's degree and most are at A4.
While the ratio of women to men was in 1990 almost 20:1 in the categories D, C and B, it was 1.7:1 in the four A categories. In 1990, salaries in the lowest D category ranged from $16 593 for step 1 to $24 821; since by provincial regulation no one could have been hired

into the D category since the early 1970s, all of the 22 teachers in this category would have been in step 6
6. Data from the Censuses of Population of 1971, 1981, 1986 and 1991 were used. Pagliarello (1995) notes, "Average income includes employment income of all person who worked full time, full year or part of the year, and all part time workers" (p. 10). Hence, teachers who work in private schools (about 5% of the total), supply teachers and the like are included in the data set, along with full-time teachers in publicly-financed schools.
7. From "Comparative Analysis of Teacher Incomes Based on Taxation Statistics," in the Canadian Teachers' Federation *Economic Service Bulletin*, June 1994. CTF *Economic Service Bulletins* are not publicly available.
8. The salary levels in table 9.5 cannot be compared directly with those in table 9.2 since salaries in the latter were adjusted upwards using the Consumer Price Index to their value in terms of 1990 dollars. A conversion is given for the maximum figure, demonstrating that teachers have maintained purchasing power at the top of the pay schedule for pre-tax income.

10

Teacher Pension Plans in Canada

"Goodbye, Mr. Parley: a teaching generation moves on."

The Globe and Mail

The *Globe and Mail* story, headlined above, reports that Mr. Parley, 54, a geography teacher for 31 years, is one of an estimated 9000 Ontario teachers who will participate in the "early-retirement deal between the provincial government and the Ontario Teachers' Federation" roughly 1 in every 14 teachers.[1] The program is funded "by a pension-plan surplus" and has the "potential to open up an estimated 18 200 new jobs for young teachers over the next 4 1/2 years."

As Auriemma, Cooper and Smith (1992) suggested in *Graying Teachers*, teacher pension plans have become a major tool for the management, restructuring and renewal of school systems. Yet, considering the extensive literature on school finance, educational politics and management, pension plans receive incredibly little attention. This is changing, of course, due to concerns about the impact of the pending retirement of baby boomers, but as the *Globe* article makes clear, the teachers who taught the baby boomers are already in their peak retirement years.

This chapter has three purposes, the first of which is to summarize the status of teacher pension plans in Canada's ten provinces. The second purpose is to consider their financial health, their current use in renewing and downsizing educational systems, and their potential value as economic instruments for provincial and national development. The final focus is to raise questions about some of the assumptions underlying the celebratory rhetoric about their current contribution to our collective good.

What Is a Pension?

One interpretation of pensions is that they are nothing more than deferred income – the payment of money earned this year but paid at a future time. Typical teachers in Canada earn pensions equal to two percent of their average salary during the last five years of service. In fact, over 93% of full-time public employees in Canada accumulated pension benefits at a rate of 2% of salary 1996, while only 21% of full-time private sector employees had an accumulation rate this high (Statistics Canada, 1996). If the average salary during a teacher's last five years equals $65 000 – a typical maximum for experienced teachers in major urban centres in Canada – the teacher would earn the right during the last year of employment to be paid $1300 per year for the remainder of his or her life. That income stream can be translated into its net present value – i.e., the amount of money needed at present to provide the payment over a certain number of years – which is easily calculated on most spreadsheet programs. If one assumes the individual has a life expectancy of another 25 years, that a discount rate of 7% applies, and that the employer pays the cost of the pension, then the current lump-sum or commuted value of the pension earned in the last of year of teaching is $15 150. Deducting a teacher's contribution (8.9% of salary in Ontario) means that, in the last year, the teacher earned about $9400 in deferred income. That is, the total income earned during that final year, *including deferred income*, is about $74 400.

Of course, a pension of $1300 per year is unlikely to keep one in champagne and caviar, but after 32 years of teaching, an individual would receive about $42 000 annually, an amount equal to roughly two-thirds of final pay. Normally, a person who retires early would receive a reduced pension; however, this reduction is waived or lessened by Ontario's special early retirement benefit. A very nice benefit indeed, although not as generous as some of those reported for U.S. states by Auriemma, *et al.* (1992).

The type of pension plan outlined above is typical for public sector employees in Canada where, at the beginning of 1996, 5.1 million workers contributed to registered pension plans, including 2.5 million in the public sector and 2.7 million in the private sector. Virtually all public sector members contributed to their plans, with 76% of these employees contributing 7% or more of their salaries. Only 55% of private sector plan members contributed to their plans and less than one percent paid 7% or more of earnings. Overall, 73% of registered pension plan members contributed to their plans, which on January 1, 1996, held $485 billion.

The type of pension described above is a *defined benefit plan* in which the employer has promised a specific amount of money per year after an individual retires. Ninety-five percent of public sector members participated in defined benefit plans in 1996 versus 81% in the private sector. Seventy-six percent of public sector defined benefit plans in Canada also offer some level of protection against inflation by indexing pension values to the Consumer Price Index, while only 14% of private sector plans do so (Statistics Canada, 1996). When government or an agency of government makes that promise, the good credit of the government (and that of its taxpayers) underwrites the guarantee. To help pay the bill, governments often require employees to help fund the plan, even though these contributions may simply go into general government revenue. Who actually pays these pensions, and when these payments are made, is a complex issue discussed later.

An alternative form of pension is the *defined contribution* or *money purchase plan* in which the money used to fund the pension is deposited by the employer and often the employee into an investment account. These funds are typically annuitized at retirement, a process equivalent to the reverse of calculating the net present value, in order to determine the value of the annual pension that can be purchased. No guarantees are given with defined contribution plans; a poor investment climate can result in a low pension while a good climate can result in an excellent pension. Also, laws require them to be converted into annuities on the recipient's 80th birthday; thereafter, no inflation protection is provided. Often, employees will be able to select what types of investments the funds will purchase. In the case of one large Ontario university, faculty members with a money purchase plan who bet on the stock markets during the inflationary 1970s and 1980s were sorely disappointed when their rate of return averaged just 9 percent, considerably less than the 12 percent earned by those who invested in bonds.

Auriemma, Cooper and Smith (1992) emphasize that states (and provinces) began teacher pension plans as teacher welfare systems. Teachers retiring in the first half of this century, after a lifetime of low salaries and few benefits, were indigent, and governments promised to pay them a modest reward for their years of dedication. With growth in the economy and lobbying by teachers' organizations, these promises were transformed into increasingly generous defined benefit pension plans that often include elements of inflation protection.

Survey of Canadian Teacher Pension Plans

Table 10.1 provides an overview of pension arrangements in each of Canada's ten provinces, listed in geographical order from Newfoundland in the east to British Columbia in the west. Eleven headings designate key features of the plans.

Plan governance indicates who has responsibility for the operation of the fund, including the improvement in benefits such as inflation protection or use of funds for early retirement. In all provinces, provincial statutes have been passed which detail these legal responsibilities. While in practice teachers' federations are consulted in drafting and revising these acts, in most cases the

Table 10.1
Summary of Teacher Pension Plans Across Canada, 1998

Province	Plan Governance	Pension Negotiations
Newfoundland	Provincial government	Negotiated province-wide
Prince Edward Island	Provincial government	Not negotiated
New Brunswick	Provincial government	Not negotiated
Nova Scotia	Provincial government	Not negotiated
Quebec	Provincial government	Not negotiated
Ontario	Government-teacher partnership	Negotiated province-wide
Manitoba	Provincial government	Not negotiated
Saskatchewan	Provincial government	Negotiated province-wide with salaries
Alberta	Government-teacher partnership	Negotiated province-wide
British Columbia	Provincial government	Not negotiated

province is designated as the party with governing responsibility. In two provinces, Alberta and Ontario, the legislation formally creates a commission with representatives from both government and teachers' unions to be responsible for the operation of the plans.

Pension negotiations occur on a province-wide basis in four provinces and are set by governments in the remaining six, although discussions between governments and teachers' federations also occur in these cases. Typically, pension benefits are set independently of salaries, although obviously the two are linked in that higher salaries will increase pension plan obligations. In the 1990s, however, salary freezes and reductions had the opposite impact, decreasing plan obligations below levels that had been predicted.

Salary negotiations are conducted provincially in seven provinces, with only Saskatchewan reporting a "total compensation" approach to bargaining in which salaries and benefits, including pensions, are on the negotiating table at the same time. In Ontario,

Table 10.1
Summary of Teacher Pension Plans (cont.)

Salary Negotiations	Contribution Rate – Member	Contribution Rate – Employer
Province-wide	7.90% up to YMPE 8.50% above YMPE	7.90% up to YMPE .50% above YMPE
Province-wide	7.20% up to YMPE 9.00% above YMPE	7.20% up to YMPE 9.00% above YMPE
Province-wide	7.30% up to YMPE 9.00% above YMPE	7.30% up to YMPE 9.00% above YMPE
Province-wide	8.30% up to YMPE 9.90% above YMPE	8.30% up to YMPE 9.90% above YMPE
Province-wide	RRE: 8.08% RREGOP: 7.95%	RRE: 10.14% RREGOP: 7.95%
Local level	8.90%	8.90%
Local level	5.70% up to YMPE 7.30% above YMPE	None
Province-wide	6.05% up to YMPE 7.85% above YMPE (to 9.00% by 2000 for STRP)	6.05% up to YMPE 7.85% above YMPE
Local level	8.86% up to YMPE 12.06% above YMPE	11.23%
Province-wide	6.00% up to YMPE 7.50% above YMPE	9.13% up to YMPE 10.63% above YMPE

Note: for Quebec: RRE=régime de retraite des enseignants (teachers' retirement plan), RREGOP=régime de retraite des employés du gouvernement et des organismes publics (retirement plan for employees of government and public organizations). For Saskatchewan: STRP=Saskatchewan Teachers' Retirement Plan; SSTSC=Saskatchewan Teachers' Superannuation Commission.

salaries and other benefits are negotiated at the school district level, while pensions are negotiated provincially. Since Alberta and Ontario have moved to province-wide funding of schools, the actual range of discretion for salary negotiations is now relatively narrow. Only Manitoba retains the tradition of shared province/local funding with local collective bargaining. All other provinces have centralized funding or salary negotiations, or both.

Contributions by governments and active members of pension plans generate the capital needed to fund pensions. Typically, each party contributes a certain percentage of salary. A key figure in determining contribution rates in most provinces is the Yearly Maximum Pensionable Earnings, or YMPE, an amount set by the

Table 10.1
Summary of Teacher Pension Plans (cont.)

Province	Employer for Matching Contributions	Annual Employer Matching Contributions
Newfoundland	Provincial government	$29 million plus $160 million toward liability
Prince Edward Island	Local school boards (100% provincially-funded)	$4.7 million
New Brunswick	Provincial government	$32 million
Nova Scotia	Provincial government	$44 million
Québec	Provincial government	$418 million
Ontario	Provincial government	$667.4 million (plus $465 million for initial liability)
Manitoba	Provincial government	Pay-as-you-go
Saskatchewan	Provincial government	STRP - $14 million STSC - $20 million
Alberta	Provincial government	$98 million plus $59 million for liability
British Columbia	Provincial government	$76 million

federal government to indicate the amount of salary on which the governments of Canada and Quebec will pay pensions. In 1998, approximately 3.5 percent of salary was paid to fund these plans, so provinces often set a *lower* rate for teachers' contributions to their provincial teachers' pension plans based on amount of salary up to the YMPE and a *higher* rate on the balance of salaries. There is also a maximum salary level above which deductions for pensions are not tax deductible. This provision affects salaries of about $90 000 or higher – an amount of concern to some principals and most superintendents in the wealthier provinces.

In 1998, employee contributions ranged from a low of 7.5 percent above YMPE in British Columbia to a high of 12 percent in neighboring Alberta. Employer contributions ranged from a low of 0% in Manitoba, which operates the government contribution on a "pay-as-you-go" basis, to a high just over 11% in Alberta. Combined contributions ranged from lows of 7.3% above YMPE in Manitoba and 13.9% in Saskatchewan to a high of an incredible

Table 10.1
Summary of Teacher Pension Plans (cont.)

Amount of Unfunded Liability/Surplus	Early Retirement Benefit	Number of Active Members
$1.5 billion	Full pension after 30 years	7800
Less than $127 million	Full pension after 35 years or age 55 with 30 years	1435
$337.6 million (86.3% funded)	Full pension if age+exp. =87 or 35 years experience	8575
$144 million (95% funded)	Full pension if age+exp. =85	13 000
RRE: $6 billion (1993) RREGOP: $9.4 billion surplus (1993)	Age 55 with 35 years; age 60 with 20 years	95 809
$4.4 billion surplus	Full pension if age+exp. =80 to 12/31/2002	155 000
Estimated $1.5 billion	Full pension 55 & age+exp.=80 and 70 factor over 60	14 000
STRP fully funded STSC - $2 billion	After 30 years or age+service at 55	STRP - 5100 STSC - 6900
$3.89 billion (2/3 gov't., 1/3 teachers)	Age+exp.=85 at age 55	32 000
Fully funded	Age+exp.=90	40 700

23.29% of salary over YMPE in Alberta. The variation in rates reflects very different sets of assumptions, policies and histories toward the funding of teachers' pensions. Auriemma *et al.* (1992) found similar, if not greater, variation among the U. S. states in terms of how pension obligations were to be met.

Employer matching contributions are made by the province in all but one case, Prince Edward Island. However, P.E.I.'s three school districts are fully funded by the province, implying that the province is ultimately responsible for the employer's share of pensions. Nevertheless, Prince Edward Island's accounting practice means that the full costs of salaries – current and deferred – are evident in the school districts' budgets, something than cannot be said for the other provinces.

Annual employer contributions range from a modest $4.7 million in Prince Edward Island to two-thirds of a billion dollars in Ontario – excluding a half-billion dollars in special payments to cover an earlier fund deficit. Amounts vary among provinces, obviously, due to differences in contribution rates, salaries and numbers of teachers. Amounts per active teacher (for all provinces except Manitoba) range from about $3300 to $4300, although the amounts are difficult to calculate due to differing arrangements for making good on unfunded liabilities. The largest pension fund, that of Ontario, now exceeds $50 billion in value and is one of the largest and most influential pools of capital in Canada.

Unfunded liabilities and the actuarial soundness of pension plans is a matter of concern to governments and teachers alike. This issue rose to prominence during the inflationary years of the 1970s when funds that had been set aside to meet pension obligations began to look depressingly small. At the same time, the "baby bust" was cutting into school enrolments and the assumption that "pay-as-you-go" pension systems could be funded from the ever-growing base of the population pyramid, with each new generation outnumbering the old, came into question. Provincial policies of borrowing from public sector pension plans, often at below-market rates, to meet their own capital needs also seemed increasingly risky.

Several teachers' pension funds are fully funded at present, including those for British Columbia and Ontario, although Ontario continues to make payments for the "initial liability" that existed at the time the current pension plan structure was adopted in the late 1980s. Estimates of liabilities require many assumptions concerning rates of return on investments, retirement dates and life spans. Several provinces, including Quebec and Saskatchewan, approached the issue by taking on the liability of the existing plan as a provincial responsibility and creating an altogether new fully-funded plan for future pensions. Manitoba does not officially estimate its pension liabilities. The employees' contributions are set aside in a separate fund that is used to pay half of teachers' pensions and to provide inflation protection and other pension improvements. Judging from other provinces, Manitoba's current unfunded liability for teachers' pensions must be on the order of $1.5 to $2 billion. Alberta, with a substantial unfunded liability, is unusual in that it has assigned two-thirds of the burden for funding its shortfall to the government and one-third to the teachers, which helps to account for the very high contribution rates for that province.

In late 1998, the government of Newfoundland and Labrador reached an agreement with the provincial teachers' association to make the teachers' pension fund actuarially sound. Pensions had been paid on a pay-as-you-go basis but the accrued liability for current and future pensions was about $1.5 billion. The province agreed to pay a total of $815 million over 14 years, with payments of $166 million in 1998 and 1999 and $76 million in each of the following twelve years. Interest paid on the funds, employee contributions and savings from integrating the plan with the Canadian Pension Plan should remove concern teachers had over the soundness of the plan.

Early retirement benefits are or have been a feature of most provincial education systems during the current decade as governments have downsized their educational systems, particularly in Quebec and the Atlantic provinces where school enrolments continue to decline. Federal law allows the use of pension funds to enhance retirement benefits for those 55 and over. The most common use of surplus funds is to eliminate the "early retirement penalty" which is a deduction ranging up to 6 percent of pension per year for those retiring before age 65 (Delaney, 1998). Reduced pensions make actuarial sense since early-retirees will be on pension for a longer period of time and invested funds will have less time to grow; nevertheless, they deter older, highly-paid teachers from retiring. The most common early-retirement arrangement is to provide "full pension" at a combination of age and experience equal to a number between 80 and 85. A "full pension" for those retiring early is usually not equal to what the person would receive at age 65, the normal retirement. If a person meets the 85 factor with 30 years of experience but the plan allows up to 35 years of credit, the full pension will be 60 percent rather than 70 percent of average salary over the last five years. Also lost are pension increases attributable to the higher salaries that might have been earned during the years of forgone employment.

Normal retirement policies vary across the provinces so that what is "early retirement" in one may be "normal retirement" in another. An "85 factor" is required for an Ontario teacher to take advantage the agreement between the province and teachers' unions to use $2 billion of the surplus in the teachers' pension plan to fund an early retirement plan. In Manitoba, however, normal retirement at full pension is allowed with an "80 factor." Even with this generous provision for regular retirement, Manitoba's teachers' unions have approached the government to negotiate an early retirement scheme.

Enrollees in teachers' pension plans fall into three categories: active members, who are currently employed and paying into the plan; inactive members, who are not teaching but have vested benefits that are due in the future; and retirees, who are collecting pensions. The number of active numbers determines the future level of contributions and the growth in liabilities. Currently, teacher pension plans in Canada have about 375 000 active members.

To communicate to their members and the public, several pension plans have initiated web-sites. At various stages of development are those for Ontario (www.otpp.com), Saskatchewan (www.stsc.gov.sk.ca) and Alberta (www.atrf.com). The British Columbia Teachers' Federation and Newfoundland and Labrador Teachers' Association maintain excellent sites that have detailed sections on pensions and retirement (www.bctf.bc.ca and www.nlta.nf.ca, respectively).

Pension Policy Issues

There are at least three major issues concerned with teachers' pensions that bring debate, concern and action: their financial health, their use as a tool for assisting in the restructuring of school systems and their use as agents of economic development and/or social reform. Each of these is touched on briefly.

Provincial governments initially assumed the financial obligation for paying pensions, making the pensions as sound as the governments which promised them. How sound are our provincial governments? During the recession that commenced in 1990-91, several provinces were incurring huge deficits and Bob White, President of the Canadian Labour Congress, confidentially suggested that Ontario could just declare bankruptcy, paying 50 or 60 cents on the dollar (Rae, 1997, p. 242). Just how such an action would have affected teachers' pensions in a province is anybody's guess, but the crisis created in Brazil when one of its states defaulted in early 1999, setting off a 40 percent devaluation in Brazil's currency, gives an idea. It is assumed that the government of Canada stands behind its provinces and guarantees their bonds, but whether this means that it stands behind their public employees' pensions is another matter. In any case, good fiscal management would seem to require that funds be set aside to pay for pensions, although there are several sides to this issue.

Pension Liabilities

Most provinces have moved toward making pension funds actuarially sound, although some have stopped short of this goal out of concern for the immediate impact that increasing payments would have on taxpayers and active pension plan members. The three Prairie Provinces are taking contrasting approaches. Alberta is committed to full funding of the liability and, as a result, is paying more as the employer and demanding more from teachers: the result is Canada's highest rate of contribution for both parties. Saskatchewan, in contrast, isolated the existing liability in the mid-1980s but has not tried to fund it, instead creating a new, fully funded pension plan for all new teachers. The province plans to meet the costs implied by the liability on a pay-as-you-go basis, a burden their treasury department believes is within the province's capacity. Finally, Manitoba has made no formal estimate of its liability nor set aside funds to meet it, in spite of the very generous retirement terms. However, the province has adopted "balanced budget" legislation and is using a modest surplus to repurchase outstanding bonds, thereby reducing the province's official debt. In a sense, one could argue that the province is "borrowing" from the employers' portion of the teachers' pension fund at 0 percent interest in order to repay loans on which 5 or 6 percent interest is paid. All three approaches can be defended although each choice has very different implications as to who will, in the end, pay the pensions promised: employees, provincial taxpayers, domestic firms or international firms and their employees.

Ontario followed yet another course in the late 1980s, changing to a jointly managed pension fund, with the government committing itself to make annual payments of about $500 million for 20 years to make up the existing shortfall, now referred to as the "initial deficit." In practice, the well-managed fund has grown so rapidly that it is now in surplus – yet the government still had the legal obligation to continue payments on the initial deficit. To escape from this now embarrassing commitment, the province negotiated a termination of the payments with the teachers' unions with the understanding that $2 billion of the current surplus would be used for an early retirement package over four-and-one-half years and that the next $6.9 billion in surplus would be used to improve the pension plan (Ruimy, 1998). For their part, teacher federations agreed to a reduction in the payments for the "initial deficit" and publicly proclaimed that they had made a $10 billion gift to the province by not holding it to the original agreement. In effect, Ontario's *defined benefit plan* had become very much like a *money purchase plan* in that gains in the investment pool will be used to benefit employees, while, of course, the province retains all of the risks. Should the fund decline in value, the province would still be obliged to honor the pension guarantees.

Given Ontario's experience and recognizing that liability estimates are just that – estimates – perhaps Saskatchewan and Manitoba are wise in not trying to fully fund their teacher pension obligations. Otherwise, they would run the risk that any gains in the investment value of money set aside for the purpose would be used to the benefit one select group, teachers, rather than all taxpayers in the province who now benefit from reductions in provincial debt.

Early Retirement and Restructuring

Pension plans may, within certain legal restrictions, be used to make "bridging" payments to facilitate early retirement of employees. The Ontario case is particularly notable in that its early retirement plan coincides with two major secondary school regulatory changes. The first change will increase teachers' classroom time by about 15 percent and the other will compress the five-year secondary program, which includes "grade 13," into the four-year program common in the rest of North America (Quebec excluded). The first initiative was part of Bill 160, discussed in chapter 7. Assuming the announced changes are implemented, perhaps 6000 fewer secondary school teachers will be required. The early retirement plan funded from the Ontario Teachers' Pension Plan will facilitate this downsizing.

At first glance, using a teachers' pension plan to assist in restructuring would seem to be a cost-effective proposal. At "no" cost to the province, highly paid senior teachers retire with only three out of four being replaced. New teachers, presumably, would be earning lower salaries than did those who they replaced. However, the scheme may not be such a bargain (Brown & Repa, 1993). Early retirement plans do not always achieve the desired effect of removing groups from the teaching force. The Texas State Pension Board (cited in the National Education Association, 1994) studied 24 public sector early retirement incentive plans implemented between 1984 and 1988. The board concluded:

> *Many states felt that an early retirement incentive program was useful in meeting initial state goals of reducing the workforce, avoiding layoffs, and providing payroll savings. At the same time, most states indicated disappointment in the long-term reduction of employees and costs. It appears that in some cases the costs were considerably more than the savings, with the costs of the incentives wiping out any financial gains.*

First, historical data indicate that four to five thousand Ontario teachers retire or leave teaching in any one year *without* incentives, yet all those who leave during the early retirement window will receive early-retirement incentives. Second, many of those retiring will receive retirement gratuities of up to $30 000 reflecting the value of accumulated sick leave. Third, many if not most of those who leave will cease to be full-time employees. No longer will they be engaged in the productive economy earning income, creating wealth and paying taxes. Instead, they will be supported by pension funds that hold government bonds, whose interest is paid by taxpayers, and equity in companies most of whose employees work at wages lower those of beginning teachers. It is not clear that there is any net gain for the people of Ontario and Canada in pensioning off employees early and paying them higher pensions rather than encouraging them to work productively until normal pensionable age. It is important to recognize that pensions are *not* paid out of vault full of gold coins; they are paid out of a *transfer of income* from working persons to non-working persons.

Investment Practices

One can praise many of Canada's teacher pension plans for being effective capitalists in managing their funds for the best economic return. Since by federal law 80 percent of pension plan holdings must be in Canadian investments, public sector pension funds offer major support and active management for the Canadian economy. The funds also help to support the value of our currency. Were pension plans not required to invest in Canada's domestic economy, a major source of capital might become unavailable as its managers sought better investment opportunities in less regulated economies elsewhere.

Pension plans invest both "actively" and "passively" in equity markets. The British Columbia pension plan, with about $8 billion in 1997, invests in both equities and bonds. Thirteen percent of the fund was invested in specific Canadian companies (active management), 28% in Canadian equity index (passive management), 4% in U.S. (active), 6% U.S. (passive), 7% non-U.S. foreign (active), and 4% non-U.S. foreign (passive). Also, 6% was placed in Canadian real estate, 22% in government bonds, 5% in corporate bonds, 3% in the money market, and 2% in mortgages (British Columbia Teachers' Board, 1997).

It is in active management of equities that social issues come to the fore. Federal and provincial policies require that pension funds work to maximize their rates of return, within the foreign content restrictions. The restrictions on foreign investment reflect a national and provincial intent that funds be used for domestic economic and social development. For some, this is not enough. They believe that some types of investments ought not to be made because of a perceived negative impact of the business on society and, conversely, they believe other investments ought to be made in order to promote perceived positive effects. Holdings of tobacco stocks, of firms with poor records of environmental protection and media outlets that oppose unions have been identified by union activists as being "unethical" for educators' pension funds. In one case, the Ontario Teachers' Federation passed a motion calling for the Ontario Teachers' Pension Fund to sell its interest in Sun Media, which published the anti-union *Financial Post* and *Toronto Sun* newspapers. The fund did not sell: Sun Media proved to be an excellent investment. Conversely, others argue for investments in renewable energy, public transportation and the like since these are deemed to be beneficial to society, even though they are likely to generate low rates of return.

A practical problem has been finding enough investment opportunities within the small Canadian economy. Active participation in small-capitalization public companies is virtually impossible for funds without creating an excessive impact on stock prices. The Ontario Teachers' Pension Plan has become a very aggressive owner of businesses since entering the merchant banking business in the early-1990s (McNish, 1995). In one case, it partnered with Onex Corporation in a hostile takeover bid for John Labatt Ltd., owner of the Toronto Blue Jays at that time. The Teachers' (as the Ontario plan is referred to in the business pages) held stock in Labatt's, but was disenchanted with its management. In the end, Onex lost out in a competitive bid for the firm to Interbrew SA, Belgium's biggest brewer (Corcoran, 1995). Hardly the way to build a Canadian corporation, but very profitable for the fund.

Another investment by Teachers' helped Wallace McCain of New Brunswick's McCain clan to make a bid for Maple Leaf Foods Inc. Investing $150 million gave the fund part ownership. Subsequently, Maple Leaf endured a bitter strike, taking "on the unions at its hog killing and cutting plants in an effort to bring labor rates and rules there in line with U.S. competitors. The company succeeded, but only after it permanently closed a plant in Edmonton and suspended operations at two bacon plants for months" (Mahood, 1998). One might argue such activity is itself ethically questionable, but if the alternative is to have the companies declare bankruptcy, perhaps pension fund actions like these contribute positively to the Canadian economy. In any case, federal and provincial pension laws mandate that pension funds seek to maximize their investment returns for the benefit of their members. To do less might be considered dereliction of duty.

Nevertheless, the irony is palpable. Successful firms that are owned in part by teachers' pension plans, including big banks and multinational corporations, are the keys to the plans' ability to meet their obligations to provide secure pensions to teachers. Yet, these teachers' own unions are campaigning nationally and internationally against agreements such as the North American Free Trade Agreement (NAFTA) and Multilateral Agreement on Investment (MAI) that are supported by these very same businesses which believe freer trade and the protection of overseas investments will help them to grow and become more profitable.

Conclusion

Reforms made to most Canadian teachers' pension plans adopted in the mid-1980s, combined with restraints on salaries in mid-1990s, have worked together to ensure the fiscal viability of most provincial plans. In a few provinces, especially Prince Edward Island and Manitoba, a close review of present policies is probably warranted in view of what appears to be substantial pension liabilities. As well, the tendency of fully funded plans to become *de facto* defined contribution plans raises questions of social equity and of just how much in deferred salaries teachers may in fact be obtaining. Relative to Canadians in the private sector, teachers maintain excellent retirement benefits. Is it fair for the public to underwrite the pensions without being able to benefit fully from pension plan surpluses?

As major players in the Canadian economy, teacher pension plans, as well as other public sector plans, are becoming increasingly visible. In provinces which formally share power in managing the plans, teachers' federations are likely to try to exercise politically motivated economic power to promote a particular vision of investment that may or may not be to everyone's liking or to the benefit of the plans. At some point, the economic power of the plans may elicit a reaction, with a move made to privatize them by dividing them into individual money-purchase retirement accounts for teachers. One advantage, from a public accountability standpoint, of such a change would be the possibility of moving toward a more accurate presentation to taxpayers of the total employment cost of teachers. Annual school budgets could include the total cost of salaries, pensions and other benefits.

Whether the lessened power to actively manage equities in pension portfolios would be good for the Canadian economy or whether such a change would remove an important source for improved management and capital investment would need to be debated. Alternatively, if the funds remain intact, they may become a major lobbying agent for an increase in the amount of foreign investment in pension funds, a reform that might well benefit all

Canadians by allowing everyone to better diversify their RRSPs and pensions beyond Canada's borders. While such a change may increase the domestic cost of capital, it would increase Canadians' economic security and reduce the burden of retirement on taxpayers and employees.

References

Auriemma, F. V., Cooper, B. S. & Smith, S. C. (1992). *Graying teachers: A report on state pension systems and school district early retirement incentives*. (ED 347 620). Eugene, OR: ERIC Clearinghouse on Educational Management.

British Columbia Teachers' Board. (1997). *British Columbia Teachers' Pension Plan Annual Report*. Victoria: The Board.

Brown, H. R. & Repa, J. T. (August 1993). Do early outs work out? Teacher Early Retirement Incentive Plans. *School Business Affairs*, pp. 12-16.

Corcoran, T. (June 2, 1995). Teachers' backroom role in Labatt attack. *The Globe and Mail*, p. B2.

Delaney, T. (June 10, 1998). Massive pension plan surplus creates a bonus for teachers. *The Globe and Mail*, p. C3.

Mahood, C. (August 12, 1998). Strike hurts Maple Leaf profit. *The Globe and Mail*, p. B3.

McNish, J. (June 17, 1995). Pension fund power. *The Globe and Mail*, pp. B1 & B3.

National Education Association. (1994). *Early Retirement Incentive Programs: Independent Considerations for State Associations*. Washington, DC: NEA.

Ruimy, J. (July 12, 1998). Ontario's pension coffers runneth over. *The Toronto Star*, p. A10.

Statistics Canada. (January 1, 1996). *Pension Plans in Canada*. Ottawa: Statistics Canada. Catalogue no. 74-401-XPB.

Notes

1. An earlier version of this chapter was published as, "Teacher pension plans in Canada: A force to be reckoned with," *School Business Affairs*, January 1999, pp. 20-26.

2. Technically, grade 13 was abolished in Ontario years ago, but with 30 credits required for graduation, most students take 12.5 or 13 years to complete. In Quebec, secondary school typically ends after grade 11, with students thereafter attending community colleges (CEGEPs). Ontario plans to begin phasing out the current system and introduce a four-year program in September 1999.

11

Who Benefits?

Caveat emptor. Cui bono?

Anonymous; Cicero

Buyer beware and who benefits? The public, through its government and elected school boards, purchases the services of teachers to instruct its members' children. We readily recognize our own critical personal interest in having schools that succeed, but schools can succeed only if the teachers do so as well. Public schools have been an innovation developed largely in North America – with deference to Scotland and Scandinavian countries – and copied the world over. Part and parcel of this innovation is a large-scale public bureaucracy that includes teachers' unions, with whom the public's representatives negotiate. Our question, in this penultimate chapter, is whether we have attended sufficiently to the Latin maxims quoted above. We turn first to the question of the benefits to the public interest of collective bargaining in education. Subsequently, we turn to the benefits for private interests.

Collective Bargaining and the Public Interest

The public interest is a fuzzy concept that does not yield to easy definition. The Canadian *Constitution Act* speaks of the need for "peace, order and good government"; the United States *Declaration of Independence* of "life, liberty and the pursuit of happiness." In the preamble to the *Canada Labour Act*, reference is made to "promotion of the common well-being" and "fruits of progress to all." At least two dimensions of public interest are evident in these visions, one concerned with safety from harm and the other concerned with economic, social or personal welfare. The first question, then, is whether collective bargaining and unions, in the public and private sectors in general and in education in particular, have in fact advanced these aims.

There are four ways in which the unions and collective bargaining can affect the general welfare of the populace, including the problem of civil unrest, their impact on the political economy of the nation, their success at the bargaining table and its spillover effects, and their impact on democratic governance.

Violence and Safety

Economic disputes, including those between employees and employers, have within them the seeds of revolution and civil war. Just as democracy has been termed institutionalized revolution, so can contemporary labor legislation be considered to be institutionalized – and domesticated – class warfare. Occasionally, particularly when aggressive unions confront strikebreakers installed by aggressive management, the underlying passions become evident. For example, in 1992, in a labor dispute at the Giant gold mine in Yellowknife, nine replacement workers died in a mine explosion set off by a bomb planted in a mine shaft by a disaffected striker (Maley, 1997). In disputes involving teachers unions, where both antagonists employ moderate tactics and restraint, such events are unknown. Still, during the recent work stoppage among educators in Ontario, a bodyguard composed of three police officers flanked one teacher who crossed the picket lines. Another teacher, the spouse of a Tory MLA, called police because the pickets weren't playing by the rules: "They grouped in front of (the doors) and they have been told not to do that. ... they would not allow me to pass" (*The Toronto Sun*, October 28, 1997, p. 19).

Government is put in a difficult position during strikes and the police, who are charged with the preservation of safety, often are sent to save both sides from one another. It is a difficult challenge. If preserving the safety of those who cross the picket lines means opening a path through striking employees, then police are likely to be seen as siding with employers against the aggrieved workers. If they do not, then they are likely to be seen as siding with employees. If government is to represent all people, it requires a role that keeps it at a distance from specific situations. Labor laws evolved to define this role and to promote the peaceful management of economic relationships. Their development was a major social and political innovation of the 20th century and their history warrants consideration.

In the 19th century and into the 20th, governments tended to side with employers against employees. It can be debated whether or not this tendency reflected the interests of those in government – i.e., business interests – or simply the application to new situations of existing laws that protected private property and outlawed conspiracies. But the facts are clear. Attempts to organize labor associations were often found to be illegal conspiracies by the courts, which repeatedly sided with employers in labor disputes. Court injunctions against strikes meant that the power of government, including the courts and police, seemed anything but neutral.

After World War I, widespread general strikes, such as those in Winnipeg and Calgary in 1919, embodied a revolutionary agenda that sought to capture the benefits of the modern economy for common workers. Craft unions reminiscent of medieval guilds were rejected and industrial unions, including both the skilled and unskilled workers, were promoted. In the case of the One Big Union, founded two months before the Winnipeg General Strike, the union opposed not just "capitalist war" but capitalism itself. Delegates at the founding convention passed resolutions supporting: the Bolsheviks in Russia, a six-hour working day, equal pay for women, free public education, health and safety legislation for industry and the nationalization of major industries including railroads and utilities (Plawiuk, 1994, p.1). The violent confrontations between police and strikers, notably in the Winnipeg strike, remain critical events in the history of Canadian unionism and the development of the Canadian state. Much of the radical agenda summarized above has come to pass over the ensuing 60 years, while some of it has come and gone. But the nexus of the problem for life in civil society remains: how to cope with conflicting goals in a peaceful manner that respects the humanity of all parties.

The prevention of civil violence was, and remains, a major objective of labor laws that determine the framework and process of collective bargaining. Instead of viewing an association of employees as an illegal conspiracy created in order to blackmail businesses and industrial owners or to overthrow government, labor laws hold that employees, as citizens, have the right to free association. The bridge from an association that reflects a "community of interest" – such as a common line of work or a common employer – to collective bargaining can be explained as an act of social and political pragmatics. All governments desire civil peace and democratic governments value a peace in which the citizens do not require the surveillance of police in order to behave in an orderly fashion. By setting up a balanced, monitored process for dispute resolution and accommodation of conflicting interests, government can minimize the likelihood of violent confrontation.

Political Economy

Even a peaceful strike or job action can have an impact on the general economy or public services. While the effect of a strike at a small business in a competitive sector of the economy, such as retailing, would be negligible, in a crucial sector such as transportation widespread economic harm may occur and many employees may be laid off due to the impact of the strike on other sectors. At a certain point, the government, believing that damage to the welfare of citizens is too great and that the public's interests override those of employees or employers, may mandate that workers return to work and that employers open their doors. In other sectors, such as law enforcement, government may believe that the risk to citizens of even a short strike is too great and therefore choose to outlaw strikes altogether, mandating arbitration for the settlement of disputes.

Unions also can affect the general welfare, positively or negatively, through their efficacy in implementing their economic, political and social agendas. One type of unionism, sometimes called "bread-and-butter" unionism, occurs when unions bargain with employers to obtain the best possible wages and benefits, while allowing the business and its owners/shareholders to make a reasonable rate of return on their investments. This approach accepts the present mixed economy as the appropriate framework for relations between employees and employers; i.e., for relations between labor and capital. Bread-and-butter unionism is supportive of a competitive private sector in the expectation that greater economic growth will provide more benefits for both members and non-members than would alternative economic and political arrangements.

"Social unionism," in contrast, promotes a social and political agenda to rearrange the economic order to make it more favorable to employees, perhaps shifting the means of production into the hands of governments and employees and away from the private sector and, especially, from multi-national firms. Social unionism is identified with support for social democratic governments, inclusive social programs and, on occasion, deficit financing and the "ethical" investment of pension funds. In political terms, social unionism is usually supportive of neo-corporatist forms of government in which government, representatives of unions and representatives of management guide a nation's economy. Also, it often embraces international action to promote labor standards, compulsory education and bans on child labor in order to benefit workers abroad and reduce the competitiveness of other countries relative to their own, thereby moderating extreme affects that unbridled capitalism or government imperialism may have. Most unions will probably embrace elements of both extremes, depending upon the character of their members, the nature of the occupations' represented, and the current challenges faced by both unions and employers.

Collective Agreements

The third affect of unions and collective bargaining on public welfare is the impact that their successes at the bargaining table and in lobbying government for labor-friendly laws has on the distribution of wealth and income in society. One objective of labor legislation in Canada is to assure that employees receive a "just share of the fruits of progress." It is quite possible, however, that the laws either fall short of this goal or overreach it; that is, labor may acquire either too few benefits from a growing economy or it may become so powerful that it acquires a disproportionate share of national income. In the latter case, organized labor may be instrumental in slowing economic growth by reducing the rates of return for capital investment or by capturing most of those returns for itself, leaving less for the general public. In these matters, judgment plays a major role in that the notion of "just share" is by no means objectively defined.

Democratic Government

The final challenge of unions and collective bargaining to public welfare is specific to bargaining in the public sector: does public sector negotiation of contracts amount to the making of public policy in secret, thus violating the tenets of democratic governance? Were teacher union contracts simply agreements on wage rates, this argument would have little merit. However, today they are much more than that, often designating staffing levels, types of positions, procedures for staffing and evaluation, and the like. In short, they effectively define who does what, where and when (Lieberman, 1997; Stern, 1997). Decisions on these matters is the rightful province of legislatures and school boards and, according the principles of democratic government, ought to be decided as a result of legislative debate held in public. Collective bargaining can short-circuit democratic decision-making by taking into the back rooms decisions that should be made in the light of day. Gandz and Beatty (1986, p. 20) report the following events in one of the school districts they studied:

> In the ensuing, high-pressure negotiations, the board capitulated to the teachers' demands and the result was widely hailed as a victory for the teachers... [who] won a "one-for-one" C.O.L.A. [cost of living allowance] clause and an increase in salaries of 27 percent. The parties agreed to a new clause in the 1975 agreement which, in effect, removed the right of management to change existing practices and policies.
>
> 19.01 All existing determination, authorizations, by-laws, regulations, rules, rulings, resolutions, certifications, orders, directive and other actions

made, issued or entered into by the board of education governing or affecting salary and working conditions of the members of District , O.S.S.T.F. [Ontario Secondary School Teachers' Federation] shall continue in force during the term of this Agreement and after the term of this Agreement until a new Agreement is settled between the two parties.

In the words of one administrator, this clause, "took away all the rights of the board to change anything that was going on in the schools, almost to the point . . . where you couldn't change a light bulb without being subject to a grievance."

Even though the school board had made its initial offer public and formally approved the negotiated contract at a public meeting, the private negotiation process had led to a contract that effectively delegated the board of education's authority to the union. The board was quite unclear about what they had done and succeeding boards fought for a decade through a number of strikes in order to reclaim the management rights they believed essential to ensuring that the views of the public they represented could be translated into school board policy and action. This experience is not unique. In their analysis of three decades of bargaining in Milwaukee, Wisconsin, researchers Fuller, Mitchell and Hartmann (1997, p. 2) reported that the norm was for the negotiating team to agree to the contract months before the agreement was approved by the board. An approval given in a *pro forma* manner before the negotiated agreement had even been printed – if it was printed at all: "the 1995-97 contract [between the Milwaukee Public Schools and the Milwaukee Teachers' Education Association] expired without copies ever having been printed."

In 1998, the norm is little different from these two examples. The memorandum of settlement referred to in chapter 7 is stamped, "DRAFT – CONFIDENTIAL TO OSSTF MEMBERS ONLY. This information is confidential until after ratification by the Bargaining Unit and the District School Board." In the contract, the school trustees had yielded the right of principals and management to allocate teachers to and within schools in the manner they believed best and, in the process, eliminated most counselling and many teacher leadership positions. When, in the battle over the *Education Quality Improvement Act*, the government had proposed making decisions on pupil/teacher ratios within the Ministry of Education and Training, teacher unions had protested that to do so was undemocratic. In response, the government introduced legislation that was debated in the legislature, with the government introducing amendments so that class size and pupil teacher ratios would be set in legislation. Subsequently, the unions and school trustees proceeded to redesign the province's publicly-financed schools behind closed doors, informing the public of their decisions only after the fact.

Collective Bargaining and the Individual

Unions are by definition collective affairs that are meant to benefit, to the extent possible, all those that share a particular community of interest. Often, these interests will coincide with those of the individual, since collective action usually arises from individual needs that cannot be met through individual action. A single employee typically has little or no bargaining power with the employer, who can easily find a person to replace another individual who resigns due to dissatisfaction with the level of compensation or treatment at work. It can be argued that for many, if not most, employees, unions provide individual benefits that equal or exceed any direct cost of dues or indirect costs due to a lack of alignment of the individual's preferences with those reflected in a collective agreement or by a union's political activities. However, there is another side to the argument.

Historically, one of the great achievements of Western society was its recognition of the individual's right to contract his or her own labor. In feudal society, the mass of people were serfs tied to the lands of their lord; later, indentured servantry was common, as was slavery; only a relatively small proportion of society had the status of freemen, able to enter into contracts and, later, to vote. Even today, many people in the world do not have the legal right to resign from their jobs, move to another city and take up new positions.

The personal right of contract implies that individuals have a right to sell their labor and skills to the highest bidder. Yet, labor laws restrict the ability of individuals to exercise this right. The shortage of math and science teachers generally evident in North America has been ascribed to the ability of individuals in these fields to command higher salaries in the private sector than in the public schools that have uniform salary scales. Were these specialists free to negotiate higher salaries with school districts on an individual basis then the shortage that exists at current wage rates would disappear. However, they are denied this right of contract by restrictive labor practices promoted by teachers' unions and, today, by Canadian governments and the courts.

Another achievement of Western society is recognition of the individual's freedom of conscience. Applied particularly in the case of religion, the individual is recognized as being free, without interference from the state, to believe what he or she wishes. A corollary of this principle is that individuals ought not be forced to support, through their labor or the products of their labor, beliefs that are contrary to their own. Recognition of rights of conscientious objectors during times of war is reflected in arrangements for them to provide alternative service. These rights of conscience are matched by a responsibility to act according to the principles of justice and ethical behavior. Yet, labor laws may force an individual into joining associations which, in some cases, act in a manner which violates the individual's beliefs – an action in direct contradiction to Article 20 Section 2 of *The Universal Declaration of Human Rights*: "No one may be compelled to belong to an association." Yet across Canada all school teachers employed in publicly financed schools, by law, must belong to a teachers' union dedicated to a form of social unionism or codes of ethics that forbid teachers to follow their consciences and serve their students during union-called strikes. Union members who support a government to which their union is opposed are required, through their union dues, to support a political action that they personally believe is not in the public interest.

The relation of the individual to a union involves such issues as mandatory/voluntary membership, mandatory dues and dues check-off. In some cases, unions allow conscientious objectors who cite religious reasons to refrain from joining, but rarely are political grounds recognized. Even in these cases, non-members are still required to pay dues under the "Rand Formula."

The Rand Formula

The late Ivan Cleveland Rand was a former Justice of the Supreme Court of Canada with a background as a former labor arbitrator. He was of the social activist school of legal interpretation and was strongly influenced by the views of his mentor, United States Supreme Court Justice Louis Brandeis. The "Rand Formula" is based on Rand's 1946 arbitration decision involving a strike at the Ford Motor Company. In his decision he provided for a form of security for the union by requiring an employer to deduct a portion of the employees' salaries (i.e., dues check-off) for all those represented by a bargaining unit, whether they were union members or not. This formulation is based on the assumption that the union is essential for all workers and that a union must be responsible for the welfare of all those who it represents.

Two additional provisions have been inferred since the original decision: 1) although the check-off is deemed to be necessary for the union to carry out its programs, financial penalties should be established for employees and unions who engage in work stoppages or illegal strikes in defiance of existing contracts; and 2) for employees these sanctions could consist of daily fines and loss of seniority; for the unions, sanctions could mean the suspension of the collection of union dues.

Collective agreements have spread a modified Rand Formula throughout Canada and some provinces have given it legal force. In some cases, such as the recent debate over dues check-off at the University of Toronto (*UTFA Newsletter*, October 6, 1997; April 3, 1998), application of the Rand Formula is seen as an alternative to formal certification as a unionized bargaining agent.[1] It is argued that the Rand Formula preserves freedom of association and dissent in that persons are not required to become members of the union, even though they pay dues. Adopting the Rand formula without unionization is seen as a middle path for associations in organizations where formal certification as a union is controversial.

Objections to Rand

There are at least three major objections to the assumptions underlying the Rand Formula and dues check-off. First is the assumption that all individuals are better off under collectively negotiated agreements than they would be with privately negotiated contracts and that, therefore, all individuals should contribute to the cost of negotiations. Although this may be the case for a majority of individuals, it does not hold for everyone.

In bargaining, union leaders must determine a set of priorities. How this process is carried out may result in a set of objectives which is widely supported but which invariably ignores or even harms the interests of some of its members. If, for example, the majority of members of the bargaining unit are senior members at the top of the pay scale, it will be to their advantage to lobby for across-the-board percentage wage increases. As a result, junior teachers may be laid off, as mandated by the traditional union rule of "last-in and first-out." It would be difficult to argue that the union has acted in the junior teachers' best interests.

Put another way, the utility function of a union negotiating committee is never going to represent the utility functions of individual members. The Rand Formula assumes that the strength in numbers is sufficient to generate a benefit for all members that offsets the lack of fit between individual and collective preferences. But if the added benefits are not sufficient to provide net gains to all members, then the whole argument that non-paying members are "free riders" must be laid aside. Many of the supposed "free riders" would in fact be individuals whose interests are harmed by the outcomes of negotiations, including both those who could negotiate a better deal individually and those whose interests are sacrificed for the "good of the majority." Requiring individuals in these circumstances to pay for the "service" of having their level of compensation limited or jobs eliminated is perverse, to say the least.

In some cases, a minority group (e.g., medical school faculty in a university) may be able to exercise sufficient influence within the bargaining unit to bring about a supplementary benefit that recognizes their special skills or it may successfully form a distinct bargaining unit. In the latter case, the group would need to demonstrate that it does not share a community of interest with other bargaining unit members. If neither of these options is successful, an individual or group may file a complaint with the relevant labor relations body claiming that their union representatives acted in bad faith by failing to offer appropriate representation.

The second and third objections to the Rand Formula relate to the broader mission of the union and the problem of violating the conscience and beliefs of the individual. Both objections relate to concerns with the political aspects of collective bargaining.

The political mission of "bread-and-butter" unionism is relatively narrow and relates to improving the labor laws that affect the ability of unions to serve their members. In the private sector, unions have been provided unfettered rights to negotiate with employers who face budget constraints brought about by free-market competition. In the public sector, constraints are primarily political rather than economic, although certainly economics has a role in politics (Thompson & Fryer, 1994; Swimmer & Thompson, 1995). As long as union political activity is narrowly focussed on matters with a close connection to the immediate economic interests of union members, one can argue political activity is a direct extension of collective bargaining. In this case, there is no problem with requiring individuals to pay dues that are used, in part, for political action.

However, in practice, union objectives are much broader, including both "moderate" and "radical" models of social unionism. Requiring individuals to contribute to these political agendas can be a gross violation of the individual's political rights by requiring contributions to activities that, in the individual's views, are opposed to the public interest and his or her own personal values and beliefs.

The moderate model of social unionism has as its mission the preservation and extension of government-funded and government-provided services; traditionally, it could be termed a social democratic or socialist view of the role of government. This agenda is not necessarily based on the ideological belief that such a government is in the public interest, although no doubt some persons believe that this is the case. More to the point is that such types of governments are best for public sector unions, in general, and teachers' unions, in particular. Public sector unions, individually and jointly, will support extensions of government provided services of all types – child-care and elder-care, for example – and fight to maintain existing government services, including the production and distribution of electricity, liquor and wine distribution, parks and recreation, etc.

Expanding public employment increases union power at the bargaining table, builds membership, and increases revenue. Unions quite rightly perceive that the international economic environment has forced governments to control expenditures and encouraged them to import the discipline of the private sector into the public sector through means such as contracting out, privatization and performance-based assessment of publicly provided services. As emphasized in chapter 5, teachers' unions oppose initiatives such as charter schools, school charitable foundations, school-based management, student testing and many other reform projects. They oppose these actions even if a sound argument can be made that such initiatives are in the long-term public interest or are preferred by the democratically elected representatives. A major factor in their opposition is the concern that such initiatives are not in the unions' institutional interests or those of a majority of their members.

Individual union members may still support government restraint and restructuring, charter schools and other schemes either because they believe that these changes are in the public interest or because they believe that a more competitive provision of services would be advantageous to them personally. The Rand Formula, however, requires that they contribute to massive local, provincial, national and international campaigns that oppose fiscal responsibility, competitive provision of services, competitive international markets and the like.[2]

The radical model of social unionism is tied less to economic interests and more to narrow sets of often-controversial agendas that arise from internal interest groups within unions.[3] One example is provided by those who use position and power within public sector unions and organizations to advance minority causes such as the allocation of a proportionate share of jobs to specific groups, including women and visible minorities, or "equal pay for work of equal value."[4] The formation and achievements of such an interest groups played a key role, for example, at the 1997 York University Strike (Briskin, 1998). One professor stated, "'Equity' was what kept members of my Department out on the picket line. It will bring them out again if necessary." As a reward for women's caucus' support, the negotiated contract included a "modest pay equity plan" and the union's constitution was changed to create a Standing Committee on Equity. York University has 34% women on its faculty, in part due "to a negotiated affirmative action clause in the 1987-89 collective agreement." Briskin comments that,

> Calls for democratic governance invariably invoke issues of representation, which are, by definition, about equity – not only equal numbers but also equitable access to voice. Since women and men have unequal status in the university, they do not experience democracy, or the lack thereof, in the same way – yet another reminder of the need [for] gender strategy and analysis. . . . The groundwork has been laid for broad-based alliances with other equity-seeking constituencies, and the possibility increased that the voices of marginalized women will be heard – women with disabilities, women of color, and lesbians (p. 19).

The results of coalition politics between interest groups within unions are policies and actions like those of the British Columbia Teachers' Union which, for example, opposed certification of the teacher graduates of a fully accredited liberal arts university because the university required its students "to observe, although not to necessarily agree with, a code of conduct which proscribes '. . . premarital sex, adultery, and homosexual behavior'" (Benson & Miller, *Lex View*, 11). The fact that the students had excellent academic records, impeccable student teaching and were sought after by school districts was beside the point. The "independent" British Columbia College of Teachers, whose board is composed primarily of candidates promoted by BCTF, agreed with the union and refused to certify the graduates. The British Columbia Court, in *Trinity Western University v. The British Columbia College of Teachers*, did not agree. While the BCCT "feared that the TWU-trained teachers would not be able to sympathetically or adequately respond to the needs of students who are homosexual, it did not offer any evidence to support this concern." The Court observed that a number of its graduates had "gone on to successfully teach in multicultural situations, First Nations schools, prisons," public schools and Third World settings, and concluded that the BCCT had not made its decision based on the evidence before it, and quashed the BCCT decision not to accredit TWU's teacher education program (*op. cit.*).

Whether one agrees with these examples of union actions or not, the point is that *individuals have no choice* as to whether or not they provide financial support for these actions under the Rand Formula as it is applied in unions. Although it is the radical left that currently holds sway in some teachers' unions, it is not beyond imagination that a union could act in support of radical right agenda, such as the exclusion of immigrants who threaten the security of blue collar workers. In that case, it would be left-leaning members who would find their mores violated by the mandatory payment of dues.[5]

Legal Challenges

The Rand Formula was challenged in *Lavigne v. Ontario Public Service Employees Union* (1991), with the plaintiff arguing that mandatory dues check-off for all bargaining unit members is a denial of freedom of association and of freedom of expression under *The Charter of Rights and Freedoms*. "More precisely, he objected to the union's expenditure of funds on various political issues, including contributions to the New Democratic Party, opposition to the use of public funds to build a sports stadium in Toronto, and support for freer access to abortion. . . . Had his argument been accepted, there would have been an important new judicial role as supervisor of the internal affairs of trade unions, since the court would have to scrutinize union expenditures to determine whether they had a political or collective bargaining basis" (Swinton, 1995, pp. 66-67; see also Thornicroft, 1992). What is more, the court required that he pay the costs of the intervenors, which came to $1 million on top of his own costs of $500 000. The National Citizens' Coalition, which supported Lavigne, eventually settled for $350 000 (*Vancouver Sun*, February 18, 1995).

Courts in the United States came to a different conclusion in the case of *Abood v. Detroit Board of Education* (1977) and held that such forced support of causes against one's beliefs violates the *Constitution of the United States*. As Swinton suggests, however, this conclusion is turning out to be a messy process, with estimates running from just 5 percent to as much as 50 percent of union funds being used for political purposes. Thornicroft (1990), in a detailed comparison of Canadian and U.S. legal stances on the question of the use of union dues for political activity, endorses the lower estimates. However, one problem that is especially acute with public sector bargaining is that one can argue that the whole process is political—i.e., that collective bargaining is political bargaining since elected officials face political, not economic, constraints. As well, teachers' unions can and do use their organizational capacity which quite literally extend into every school. How does one put a price tag on this?

The words of Premier Clyde Wells, when he called the 1993 provincial elections, sum it up. He asked "voters to decide if the province should be run by government or the NTA [Newfoundland Teachers' Association]" (Thompson & Fryer, 1994, p. 15). One cannot get any more political than that. Premier Wells and his Liberal Party were reelected.

The Supreme Court of Canada, in deciding to remain outside the inner workings of unions, has not precluded legislative action in this arena. If legislatures were persuaded that the Rand Formula violates the rights of individuals beyond what is reasonable in a free and democratic society, they could consider statutory measures to change the situation.

Conclusion

In late 1998, when the National Hockey League Players' Association was lobbying for a tax break for Canadian-based NHL clubs, an Ottawa parliamentarian expressed surprise to learn that players' lobbying efforts were supported by tax-deductible dues that had helped to fund the NHLPA's $80 million "rainy day" fund (Joyce, 1998). In fact, substantial portions of all unions' budgets are paid for by all Canadian taxpayers in the form of "tax expenditures" – i.e., the value of the taxes not collected on dues that are paid to unions. Of even greater concern is that individual members who disagree with their unions' agendas are required to contribute to the union if they wish to work in their chosen occupation. While the history of unionism does demonstrate that the right of association, including the right of employees to associate, was not always recognized and protected, many legislative actions envisioned by unions decades ago are now law and now protect all employees. Employment standards legislation and administrative law now provide for vacation time, minimum wages and protection against dismissal without cause; employment safety legislation assures safer workplaces; employment equity laws ensure equal pay for equal work; the list goes on. While most non-unionized employees, particularly in the private sector, may not share the same level of benefits employed by unionized employees, there is no longer as great an imbalance in power that the courts perceived, in past decades, in need of correction. Now of concern are the infringement of individual rights and the disproportionate power of tax-supported lobby groups that influence government. Should a new balance be struck so that unions must solicit financial support from their members and individuals are free to select their own agents in employment and political matters?

References

Abood v. Detroit Board of Education. (1977), 431 U.S. 209.

Benson, I. T. & Miller, B. (n.d.). Back to school with the BC College of Teachers. *Lex View*, 11.

Briskin, L. (Spring 1998). Equity in the 1997 York University strike. *OCUFA Forum*, Ontario Confederation of University Faculty Associations.

Corcoran, T. (July 31, 1998). Radical feminism's absurd legacy. *The Globe and Mail*, p. B2.

Fuller, H. L., Mitchell, G. A. & Hartmann, M. E. (October 1997). *The Milwaukee Public Schools' Teacher Union Contract: Its history, content, and impact on education.* Milwaukee, WI: Institute for the Transformation of Learning, Marquette University.

Gandz, J. & Beatty, C. (1986). *Changing relationships in educational bargaining.* Toronto: Education Relations Commission.

Joyce, G. (December 2, 1998). Report on sports business treads lightly on players. *Financial Post*, A1-2.

Lavigne v. Ontario Public Service Employees Union. (1991), 81 D.L.R. (4th) 545 at 619 (S.C.C.)

Lieberman, M. (January 1997). Do school boards still have options? *School Business Affairs*, pp. 3-13.

Maley, D. (October 20, 1997). Canada's top women CEOs - Peggy Witte, Royal Oak Mines Inc. *Macleans*. www.macleans.com

Plawiuk, E. W. (June 1994). Calgary 1919: The birth of the OBU and the general strike. *Labour News*. WWW: Plawiuk Pontificates - Voice of the Rebel Worker located at www.geocities.com/CapitolHill/5202/index.htm

Stern, S. (Spring 1997). How teachers' unions handcuff schools. *City Journal*, pp. 25-47.

Stirling, J. (June 22, 1998). New faculty to pay dues. *The University of Toronto Bulletin*, p. 1.

Swimmer, G. & Thompson M. (Eds.). (1995). *Public sector collective bargaining in Canada.* Kingston, ON: Industrial Relations Centre, Queen's University.

Swinton, K. (1995). The Charter of Rights and public sector labour relations. Chapter 3 in G. Swimmer & M. Thompson (Eds.). *Public sector collective bargaining in Canada.* Kingston, ON: Industrial Relations Centre, Queen's University.

The Globe and Mail. (August 1, 1998). Pay equity: The casino is open. Editorial, p. D6.

Thompson, M. & Fryer, J. (1994). *Collective bargaining in Canada's public service. Discussion Paper Series #94-15*, Kingston, ON: Government and Competitiveness, School of Policy Studies, Queen's University.

Thornicroft, K. W. (1990). Unions, union dues and political activity: A Canada/U.S. comparative analysis. *Labor Law Journal*, 41(12), 846-855.

Thornicroft, K. W. (1992). Case comments. *Lavigne v. The Ontario Public Service Employees Union, (1991),* 81, O.L.R. (4th) 545 (S.C.C.). *The Canadian Bar Review* (71 Can. Bar Rev.), 155-166.

UTFA Newsletter. (October 6, 1997; April 3, 1998). University of Toronto Faculty Association.

Vancouver Sun. (February 18, 1995). Charter challenges must not break litigants. Editorial.

Notes

1. The payment of dues question was submitted to a three-person arbitration panel. Management and labor each appointed one member and the third, retired Chief Justice Alan Gold, was mutually agreed upon. Gold formerly served on the labor relations board in Quebec; labor boards are almost always sympathetic to labor. Not surprisingly, the panel found in favor of mandatory dues or "an equivalent payment to charity" for all faculty and librarians hired after July 1, 1998. "In the landscape of Canadian universities, this [dues check-off (the Rand Formula)] is a well-known position. I have no trouble recommending this," said President Robert Prichard, as if the actions of others could justify his own (Stirling, 1998).
2. Where provisions are made for dues to go to charities instead the union, the charities to benefit require the consent of the union. As a result, the union can veto the use of funds for purposes that conflict with the union's own agenda.
3. Corcoran (1998) would argue with this view. He links "radical feminism" to the "international labor movement and the Marxist origins of the gender issue." Even the federal Liberal government is now having second thoughts about "equal pay for work of equal value" once a decision by the Canadian Human Rights Tribunal regarding women in Canada's civil service was projected to require the entire budget surplus of $3 billion. See also, "Pay equity: The casino is open," *The Globe and Mail*, August 1, 1998, p. D6.
4. At the University of Toronto, diversity and equity are used interchangeably, referring to visible minorities, disabled persons, aboriginals and women in traditionally male-dominated fields. Search committees for new faculty at OISE/UT include an associate dean to ensure that "equity" is given consideration and who collects data on the gender and color of all applicants. Such information is surmised from names, fields of research, countries of origin and personal knowledge.
5. It can also be argued that teachers' unions opposition to relaxed certification standards, charter schools, government aid to private schools and the like help to maintain the institutional structure of public education and thereby close off opportunities that a more decentralized and less regulated system might provide immigrant teachers who do not hold Canadian certification.

12

Choices

Critics paint unions as the problem that needs to be fixed, most usually by elimination.

Charles Kerchner, 1998

Is there a need for changing the legal arrangements that create teachers' unions and govern the way they operate? Are there alternative strategies for teachers' unions to adopt in meeting their members' needs and aspirations? Evidence presented in preceding chapters indicates that Canadian provinces have in fact made significant changes in existing labor legislation affecting teachers during the 1990s and that those changes have exacerbated some problems while resolving others. It is unlikely, therefore, that changes will cease and that the various parties will settle into a placid accommodation with each recognizing the other's needs and desires. The economic difficulties and budget deficits that drove economic confrontation between governments and teachers' unions are currently in abeyance, providing hope that some funds can be found to grease the wheels of collective negotiations. However, reforms touching on such issues as curriculum and evaluation remain unsettled and teachers' unions have yet to adopt policies on these and other issues that receive broad public and professional support. Until there is a meeting of the minds on these issues, rancorous debate and confrontation are likely to remain common features on the evening news.

Viewed in another light, this situation is not altogether bad: front-page news is *important* news. Conflict occurs about those things which people value most. Education is front-page news because parents, teachers, governments and unions alike know that it is of increasing importance in the contemporary knowledge-based economy. If it were easy to avoid both debates over schooling and the impact of the disruption of services, then there would actually be more reason for concern since it would imply that we care little for the future of our children and of the publicly-funded schools that they attend.

In order both to interpret Canadian teachers' unions stances relative to the political and economic ferment of the day and to provide alternative paths that may be taken both by public authorities and unions, it is helpful to consider the situation in other jurisdictions (chapter 8) and to explore various scenarios that others have developed. Three themes emerged earlier: alterations in legislation affecting collective bargaining for teachers; school choice including charter schools and aid for independent schools; and the emergence of a corporate-managerial model for education that emphasizes efficiency, measurement and effectiveness. An element of the latter is the use of standard tests to evaluate schools, school systems and sometimes students and teachers. These issues and others were also evident in the review in chapter 5 of Canadian teacher unions' opposition to funding controls and reductions, public choice in education, reducing or eliminating certification requirements, and the "new basics" that include a more explicit curriculum and external assessment. One vision of the future role of teachers' unions was put forth in Barber's advice for the National Union of Teachers in England and Wales. He advised them to pursue accountability to the community, responsiveness to members, firm positions on key issues, collaboration with other unions and an active policy role in educational debates.

Optional Paths

A number of academics have reflected on these and other problems faced by unions and governments in dealing with one another and suggest that there are a number of different scenarios that may unfold or be intentionally selected as models to follow. In some of these options, unions play a central role in defining and delivering high quality educational services; in other scenarios unions are viewed as yesterday's institutions that will fade into oblivion. The purpose of this review is to facilitate thinking "outside the box" – to imagine options that are beyond our current experience. Subsequent reflection on the contemporary Canadian situation may suggest paths that should be taken or should be avoided.

Cooper (1998) analyzed educational systems and teacher organizations in 14 different nations and distilled four broad patterns. From these he posited four theoretical models of teacher-employer relationships that assert contrasting characteristics and values for the various parties. He terms these four: *localism-communitarism* – closing the classroom door and working with students, their families and communities, while leaving the politics to politicians; *nationalist-syndicalism* – joining "big" government and "big" labor, ensuring that teachers' unions are visible, influential players in state/provincial and national decision-making; *privatization-free agency* – selling teaching services in an education marketplace characterized by vouchers, charter schools, grant-maintained schools and other autonomous forms of education; and *adaptation-redefining education* – working within the system but altering the structure of schooling and engaging in career development. Cooper's four classifications embody many of the elements identified by others, which are discussed later after a more detailed exploration Cooper's ideas.

Localism-communitarianism implies that power is held by the local community. This option is derived from a simple fact of life for teachers, Cooper suggests: "The phenomenology of teaching remains personal, local, and restricted to the teachers' classroom, students and school" (1998, p. 36). In other words, teaching is both individualistic and community-oriented, and the values, curriculum and the hiring and development of teachers is a matter that can be worked out strictly on the local level between teachers, parents and community members. This is an extreme form of decentralization, one that returns public education to the basic nexus from which it emerged over a century ago in North America. Such was the notion of schooling long before provincial and state departments evolved to impose varying degrees of centralized monitoring and control and began to lay claim to local schools in the name of the state and society. It was also long before teachers' unions developed along industrial union lines to become "job conscious," seeking uniformity and standardization in contracts, teaching conditions and compensation packages that obscured local contexts (Kerchner, Koppich & Weeres, 1997, p. 40). In the communitarian image, teachers are no longer a peculiar breed of civil servant in the employ of the state, nor are they members of a teachers' organization whose agenda is not reflective of an on-going discourse rooted in the local community. While not precluding some form of state funding to ensure some degree of equity, this model sees schools as democratic, grass-roots institutions in which the balancing of the interests of community and family take precedence over distantly-defined political and bureaucratic imperatives. Charter schools in the United States illustrate elements of this model, as does the arrangement in New Zealand.

Nationalist-syndicalism implies that power is invested in large-scale, polity-wide organizations. With the governance power of many Canadian district-level school boards being steadily emasculated by provincial governments in the 1990s (CMEC, 1996), one option is to eliminate school boards altogether, as has already happened in New Brunswick. According to this logic, provincial governments can stake out their authority as public education paymasters and as the designers of curriculum and evaluators of achievement. If this were their prerogative as employers and a reasonable reflection of their management rights, then teachers as employees would delegate to their union the exclusive power to act as their agent. Starting with the principle that management needs both the expertise and the cooperation of their professional employees, all educational matters including policy, funding, implementation, curriculum and assessment, and compensation should be "on the table" and negotiated in good faith between two sets of legitimate interests on a province-wide basis. The case study of collective bargaining in British Columbia in chapter 6 illustrates a quasi-syndicalist/corporatist approach that is implied by this model.

Privatization-free agency implies that power is in the hands of the consumer. This model reflects the values of the marketplace over those of the community or corporatist society. Schools in the "quasi-public education marketplace" (Cooper, 1998, p. 43) could be funded by provincial governments but their mission, curriculum, assessment and teaching methodologies would be designed by "educator-entrepreneurs" who sell their concepts to students and parents who may choose to purchase these professional services with vouchers. Educational consumers in this option have an extended menu from which to select, including public schools, charter schools, religious-based schools, home schools, "Internet" schools and independent tutors. If concepts do not sell and schools do not live up to their billing, consumers are free to shop elsewhere. Aside from a modest role in facilitating public choice, consumer protection and of course funding, in an ideal type of choice system school boards and ministries and departments of education would have very little role to play. Teachers' unions expecting standardized contracts would find few takers for their traditional roles since educators keen to establish successful niches in the educational market would presumably value risk-taking and performance-related rewards over collective solidarity. For their part, parents would quickly desert any school constrained by contract-driven rules about staffing, instructional time, and extracurricular activities if these rules interfered with the delivery of high quality services. While Alberta has "weak" provisions that allow for a limited number of charter schools, with numerous strings attached, under the unsympathetic gaze of school boards and the Alberta Teachers' Association, other variations of this model are proliferating in the United States, to mixed reviews (chapter 8). In any case, many parents are used to being in the marketplace for music and art teachers, sports programs, and the like and some schools already arrange for the use of school facilities by independent specialist teachers whose services complement the standard curriculum.

Adaptation-redefining education implies that teachers work within an educational system in which their union has become a "learning organization" responsive to their needs, wants and aspirations. Cooper describes this model as the more "moderate" of the four options because it leaves the existing public education system largely intact. Still, it implies a formidable exercise that requires "transforming unionism, improving the act of teaching, altering union-management agreements, and then institutionalizing the new kind of union. In other words, reconceptualize, improve, restructure, and make permanent" (1998, p. 45). This adaptation model, with its roots in organizational learning literature such as Senge (1990), receives a comprehensive treatment in the work of three American scholars, Kerchner, Koppich and Weeres (1997; Kerchner, 1998). In Canada, similar views can be found in Hargreaves and Fullan (1998).

The model proffered by Kerchner, Koppich and Weeres warrants further explication in that it is put forward by individuals who are explicit supporters of unions and who have studied systems in which the tranformation they describe has occurred. They report four sequential steps to transforming teacher unions:

1. *Changing the nature of unions in schools.* Unions are redefined from an industrial-union entity into a knowledge-based organization. Teachers are no longer perceived as white-collar laborers but rather as "knowledge workers" who "create, synthesize and interpret information" about their work in professional communities organized around individual schools of quality (1997, p. 7).
2. *Leveraging education quality.* A craft union sensitivity is instilled to improve the quality of education by redefining how union members understand and involve themselves, beyond their local communities, on a wide array of issues, some of which unions presently avoid. Issues would include goals, curriculum, training, evaluation, peer review and support, mentoring, and setting and evaluating standards (1997, p. 99).
3. *Redefining labor relations in education.* While unions should continue to bargain new-style, trimmed-down contracts and negotiate salary structures, their main focus would be on "bottom-up," "quality-agenda" approaches that feature "school-centered compacts" incorporating school goals and principles, plans of operation, guidelines and procedures for implementation (1997, p. 137). Compacts would set forth what is expected of all parties, but would not be grievable and hence not part of the labor relations legal apparatus that is sometimes seen to impede positive change.
4. *Making the labor market secure.* The labor market in which teachers work and unions function needs to be reconceptualized and made secure. "Unions are utterly dependent on the existing power structure

and power alignments within public education: a massive, rule-bound, hierarchical public bureaucracy" (1997, p. 14) which the reforms of the 1980s and 1990s have barely addressed. Instead, new labor laws should be written to reflect a move away from "job security" towards "career security" involving the use of choice, career ladders, better pension plans, a redefinition of tenure, job ownership, and a link between certification and career development.

Other models and scenarios have been developed, although none provide as comprehensive a portfolio as does Cooper in concert with Kerchner, *et al.* For example, Johnson and Kardos (1998) believe only three options exist:

1. Maintain the status quo with the industrial model of unionism, which they believe will lead to a greater variation in arrangements and the quality of education within U.S. states as some jurisdictions improve relations while others experience deterioration. In the Canadian context, their observation seems more applicable *between* rather than within provinces.
2. Eliminate collective bargaining and empower administrators to implement reforms to improve education, an approach that might work so long as administrators' judgments are better than those made by teachers and their unions in negotiations. In England and Wales and some parts of Michigan this mode of operation is present.
3. Enlarge the role of collective bargaining to provide a legitimate, collaborative process for discussing educational challenges, exploring options for improvement and tailoring strategies to meet local needs and realities. This last is their preferred choice and has many parallels with Cooper's fourth perspective, adaptation of the existing system, and Kerchner *et al.*'s proposals.

Bascia (1998) advocates a similar program, including "changes in labor law that increase the purview of their [teachers'] authority over educational policy making and practice." Teachers' unions, she argues, need to recognize the "big" picture of systemic reform and the "little" picture at the local level "by providing services and programs that are meaningful and necessary to teachers... to create avenues within their organizations for greater and more varied forms of teacher participation, representation, and innovation" (p. 22).

Fuller, Mitchell and Hartman (1997; 1998) state that collective bargaining should be strengthened because a) it is a reality, b) it shapes day-to-day school operations and outcomes and c) with more public involvement and oversight, results of the bargaining process could provide a way to hold the parties accountable. Public oversight, they believe, should include the carrying out of all negotiations in public

A final option, suggested in the 1970s by the Committee on Costs of Education in Ontario, would probably fall under Cooper's second category, *nationalist-syndicalism*. The Committee recommended that Ontario's Education Relations Commission set wages administratively using what it termed "The Principle of Fair Comparison" utilizing a consensus process that would rely heavily on information about private sector wages and wage settlements (Committee on the Costs of Education, 1976). The Committee believed that strikes were extremely disruptive and worked against the interests of teachers and students. The Hay study it commissioned on the comparability of private sector wages with those in the school system serves as a potential model, as do those currently used in Manitoba and the United Kingdom.

Current Canadian Context

Recent changes in Canadian labor legislation affecting teacher collective bargaining and impasse resolution have not been in place for a sufficiently long period of time to fully evaluate their efficacy. Nevertheless, it is clear that the two-tier systems of bargaining in British Columbia and Saskatchewan, involving province-wide management committees with both trustee and government representatives, have not been working effectively. Recent settlements were made only after government negotiated agreements directly with provincial representatives of teacher unions. In the case of British Columbia, the settlement was ultimately legislated due to its rejection by school boards.

Nova Scotia, with a similar two-tier system, reached a settlement before the last election, giving the teachers a two percent across-the-board increase (plus annual increments) and a promise not to make legislative changes in the administration of education without union consent. The sitting Liberal government lost its majority but still formed the next government. Subsequently, an impasse over the adoption of the first contract for the metro Halifax school board was resolved only when the province's Labour Relations Board ruled that teachers must follow through with the agreement which a majority had approved but which had not been supported by one of the locals representing a predecessor school district.

In November 1998, The Alberta Teachers' Association was "absolutely delighted" that delegates to the provincial Progressive Conservative party's annual convention adopted a resolution for the government to limit class size to 22 students from kindergarten to grade 3 and to provide sufficient funding for the limit. However, in January 1999, 55 percent of the province's 61 bargaining units were still without contracts for the 1998/99 school year. Those that had collective agreements received across-the-board increases of 4.2 percent (*The Edvisor*, November 16, 1998; January 18, 1999), making up much of the 5 percent roll-back experienced earlier in the decade.

It is too soon to say what Ontario's reforms will bring in terms of labor relations in the long term. The fall of 1998 saw many forms of workplace disruption including strikes, lockouts and working-to-rule as well as back-to-work legislation, problems that continued into 1999. Settlements were being made with clauses that suggest the emergence of a form of co-management; that is, some of the agreements called for school and school system advisory committees to oversee operations. Suspicions abound, however, that unions are lying low in preparation for a spring 1999 election, hoping to unseat the current government and to install a more teacher-union friendly government. Manitoba and Prince Edward Island, with their systems of binding arbitration, have avoided strikes like those that have tormented Ontario for the past two years.

Quebec's teachers pressed their case during the fall 1998 election, with 80 000 teachers staging a strike "ruled illegal by Quebec's Essential Services Council" (Clark, 1998). The largest federation, the Centrale de l'Enseignement du Québec (CEQ), demanded a $700-million pay equity settlement arguing "their traditionally female-dominated profession is underpaid." For his part, Premier Lucien Bouchard "suggested the teachers have overvalued pay-equity demands, and his eyes flashed as he rebutted a union official's suggestion that the government set aside its zero-deficit goal to meet their demands: "For them? Just for them? Just for a small group of people? ... The whole purpose of what we did for the last years is to call for all Quebecers to make a collective effort."

Making Choices

This survey of the development and roles of teachers' unions in Canada demonstrates these organizations' awesome character: the unions have 375 000 well-educated, well-organized and well-paid members, budgets in the tens of millions of dollars – and a political agenda that is demonstrably more extreme than that of their members and the general public. In spite of their strengths, they have suffered setbacks during the 1990s due primarily to the economic problems faced by governments, which were resolved to put their financial houses in order. In the process, governments trimmed not only their budgets but also, in several provinces, tightened the laws that governed collective bargaining or arbitration for teachers. While local trustees may not have been up to the task of freezing and reducing expenditures, provincial governments were. In short, the centre held.

Why were provincial governments able to assert their authority successfully, even if there was moderate social discomfort in the process? One element was that teachers' unions tended to lose even when they won. That is, in situations where they strongly opposed a government, as the Newfoundland and Labrador Teachers' Association did Premier Clyde Wells, and the Premier was re-elected, they were left with essentially no bargaining power. However, when governments they supported were victorious, as with New Democratic Party governments in British Columbia, Saskatchewan and Ontario, the party they supported expected them to place the government's interests ahead of the union's.

Why then do unions' play this high risk political game? Part of the reason may be embedded in Canada's history of social unionism. The political leadership of unions appears committed not simply to negotiating collective agreements for their members, but also to changing the character of the Canadian state by bringing about a social-democratic renaissance with a greatly expanded public sector. That is, their goals are political in the broadest sense of the word. Their dislike of neo-liberalism is as great as is their dislike to neo-conservatism. So long as union leadership remains committed to this mission, they will continue to try to play "kingmaker" by electing governments that they hope to be able to influence. But, when they lose, they will continue to lose big.

At the same time, it must be admitted that this strategy apparently worked in the past, as evidenced by the gains made by teachers' associations without benefit of unionism during the postwar period. Yet, today, this strategy constitutes a learned incapacity – i.e., a behavior that worked in previous situations but which fails when now applied. Both the capacity of the domestic economy to support social benefits and services and the changing global economic climate mean that old goals and old solutions are no longer adequate. It is not clear that Canadian teachers' unions have learned or accepted this message.

Their leaders' embrace of social unionism and special interests that are not broadly supported by union members is evidence of a second critical problem. Provincial offices – the unions' own bureaucracies – have not seen themselves as customer-centred service organizations. While most members approve of the economic benefits they perceive unions have won for them, they consider themselves uninvolved and opposed to many special interest forays engaged upon by union-central. Some teachers are unalterably opposed to controversial policies their unions pursue and consider the use of their dues for these purposes to be a violation of their individual rights. Other teachers are just embarrassed by the radical reputation that their organization brands them with in the local community.

Change ought to occur on at least four fronts for a new balance to be developed between teachers' unions and their publics.

First, teachers ought to have *freedom of choice* in their selection of an agent to represent them. With authority in the hands of individual teachers, unions and other agents would be forced to win the loyalty of individuals in open competition with other bargaining agents, union and non-union. Such a process would ensure that the agents paid attention to teachers' preferences and desires and therefore maintained acceptable services and policies. A marketplace of competing service providers would replace the monopoly currently enjoyed by current teachers' unions. In labor law terms, this would mean that provinces would discard the Rand Formula and, instead, legislate open shops so that each person could decide which union to join, if any union at all. No union would be recognized by statute as the bargaining agent for teachers, as is commonly the case at present. Freedom of choice would mean that unions would be less secure, but this is the condition that is the norm in the private sector in which the consumer, not the provider of a service, is sovereign. If a union provided high quality services genuinely desired by teachers, it would gain the security offered by the support of loyal members.

Second, *union services should be disaggreggated* so that teachers could select those elements that they desire from a menu of service options. Choices could include salary negotiations, malpractice insurance, educational programs, political lobbying on a specific issue, etc. In effect, a "public choice" model would be applied to unions much in the same way that the model is being used to "reinvent" government by disaggregating of public services. It is possible that a teacher might select a single provider for all of these services or select different agencies for different services.

Third, *unions should lobby issues* rather than try to form governments or to instigate social reform. Such a change in political strategy would lower the political profile of teachers' unions and thereby lessen public concern about the power of an institution whose members, in many ways, hold our children's and our society's future in their hands. Arms-length organizations supported by voluntary donations from members should be used to conduct any lobbying and legal action on controversial issues supported by special interest groups. General purpose dues should not be used for such purposes and statutes should be passed by provincial legislators to provide union members with the right to withhold a percentage of their dues if unions continue to operate on political issues as they do at present. Both the second and third proposals would help to restore individual rights and reduce the monolithic appearance of provincial teachers' unions.

Finally, *teachers' unions should attune themselves to the public*, remembering that public schools were created to serve students, their parents and the community. Listening to the genuine opinions of the public, parents and students would yield insights to guide the formation of new relationships between teachers and the public that are more satisfying to all than is the current situation. Many parents are interested in a clear curriculum, sound assessment and greater choice in types of programs and schools – initiatives that teachers' unions currently oppose. With a willingness to listen and to explore new options and a commitment to meeting the genuine needs of children and the preferences of parents and the community, energy that has been devoted to conflict can be harnessed to benefit all parties, including teachers' and the organizations they voluntarily support.

References

Bascia, N. (1998). Teacher unions and educational reform. *The international handbook of educational change*. New York: Kluwer Academic Publishers.

Boyd, W. L., Plank, D. N. & Sykes, G. (1998). Swimming against the current: Teachers' unions in hard times. Paper prepared for the conference on "Teacher Unions and Educational Reform," Kennedy School of Government, Harvard University, Cambridge, MA, September 24-25, 1998.

Chadbourne, R. (Winter 1996). Educational vision or self-interest? The response of Western Australian principals to further devolution. *Leading and Managing*, 2(2), 100-117.

Clark, C. (November 19, 1998). Striking teachers dog angry Péquiste leader. *National Post*, p. A6.

Committee on the Costs of Education. (1976). *Salary + Benefits = Compensation. Interim Report Number 6. Compensation in Elementary and Secondary Education*. Toronto: The Committee.

Cooper, B. S. (1998). Teacher unions, politics and organizational adaptation: An international perspective. Paper prepared for the conference on "Teacher Unions and Educational Reform," Kennedy School of Government, Harvard University, Cambridge, MA, September 24-25, 1998.

The Edvisor Canada's Weekly E-Mail Digest of K-12 Education News. (November 16, 1998). Teachers praise Alberta Tories call for class-size limits. Item 8.

The Edvisor. (January 18, 1999). 55 per cent of Alberta teachers lack collective agreement. Item 10.

Fuller, H. L., Mitchell, G. A. & Hartmann, G. A. (1998). The educational impact of teacher collective bargaining in Milwaukee, Wisconsin. Paper prepared for the conference on "Teacher Unions and Educational Reform," Kennedy School of Government, Harvard University, Cambridge, MA, September 24-25, 1998.

Fuller, H. L., Mitchell, G. A. & Hartmann, G. A. (October 1997). *The Milwaukee Public Schools' Teacher Union Contract: Its history, content, and impact on education.* Milwaukee, WI: Institute for Transformation of Learning, Marquette University. Report 97-1.

Johnson, S. M. & Kardos, S. M. (1998). Thirty years of collective bargaining in public education: Taking stock of its promise for school reform. Paper prepared for the conference on "Teacher Unions and Educational Reform," Kennedy School of Government, Harvard University, Cambridge, MA, September 24-25, 1998.

Hargreaves, A. & Fullan, M. (1998). *What's worth fighting for out there?* Toronto: Ontario Public School Teachers' Federation.

Kerchner, C. T. with Lopez-Elwell, C. (1998). Organizing around quality: Examples and policy options from the frontiers of teacher unionism. Paper prepared for the conference on "Teacher Unions and Educational Reform," Kennedy School of Government, Harvard University, Cambridge, MA, September 24-25, 1998.

Kerchner, C. T., Koppich, J. E., & Weeres, J. G. (1997). *United mind workers: Unions and teaching in the knowledge society.* San Francisco: Jossey-Bass.

Lawton, S. B. (1996). *Busting bureaucracy to reclaim our schools.* Ottawa: Renouf.

Senge, P. M. (1990). *The fifth discipline.* New York: Doubleday.

Index

accountability: 83, 117-8, 131, 140, 149, 163, 200

adaptation-redefining education: 201, 203

administrative agency: 117

agency shop: 44, 90, 123

Alberta: 10, 16, 22, 24, 28, 33, 39, 49-51, 59, 64, 72, 76, 81, 99, 115, 118, 133, 136, 144, 163, 170-4, 176, 202

Alberta Teachers' Alliance: 20, 23

Alberta Teachers' Association: 23, 25-6, 29-30, 59, 64, 66, 69-73, 76, 78-9, 81, 202, 205

amalgamation (of school districts): 11

American Federation of Teachers: 123-4

Anglo-democracy: 10, 115, 123, 129

arbitration: 21, 27-8, 32, 43, 45-8, 51-5, 58-9, 66, 77, 93, 107, 142, 158, 186, 190, 198, 206-7

assessment (see also, authentic assessment): 75, 83, 105, 126, 132, 151, 193, 202, 209

Association de l'enseignant français de l'Ontario: 23

Association des enseignantes et des enseignants franco-ontariens: 23, 26, 70, 109-10

Association des enseignants et des enseignantes francophones du Nouveau Brunswick: 23, 30, 70

Association of Prince Edward Island Teachers: 23

Australia: 123, 126—8, 132-3, 153

authentic assessment: 83

bargaining agent: 42-3, 51, 94, 123, 154, 202, 208

bargaining unit: 42-5, 47, 49, 53-62, 90-1, 107, 123, 135, 188, 191-2, 195, 206

benefits: 10, 45, 51, 57, 59, 74-5, 77, 125, 135, 145, 160, 163, 169-71, 173, 175, 181, 186-7

benevolent associations: 9

Bill 160 (Ontario): 10, 72, 76-7, 79, 103-22

bread-and-butter unionism: 186, 192

British and Canadian School Society: 16

British Columbia: 10, 15-6, 19, 22, 24, 27-8, 32, 39, 48-51, 59, 61, 76, 87, 91, 93-5, 98-100, 108, 118, 129, 136, 143, 145-6, 151, 163, 169-74, 179, 202, 205, 207

British Columbia College of Teachers: 89, 194-5

British Columbia Confederation of Parent Advisory Councils: 97

British Columbia Public School Employers' Association: 94-97, 102

British Columbia School Boards Association: 91

British Columbia Teachers' Federation: 21, 23, 28-30, 59, 62, 69-70, 75-6, 78, 80-2, 84, 89, 91, 93-7, 100, 102, 176, 194

Canada Labour Code: 41, 45, 183

Canadian Labour Congress: 80, 90-1, 100

Canadian Teachers' Federation: 7, 23, 30, 34, 40, 65-6, 68, 71-2, 80-2, 84-5, 124, 156

Canadian Union of Public Employees: 51, 62

Centrale de l'enseignement du Québec: 23, 206

centralization: 25, 50, 52, 87-8, 93-4, 98, 100, 117-8, 121, 129, 151, 171, 198

certification (of teachers): 9, 15, 22, 38, 66, 75, 78-9, 108, 126, 141, 143-5, 147-9, 151-4, 163, 187, 191, 194, 198, 200, 204

certification (of unions): 27, 43-4, 47, 135

Charter of Rights and Freedoms: 11, 15, 24, 91, 195

charter schools: 78, 82, 85, 125-6, 132, 193, 198, 200-1

class size: 45, 51, 54-5, 57, 59, 76-7, 92, 108, 112, 114, 143, 145, 151

closed shop: 28, 90-1, 129

collective agreement: 9, 43, 46-8, 55, 57, 60, 67-8, 77-8, 96-7, 127, 129, 144-7, 165, 187, 191, 206-7

collective bargaining: 8-9, 13, 20, 22, 24, 26-8, 31-2, 39, 41-2, 44-5, 47-50, 59, 63, 66-7, 69, 71, 73-4, 77, 80, 88, 91, 93, 95, 98, 104, 107-8, 117-22, 128, 141-2, 148, 171, 183, 185, 187, 189, 191-2, 195, 199-200, 202, 204-5, 207

collective resignation: 31

conciliation: 28, 45-6, 51, 53-5, 57, 107

Confederation: 15

Constitution Act, 1867: 13, 45, 111, 114, 183

contingency fund: 69, 72-3

contract: 26, 49, 123, 126, 128, 130, 187-9, 191, 202-3, 205-6

contract-stripping: 75, 77, 115

Corporation générale des instituteurs catholiques du Québec: 23

corporatism: 9, 80, 87-8, 99-100, 202

court (challenges and decisions affecting unions): 11, 22-4, 42, 44, 47-8, 52, 82, 90-1, 98, 115, 148, 152-3, 184, 190, 194-6

craft unionism: 50, 62, 90, 185, 203

curriculum: 11, 29, 31, 33, 66-7, 69, 75, 78, 81-4, 98, 105, 121, 125-6, 129, 132, 151, 158, 199-203, 209

defined-benefit plan: 168, 177

defined-contribution plan: 169, 177

denominational schools: 14-5, 38

departments of education: 16-7, 20-1, 26-7, 29, 126-8, 141

devolution: 126-8

discipline: 22, 34, 44, 54, 65, 154

dispute resolution: 42, 45, 107, 132, 184, 186

division of powers: 13

Educational Association of Nova Scotia: 17

Elementary Teachers' Federation of Ontario: 113, 115

English: 13, 15, 20, 37, 40, 53-61, 109, 111, 144

enrollment: 17, 29, 76, 141, 143, 146-7, 158, 174-5

ethics: 22, 34, 89, 190

fact-finding: 45-6, 59, 68, 119

Federation of Women Teachers' Association of Ontario: 20-1, 23, 26, 69-70, 109-10, 113

fiscally-responsible government: 118

freedom of association: 11, 41, 91, 185, 191, 195-6

freedom of speech: 195

French: 13, 15, 20, 37, 40, 53-61, 103, 111, 124, 144, 147, 158

French Education Authority: 94

funding (of education): 49, 53-60, 75, 78-9, 82, 92, 106, 113-5, 118, 120, 124, 126, 128-30, 132, 142, 171, 173, 199, 201-2

Great Depression: 22, 24

grievances: 8, 10, 19-20, 42, 45-7, 53-60, 65, 73, 97, 106, 120, 145, 184, 188, 203

Hall-Dennis Report: 30-31, 40

history (of teachers' unions): 9-10, 13, 16, 61, 63, 189, 196
Hope Commission: 29
impasse resolution: 205
in-service training: 16-7
industrial unionism: 50-1, 62, 201, 203-4
instructional time: 116, 151
interest bargaining: 95
International Declaration of Human Rights: 11, 190
Interstate New Teacher Assessment and Support Consortium: 151
Korbin Report: 87, 93
labor market: 135-48, 203
labor relations: 22-3, 41, 43-6, 48, 50-1, 53-60, 102-4, 107, 111, 123, 131, 192, 198, 205-6
law/legislation: 8-9, 13, 18, 22, 24, 26, 28-9, 31, 38-9, 41-3, 45-6, 48-9, 51, 53-61, 79, 123, 132, 138, 142, 144, 148, 170, 184, 187, 190, 192, 200, 204-5, 208
localism-communitarism; 200-1
lockouts: 32, 48, 52, 56, 59, 93, 115, 206
Manitoba: 15-6, 22, 24, 28, 48, 50-2, 57, 76-7, 118, 136, 146, 163, 170-5, 177, 181, 205-6
Manitoba Teachers' Society: 20, 23, 27, 30, 57, 69-70, 77, 81
mediation: 21, 46-8, 51, 54-60, 68, 92, 107, 119
membership: 25-8, 44, 61, 64, 70, 76, 91, 193, 209
mission statements: 62-63, 75
monopoly: 93, 138, 149, 208
monopoly rents: 138
monopsony: 93, 139, 143
Multilateral Agreement on Investment (MAI): 80, 181
National Board for Professional Teaching Standards: 151

National Council for Accreditation of Teacher Education: 151
National Education Association: 123-4
National Union of Teachers: 130-1, 200
nationalist-syndicalism: 200-1
neo-conservative: 10, 75, 78, 85, 103, 207
neo-corporatist: 88, 93, 95, 100, 186
neo-liberal: 10, 207
New Brunswick: 14-6, 22, 24, 28, 31, 33, 49-51, 54, 94, 99, 118, 126, 136, 163, 170-3, 201
New Brunswick Teachers' Association: 19, 23, 29-31
New Brunswick Teachers' Federation: 54, 70
New Zealand: 123, 128-9, 132-3, 201
New Zealand Post Primary Teachers' Association: 128-9
Newfoundland: 14-5, 24, 28, 38, 50-1, 53, 99-100, 118, 136, 144, 147, 163, 169, 170-4
Newfoundland and Labrador Teachers' Association: 19, 23-4, 30, 53, 61, 63, 70, 176, 196, 207
Normal schools: 15-8, 38, 141
North American Free Trade Agreement: 80, 181
Northwest Territories Teachers' Association: 23, 30, 70
Nova Scotia: 14-7, 22, 24, 28, 33, 38, 48, 50, 54, 77, 94, 99, 118, 136, 163, 170-3, 205
Nova Scotia Provincial Education Association: 18
Nova Scotia Teachers' Union: 18, 23, 28, 30, 38, 54, 62, 66, 69-72, 77
objectives (of teachers and unions): 10
Ontario: v, 8, 10, 14, 20, 22, 24, 26-33, 37-40, 49-51, 55, 61-2, 72, 76-

77, 79, 85, 88, 99, 103, 108, 116, 118-21, 124, 136, 143-4, 147, 151-2, 157-8, 160, 162-3, 167-79, 182, 184, 205-7

Ontario College of Teachers: 38, 40, 108, 152

Ontario Educational Association: 17, 20

Ontario English Catholic Teachers' Association: 23, 26, 63, 69-70, 77, 79, 109-15

Ontario Public School Boards' Association: 115

Ontario Public School Men Teachers' Federation: 23, 26, 38

Ontario Public School Teachers' Federation: 23, 69-71, 109-10, 113

Ontario Secondary School Teachers' Federation: 20-21, 23, 26, 62, 70, 76, 78, 84, 110-3, 115, 188

Ontario Separate School Trustees' Association: 111

Ontario Teachers' Council: 26, 38

Ontario Teachers' Federation: 26-7, 30, 38-9, 61, 109, 113, 167, 180

Ontario Teachers' Superannuation Plan: 160

open meetings: 48

open shop: 43-44, 90, 208

Parent Report: 30

parents: 9, 63, 78, 82, 85, 97, 103, 107-8, 110, 112, 115-6, 143, 150, 199, 201-2, 209

pattern bargaining: 125

pensions: 20, 25, 34, 55, 57, 66, 81, 103, 105, 114, 144-5, 155, 160, 163, 167-82, 186, 204

policy tutelage: 117, 119-20

political campaigning: 79-82

positional bargaining: 95

preparation time: 45, 51, 54-5, 103, 107-8, 110, 112, 120

Prince Edward Island: 14-6, 24, 28, 48, 51, 53, 118, 136, 163, 170-3, 181, 206

Prince Edward Island Provincial Teachers' Association: 19

Prince Edward Island Teachers' Federation: 17, 23, 30, 53, 70, 81

Prince Edward Island Teachers' Union: 23

principals: 21, 39, 44, 55-6, 61, 67, 77, 97, 106-7, 112-3, 120, 127-8, 150, 152, 160, 172, 188

private schools: 78, 82, 198

privatization-free agency: 200, 202

professionalism: 11, 63

professional development: 128

Protestant: 14-5, 27, 30, 40

provider-capture: 103, 105

Provincial Association of Catholic Teachers of Quebec: 23

Provincial Association of Protestant Teachers of Quebec (PAPT): 17, 19, 23, 30, 70

Provincial Association of Public and High School Trustees: 17

public policy: vi, 24, 63, 104, 117, 187

pupil-teacher ratios: 103, 108, 119

qualifications: 29

Quebec: 14-5, 24, 27-8, 30-2, 37-8, 40, 49-50, 52, 55, 99-100, 115, 118, 124, 136, 144, 158, 163, 170-5, 178, 182, 198, 206

Queensland Teachers' Union: 127

Rand formula: 44, 190-6, 198, 208

retirement: 20, 54, 71, 154-5, 160, 167-9, 173, 175-8, 181

Roman Catholic: 14-5, 19-20, 27, 39-40, 57, 59, 61, 64, 109-12, 114-5, 119, 144, 146

Royal Commission on Learning: 40, 107-8

salaries: 8-10, 18-22, 24-8, 32-4, 38, 45-6, 48, 50-1, 54-5, 57, 59, 63,

74-5, 77, 89-90, 97, 105, 119, 125, 127, 129-32, 135-66, 168-70, 172, 174-5, 181, 186-9, 196, 202, 208

sanctions: 47

Saskatchewan: 16, 22, 24, 28, 38, 48, 50-2, 64, 94, 118, 136, 144, 162-3, 170-4, 176-7, 205, 207

Saskatchewan Teachers' Alliance: 20, 23

Saskatchewan Teachers' Federation: 23, 25, 30, 57, 63, 66, 69-71, 73, 81, 85

Saskatchewan Union of Teachers: 19, 23

school boards/districts: 9, 17, 19-22, 28, 31-4, 39, 44, 48, 50-1, 53-60, 64, 66, 68-9, 76-8, 82, 84, 89-92, 94, 96, 98-9, 105-8, 111, 114-9, 121, 125-6, 128, 131, 133, 135, 141, 144-6, 152, 160, 165, 183, 187-8, 194, 201-2, 205

school-business partnerships: 9, 80

school day (length of): 45, 104, 107

school inspection: 132

school finance: 11

Secondary School Teachers' Union of Western Australia: 127-8

separate schools: 14, 64, 144, 162

sick leave: 20, 54, 178

social unionism: 10, 186, 190, 192-3, 207

standardized testing: 82-4, 131, 200

strike: 7, 21, 24, 26, 31-2, 39, 41, 44, 46, 48-9, 52-60, 68-9, 72, 92-3, 104, 107, 110-3, 115, 119, 124-5, 129, 131, 142-3, 180, 184-6, 188, 190-1, 194, 205, 206

students: 63, 78, 83-4, 88, 92, 105, 107-8, 110-2, 114, 116, 119, 126, 144, 147, 152, 158, 163, 190, 193, 200-2, 205, 209

subsidiarity: 119

superannuation: 20

superintendent: 13, 44, 53-60, 70, 94, 97, 172

systematic assessment: 11

teacher evaluation: 77, 96, 187, 199, 203

teacher training/education: 9, 15-7, 34, 38-9, 66-7, 141, 151, 154, 165, 195, 203

Teachers' Association of Canada West: 17, 23

Teachers' Institutes: 16, 19

Teachers' Protective Union of Nova Scotia: 18

tenure: 9, 20, 26, 90, 127, 144-5, 148, 204

trustees: 7-9, 18, 26, 28, 34, 50, 52-3, 57, 82, 85, 91-5, 97-9, 105-7, 110-1, 114-6, 118-20, 143, 149, 188, 207

unfair labor practices: 47-8

union financing: 69-73, 76, 90, 120, 123, 125, 189-91, 195-6, 198, 208-9

union security: 43

union shop: 44, 91

union structure: 61, 64

United Kingdom: 10, 88, 123, 127, 129-33, 183, 200, 204-5

United States: 42, 44, 52, 80, 88, 90, 123-7, 132, 151, 168, 173, 179-80, 183, 190, 195, 201-2, 204

values (of teachers and unions): 10, 63-4, 98, 117

vouchers: 78, 82, 85

work conditions: 20, 22, 26, 34, 41, 45, 51, 55, 57, 59, 63, 74, 77, 92, 96, 103-4, 107, 110, 131, 135, 142, 145, 188

work-to-rule: 48, 56, 107, 206

World War I: 19-21, 185,

Worth Report: 31

Yukon Teachers' Association: 23, 30, 70